D1143195

THE BOOK OF WARWICKSHIRE

The King's England

A New Domesday Book of 10,000 Towns and Villages

Edited by Arthur Mee

in 41 Volumes

NOTHING like these books has ever been presented to the English people. Every place has been visited. The Compilers have travelled half-a-million miles and have prepared a unique picture of our countryside as it has come down through the ages, a census of all that is enduring and worthy of record.

Stratford   Our Master Englishman as he sits by the Avon

THE KING'S ENGLAND

WARWICKSHIRE

Shakespeare's Country

EDITED BY

ARTHUR MEE

With 220 Places
and 215 Pictures

LONDON
HODDER AND STOUGHTON
LIMITED   ST. PAUL'S HOUSE E.C.4

First printed 1936
Reprinted 1937
Reprinted 1942
Reprinted 1947
Reprinted 1949

Printed and Bound in Great Britain for Hodder & Stoughton, Limited, London,
by Richard Clay and Company, Ltd., Bungay, Suffolk

THE EDITOR IS GREATLY
INDEBTED TO

Mr L. B. POWELL
OF BIRMINGHAM

FOR HIS ASSISTANCE IN THE
PREPARATION OF THIS BOOK

PICTURES OF WARWICKSHIRE

*When the picture is not on or facing the page given
it is inside the set of pictures beginning on that page*

vii

Many of the pictures are reproduced by courtesy of: Messrs E. Bastard, B. T. Batsford, Ltd, R. Bleasdale, W. A. Call, Philip Chatwin, Fred Crossley, Herbert Felton, E. O. Hoppé, D. Hunter, Sydney Pitcher, Percy Simms, H. J. Smith, W. H. Smith & Sons, W. F. Taylor, the Trustees of Shakespeare's birthplace, Birmingham Art Gallery, and the Victoria & Albert Museum.

It has not been thought desirable to note in this volume the lamentable changes and destruction wrought during the war.

Shakespeare's Countryside

WE must love it because it is Shakespeare's country, but we love it, too, because it is very heart of very England. It is set in the midst of the Island which is set in the midst of the greatest land-mass of the world, and we may wonder if it is not something more than coincidence that our king of men was born at the centre of all this beauty. We have no fairer scene than Warwickshire, and it was Shakespeare's home, his realm, his dear, dear land. He was born by the Avon, and, having been out into the great world and found his immortality, he came back to die by the Avon, knowing no fairer place.

A little way off from his simple grave is one of the stateliest tombs in Warwickshire, and in it lies the proud earl who burned .Joan of Arc in Rouen. Who can walk down Henley Street in Stratford, or stand by the tomb of Richard Beauchamp in Warwick, without thinking of Shakespeare and Joan, two of the greatest names that ever filled the word with wonder? Who can stand in Robert Dudley's ruined home at Kenilworth and not seem to people it with all that pageantry through which Queen Elizabeth moved for 17 days? Yet it is not Richard Beauchamp or Robert Dudley who fills Warwickshire with his name today. It was a boy in the crowd watching Elizabeth pass by who was to give her age its greatest lustre and Warwickshire its greatest fame. It was his cradle and his grave; London in all its glory could not hold him back from it when his work was done.

Nor do we wonder, for we must think of Warwickshire as Bishop Creighton thought of it—as having many claims to be considered the most typically English of the English shires. It is a central county and was long free from outside influence. It was not readily reached in early times by invasions from anywhere. The way to it was barred by dense forests, and it was late in taking part in the early conflicts of the Anglo-Saxon kingdoms.

Yet it was to play a great part in the main movement of our history. Its position was pivotal. It spoke the language which was to be adopted as written English; the men who framed our language for us lived across the central belt of the country from Gloucestershire to the Wash, and it was William Tyndale just over the border, and William Shakespeare of Stratford, who more than any other two men made English what it is. There is more of Tyndale in the Bible than of any other man: there is more of Shakespeare in our daily speech than of any other man.

And in the turbulent days when barons held their sway Warwick was the central stronghold of bold and resolute men who made their mark on the kingdom. When, in the days of the Tudors, England began to play a part in the world's affairs, and to have a proud self-consciousness, it was in Warwickshire that our great Elizabeth most gorgeously displayed her pageantry. When modern England plunged into the furnace of the Civil War it was in Warwickshire that King and Parliament first clashed in battle array and began the fight which laid the foundations of Democracy. When England emerged as the greatest industrial nation in the world it was Warwickshire that step by step built up, through a marvellous diversity of trades, the most populous of our provincial cities. Not only has Birmingham more than a million people, but Warwickshire adds a tenth to her numbers every ten years.

It is true that she has no very impressive scenery, that she has coal and iron within her borders and some of the grimmest regions in her neighbourhood, but she has the kind of beauty most distinctively English, for the very essence of the charm of our scenery comes from the woodland stream and meadow so rich and restful; and where can this be found if not on the quiet reaches of Shakespeare's Avon?

About the middle of our 40 counties in size, with less than 600 square miles, Warwickshire is sixth in population, with about 400,000 outside its great city of a million. It is compact as a county, about 50 miles from south to north and nearly 40 in its central breadth.

Through nearly its whole extent Warwickshire is a wonderful mixture of the old and the new. Its most completely typical place is the fine old city of Coventry, with about 170,000 people. The home of old romance dating back to Saxon times, it has played a great part in all the changes of our social history, and has shown a remarkable adaptability in changing its industries to suit changing circumstances. It has more than doubled the population it had 20 years ago, and with the experience of the old and the enterprise of the young it has a knack of helping itself to any business that may be astir. It was a bishopric in the 7th century; in the 20th it is the heart of the most tremendous business of our time, Transport.

Warwickshire indeed is a wideawake county, with Birmingham as the proof of it for all to see. England's second city has no claim to the veneration felt for age, but since metal became a great base of civilisation Birmingham has taken for its province all that is included in what we call Hardware. Over that province, ever widening and ever growing more complex, the city has borne increasing sway, and with its industrial growth has grown a public spirit rarely equalled in any city, so that civically, educationally, and commercially Birmingham stands in the front rank of the world.

To Edmund Burke it was the toyshop of the world, but to us it is the big wonder city of our wonder age. To John Leland, sent round England by Henry the Eighth to look at everything, it was a place where "there be many smiths to make knives and all manner of cutting tools, and many loriners that make bits, and a great many nailors"; to us it is the mother of a thousand industries.

After Birmingham and Coventry, two of the most remarkable industrial towns built up by the English-speaking race, come two towns which must ever be places of pilgrimage for those who speak the tongue that Shakespeare spake. Has any country two more attractive towns than Stratford and Warwick?

Of Stratford it is enough to say that it is Shakespeare's home.

3

We see the room he was born in, the little schoolroom in which his imagination must have begun to stir, the hall in which he must have seen his first play, the garden in which he died, and the grave in which he lies. We walk about these streets and see the things that Shakespeare saw. We open doors in Stratford and see the chair he sat in, the fireside where he sat talking with Anne Hathaway, the very gloves he wore. It is said to be astounding that we know so little of Shakespeare, but here we are in his steps, following him in his intimate places, and we feel his spirit about us.

Of Warwick it is enough to say that it is perhaps as fine an epitome of England, of its long story and its ancient beauty, as we shall find in all our island. He who would see England in an hour or two had better go to Warwick, for there is no truer concentration of it anywhere than in this ancient town on a beautiful river, dominated by a marvellous castle which has never been uninhabited since Alfred's daughter began it; with one of the noblest churches in the land, and one of the rarest of those ancient hospitals which open a door leading us into the centuries.

When the Conqueror came he found this site chosen for him, and adopted it, and he set in it stout Norman warriors who became Earls of Warwick for many generations: Beaumonts and Beauchamps who merged into Nevilles and Dudleys. They built this great castle, the only one of the very few castles of such an age which yet remains inhabited, dominating an area which has seen more history than any equal area in the land.

And after Stratford and Warwick are such towns as Leamington and Rugby and Nuneaton. Leamington is a trim and garden-like city near some of the finest scenery in the county; it is proud of itself, and rightly so. Nuneaton was George Eliot's town, where she found the knowledge of rural life on which her fame as a novelist rests. Rugby has sent its name throughout the world and has woven itself into the life of more English boys and more English men than have been touched by any other single town. Everybody has heard of its great school,

4

everybody has heard of Tom Brown's schooldays there, everybody has heard of the great game Rugby has sent out into the world, and everybody has heard of the fine spirit of Rugby built up by Dr Arnold, carried on by two masters who became Archbishops of Canterbury, and kept alive by Rugby men who have found their way to every corner of the globe.

For those who do not care for towns so much, but love the quiet ways of our secluded countryside, Warwickshire has a glorious group of villages and hamlets. It has areas where we feel that we are in Shakespeare's Forest of Arden, which stretched in his day for 20 miles by 10, with a few heights of 400 feet. It was the home of his mother, and well he must have known it. Whenever he wills that the creatures of his fancy shall "fleet the time carelessly as they did in the golden world," it is to a forest that he takes them, and we feel that Arden is the place. Here is As You Like It, and it is as we like it.

It was probably at Hampton-in-Arden that Shakespeare laid his scene; it is one of the group of villages that seem to belong to Shakespeare, and it is fine to see the splendid group of poets in its church window. In this group of villages comes Wilmcote, the home of his mother, with the marvellous beams still in the farmhouse; Aston Cantlow, where his father and mother were married; Charlecote, with the great house from which Shakespeare walked out to fame and immortality, and the church with the quaint and lovely figures of the Lucys; Snitterfield, home of his uncle Henry, the village that just missed Shakespeare; Christopher Sly's village of Barton-on-the-Heath; Luddington with the fields where Judith Shakespeare used to walk; Barcheston, the home of a fat man the poet knew; Rowington, the village with four William Shakespeares living in his day; Bidford, with the Falcon Inn where Shakespeare was last seen among his friends. In the village of Alveston we have found in a ruined church a queer statue of a man who knew Shakespeare, Nicholas Lane, and in the village of Wormleighton we have found the curious fact that there was living a George Washington not far from William Shakespeare in 1595.

Nowhere in Warwickshire is history far away from us. At Atherstone is the inn where Henry Lancaster slept, and the church in which he received communion on the eve of that day which he prayed would make him King of England; and at Maxstoke is the house where Richard of York was sleeping that night, dreaming fearful dreams of Bosworth Field. At Baginton is the ruin of the castle from which Bolingbroke set out to meet Thomas Mowbray for the duel we read of in Richard the Second. At Combe Abbey, near Binley, was brought up that Princess Elizabeth through whom was preserved the link of our monarchy with King Alfred. Near Kineton was fought the Battle of Edgehill beginning the Civil War, with William Harvey sitting on the hillside with the king's sons while the king fought for his life. At Little Compton is the church to which came Bishop Juxon, to whom his master had spoken his last word on the scaffold; here through many sad years the bishop would sit and Remember. At Astley is the little churchyard on which Lady Jane Grey used to look from her window.

We may think, perhaps, that Warwickshire's historic events come into a brief and well-defined period, but at Long Compton there is a veritable little Stonehenge, with the Rollright Stones running over the Oxfordshire border. At Wootton Wawen is one of the very queerest churches with Saxon work in its walls, and at Tredington we handled a piece of Saxon timber and found a doorway set up high in the walls by Saxons afraid of Danish invaders. The great house of Stoneleigh, one of the most wonderful treasure houses in the county, has enshrined within its stately walls something of an abbey of about 1000 years ago. At Ettington the enchanting ruined church lost in a park is part of an estate which has been in the same family for eight or nine centuries; no other family in the land, it is said, has held its tenancy since Domesday Book.

To not a few pilgrims of the countryside it may seem that a grave and a cottage on two sides of a lane at Barford are among the Warwickshire haunts that cannot be forgotten. Above the grave is a picture of a plough; in the cottage lived a ploughman of whom it may be said that he raised the status of every ploughman in the land. He was Joseph Arch, and to one who remembers his work, the fire he lit on behalf of the helpless agricultural labourers of England, it is a thrilling thing to see his cottage standing here, and to peep through his window to see his little library of books still on the wall. In this cottage there came into life a great hope which was to be fulfilled in the lives of our farm labourers, and we are reminded, as we think of it, that hereabouts was built up also something of British influence across the earth, for it was at Lea Marston that the first Constitution of New Zealand was drawn up, and in a hamlet by Coventry, on the Stoneleigh estate, was born the Warwickshire boy who was to stir up the enthusiasm which founded Australia's Commonwealth.

There may never have been a Lady Godiva, saving her people from tyranny by her famous ride through Coventry, but Warwickshire has a host of famous names, and with them are some we meet a little unexpectedly. Here was Handel playing on church organs. Here lies Addison's only daughter, living on sadly for 70 years after him. Here Michael Johnson married Sara Ford, who became the mother of our great Samuel Johnson. Here we come upon the work of Inigo Jones, Nicholas Stone, and Grinling Gibbons. At a lonely cross-roads at Copston Magna sleeps Claudius the Roman. At Kenilworth is a house where Latimer lived. At Yardley sleeps St Edburgha.

For people, for events, or for those quiet scenes that are the charm of our English countryside, the county is renowned. We come upon Little Red Riding Hoods and Little Boy Blues going home from school in one of its villages. We come in another upon a marvellous company of yews representing the Sermon on the Mount. We come upon a village which has the most magnificent brass in Warwickshire in its church and the oldest yew in the county beside its walls. We come upon villages like Alcester with lovely black-and-white streets and upon the mile-long street of Henley-in-Arden like a museum of domestic architecture with its gabled houses, crazy roofs, and timbered walls. We come in these two hundred villages upon enchantment after enchantment, delight indoors and out, and we felt again and again that it was more than chance that Shakespeare came to us this way.

Alcester   Henley Street

Alcester   Panel on Fulke Greville's Tomb

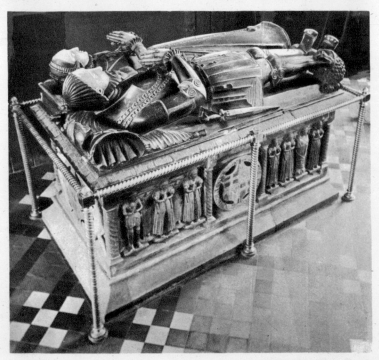

Alcester   Fulke Greville's Tomb

A Warwickshire Lane in Winter

A Warwickshire Lane in Summer

Beaudesert
Church Vane

Monks Kirby
Gates of Newnham Paddox

Fenny Compton
Signpost

Chesterton
Inigo Jones
Windmill

Lillington
Oak, in the Middle of
England

Wasperton
15th Century
Dovecote

Maxstoke
Priory Gateway

Wroxall   Stocks

Aston Cantlow
Arrow Marks

Coleshill
Pillory

Dunchurch
Old Smithy

Kenilworth
Leicester's Barn

Here is Treasure Rich Indeed

ALCESTER. It is charming whichever way we come to it, and it grows more beautiful the longer we stay. Its byways are delightful, and for those who love a natural scene there is the road to Stratford over a bridge where the Alne and Arrow rivers run together, a group of timbered cottages near by, and, a little farther on, a lovely wood and a peep of the Cotswolds with the spire of Shakespeare's church.

It has lost much that was old and beautiful, but has kept enough to make it fascinating. All but one of its churches have vanished; but this one, its venerable tower looking weary with age, stands at the meeting of the streets, with Tudor cottages all about it and with cottage doors opening on to the grass of the churchyard. Nothing remains of its ancient abbey; gone are the relics of Roman times; and the exquisite ivory crozier dug up in the rectory garden is housed in the British Museum, an example of 11th-century craftsmanship.

But, if it has not the material things, Alcester has kept the spirit of its wondrous past. This old town which wears its centuries so serenely has not forgotten that its mills made it a busy place before its needle-making passed to Redditch. Today it is content to captivate those of us who love old windows, doors with massive knockers, broad steps, and the overhanging storeys of gabled houses.

Its rows of cottages, with black timbers and shutters, are like a bit of the Middle Ages; and everywhere are charming Georgian façades. Many of our villages have a black-and-white corner; here we found a dozen, all fascinating. Very attractive is a 17th-century house of mellow brick with a massive doorway from its second storey leading to a quaint gallery above the street. The small walk called Butter Street is enchanting with its tiny houses; and set amid old-world wonder is the little 17th-century town hall on brick and stone columns, with a timbered top.

The great tower of the church was centuries old when the town hall was built, and, though most of the 14th-century building has been refashioned, it has kept a few things of great price. There is a Tudor screen of carved oak with roses and vines, there are four saints on the pulpit, and four scenes on the font have in them about 30 sculptured figures. There is a simple white figure by Chantrey of Francis, Marquess of Hertford, who rests on a couch with his finger keeping open the page of a book he is reading. Sitting in a chair in white marble is his kinsman Sir Hamilton Seymour, wearing the badge of the Order of the Bath.

Severely plain is the interior of the church, open like a chapel, the roof supported on 10 white columns; but in this plain place is a monument rich indeed, the tomb of the Fulke Greville who died four years before Shakespeare was born. He was M.P. for his county, but we remember him because he was grandfather of the namesake who went as a boy to the new school at Shrewsbury, entering the same day as Philip Sidney. That day began a great friendship between these two boys which was not to end till Greville, who had enjoyed in Elizabeth's Court what he called the longest lease and the smoothest time, bore the pall at Sidney's funeral.

On this great tomb we see the grandfather in alabaster, lying by his wife, a perfectly lovely pair. They died within a year of each other and lie here in great tranquillity. He is in armour and has his head on a helmet, a short sword at his side, and his feet on a curious-looking dog with its head raised as if in lamentation. Both figures have been painted and both have 10 rings on their fingers. The wife's petticoat is folded at the bottom so that it looks like a honey-comb. Her hair is combed close back, her head rests on two cushions, her long gown is lifted at the hem by a lap dog, and round her neck a gold chain hangs almost to her feet, with a pomander box at the end. On the wall above hangs Greville's helmet, and round the front of the tomb are heraldic shields and figures of their children, a son and six daughters, one in a shroud.

In a glass case are treasured a few old things from Alcester's past: a set of stone weights and an old register of 1560 among them; and in one of the windows there is a tiny picture of the town's old cross, just under the foot of St Nicholas.

Alcester has chosen for its peace memorial, in memory of the men who live for evermore, these noble lines:

Pass not this shrine in sorrow but in pride,
See that you live as nobly as they died.

C. P.
Stratford R.D.
Hop.
329.

The Respectable Dissenters

ALDERMINSTER. Just south of Shakespeare's town, it has two features to attract the attention of Stratford cars going Oxford way. One is a remarkable row of cottages built alike and widely spaced along the road; the other is the church with a massive central tower 700 years old and the music of the Stour murmuring past.

The work of the Normans is seen in some of the walls of the church and in the four arches of the tower. There is a carved face in each corner between the arches, a good 14th-century piscina, and an altar table standing on an old altar stone with a consecration cross to be seen under the frontal. A tablet to James Kettle of 1806 has the quaint remark that he was "40 years pastor of a respectable congregation of Protestant Dissenters in Warwick."

The Leaning Spire

ALLESLEY. It has been quiet for centuries, but today the tumult of traffic is about it, for it spreads its cottages along the road from Coventry to Birmingham. Those who rush by miss a pleasant walk up the high slope to the church, passing the house with three gables and a porch which Shakespeare might have passed.

The church spire leans a little and rises on a tower from which an angel and 30 faces, old and worn, animal and human, are looking down. Two arches of the nave have Norman carving on the pillars, which were happily saved when most of the church was made new in the 19th century.

The Queer Man Who Knew Shakespeare

ALVESTON. It is one of the lovely group of villages round Shakespeare's town. He must have known it, and here is the pathetic figure of a man who must have known our great immortal. There are groups of old cottages, an inn by the Avon, a church too new to have much historic interest, and an old one sadly forgotten.

We noticed in the new church (which has a carved oak pulpit and paintings in the choir stalls) a stone telling of a little tragedy such as we have come upon elsewhere, for it was apparently not uncommon in the days when windows were rarer than now. We read on this stone that on Christmas night in 1835 an old lady of 86, her daughter, and her servant, a girl of 19, were suffocated in their sleep through having a coke fire burning in their unventilated room.

But it is down a lane that we come on our pilgrimage to find one of those surprises that never fails us in our wondrous countryside. It is all that is left of the old Norman church, a chancel sadly neglected, in a little field. The ivy was darkening its east window when we called, the carvings over two Norman doorways were crumbling so that nothing could be made of them, but inside the royal arms were bright with paint, and we found here the sculptured figure of a man who knew Shakespeare. He stands surveying the ruin of the past, the old Jacobean pulpit on the floor, the wooden seat in which the priest sat in the sanctuary, the memorials on the walls. He faces us as we enter, and we are struck by this odd ungainly figure of Nicholas Lane.

An amateur craftsman's work it must surely be, for nothing seems right. The head thrusts forward in an ugly way, the legs are stodgy, the hands are as if they had been stuck on. Yet the stone has kept marvellously well with all its details, and Nicholas, with his little group of companions about him, is a valuable witness of a man of his station in Shakespeare's day. He wears a high collar and a ruff, breeches fastened down the side, and laced shoes, and he carries a short sword. At his feet is a lion looking as playful as a lamb, and about this calm beast four small figures are kneeling. Above them all is a panel of stone with old carving looking new.

Nicholas was important. Perhaps he was the Stratford moneylender. We know he had a dispute with Shakespeare's father about a debt which John Shakespeare had taken over from his troublesome brother Henry of Snitterfield, and we may be almost certain the poet knew him.

There is a tribute in this strange place to Colonel Newsham Peers, who died in Germany after distinguishing himself in most of the battles of Queen Anne, "regretted by his king and lamented by his country"; and by the old altar is a stone which tells us of a crime of long ago, when William Hiron was slain by a villain, and his wife was brought with sorrow to the grave a month later by this melancholy catastrophe.

Close by the ruin is a bit of Alveston unspoilt, a 14th-century cottage once the vicarage; it has splendid timbers.

There lived in this village in the 18th century Francis Knottesford, a much-learned man who spoke several languages and had a library to which men would come from universities to consult him on theology and other weighty matters.

The Shining Wonder in the Tower

ANSLEY. It goes back to Lady Godiva, who owned it, and its noble Hall, which has entered on a new chapter as offices, reminds us of the 18th-century days when poets came here, and one of them wrote to another from the old hermitage:

> *Beneath this stony roof reclined,*
> *I soothe to peace my pensive mind.*

The hermitage, still in the grounds, was built from the stones of an ancient oratory, and from the same days come the oldest stones of the church of St Lawrence, framing Norman doorways and a massive Norman chancel arch. The north door is very fine, and the chancel arch has a capital with a grotesque carving of a saint torn between a wild animal and a dragon, the medieval artist's idea of the soul in conflict with the powers of evil.

There is an old stone cross from those very early days and a curious stone coffin, and from later centuries come the old oil painting of a rural scene now on the reredos, the Jacobean chair with figures on the arms and children sitting on the back, and the fragments of glass with a knight and a lady, a Madonna, and some monks.

But it is something modern which draws the eye of all who come. One modern window has Peter as a shepherd and Dorcas clothing a child, but the shining wonder of the church is the window in the massive 15th-century tower. It glows with life and gleams with bright colour. At the top is Christ in a rich red robe attended by angels, four candles brightly burning above him; in the middle St Lawrence and the Madonna stand by a beautiful angel with the glistening star of Bethlehem in her lap, shedding its light over a charming nativity scene ringed by a rainbow. Here, in front of a thatched shelter, Mary sits with Jesus, while two child angels bring children with their gifts—the modern Magi. A little girl offers a bunch of snowdrops, while on the other side a boy eagerly offers his most precious possessions, a toy motor car and his rabbit. Like the stout oak tower screen, this window was set up here in memory of a beloved father who had lived in the village for 50 years, and it is as charming a tribute as we have seen.

The Bowman and His Arrows

ARLEY. The great pyramid from a coalpit dominates its landscape, and most of its beauty is in the 600-year-old church, set amid yews which must have been here since Elizabethan days.

Between two old windows with rich tracery is a doorway to the chancel where priests came in and out in Chaucer's day; and in the walls are grooves which may have been made by the sharpening of arrows in the far-off days when our bowmen were the finest in the world. From those days comes the stone figure of a medieval priest in a recess, angels supporting his head; and a little glass in the windows, with a monk, a saint, and a crowned Madonna.

The canopied reredos is modern, with finely carved angels blowing trumpets, and there are rich modern figures in the east and west windows, showing our Lord rising from the tomb, St Chad, St Wilfrid, and the consecration of our first missionary. There is a Noah's Ark in the tracery of the west window. The modern chancel screen is a fine piece of oak craftsmanship.

The Admiral in His Pride

ARROW. Its cottages are on the busy road to Alcester, and there seems little to tempt the traveller here; but we go across a field, turning down by a lovely piece of black and white, and come upon a sculpture by a German prince encouraged in art by his English Aunt Victoria.

It is in a small church overhung by trees, with a tower Horace Walpole is said to have designed, and a plain Norman doorway and a Jacobean pulpit with unusual panels. One of the prince's sculptures is a white monument showing Sir George Seymour in his admiral's uniform. His hand is on a sword, and the statue has delicate detail on the buttons and badges. The statue is by that nephew of Queen Victoria long known in this country as Count Gleichen, who ran away from Germany, joined the British Navy, and then gave up the sea for sculpture. He carved the fine statue of Alfred standing at the top of the street at Wantage, a noble figure worthy of Alfred's birthplace.

The Seymours lived in the great house in the park, Ragley Hall; the park has 500 acres, a broad lake, majestic oaks, and an ancient heronry. It was the head of the Seymours, the Marquis of Hertford, in whose memory the reredos was carved and painted, and the Marchioness herself carved the prayer-desk in the chancel. It has beautiful foliage. In memory of Lady Hertford is a fine window of Charity giving loaves away, with an attractive group of figures, and in one of the windows is an old medallion of the Seymour crest.

Hanging on the wall in the sanctuary is one of their helmets in black and gold, with a head on it. On the wall of the nave is the wooden cross of Lord Edward Seymour, brought from his grave in France.

The oldest possession of the church is a small stone coffin lid under an arch; it has been here since 1303. We noticed two tablets to old friends of the church, a rector who preached from this Jacobean pulpit for 45 years, and a gardener who sat listening to him on Sundays for about 42.

The Friendly Wife

ASHOW. By the churchyard, with a fine old yew and a fragment of the ancient cross, flows the Avon, a rush-grown stream on its way to Shakespeare's town. In the nave and chancel are Norman traces of an earlier structure, and the tower has seen five centuries. The interior is of so old a fashion that the pulpit is in one of the roomy box pews. Over the altar hangs an old Dutch painting of the Crucifixion, and above it is a splendid modern window showing Christ enthroned, with St George in the tracery.

There is a tablet to a rector's wife "who never made an enemy or lost a friend," a homely tribute fitting in this homely place among the meadows, where we imagine the rector's wife going from door to door among the cottages, which stand with their thatched and tiled roofs and their timbered walls as if holding out a smiling welcome.

Two Queens of Sorrow

ASTLEY. Lying amid fields and bright cottage gardens, with a fascinating church and castle standing together among old trees, it speaks in countless ways of a story that began 1000 years ago.

Of that remote past in Astley we found one relic surviving. High up in a buttress of the great tower of the church, in striking contrast with the red sandstone of the tower itself, is a white stone sculptured in relief with a half-circle and several irregular rays. It is a Saxon dial, which may have come from the earlier church which Thomas Astley made new 600 years ago, and kept again when this 16th-century church was built.

We look from it to the heavy mullioned windows of the castle across the churchyard, and think how much of the story of Astley has become the story of England since men looked to this stone to mark the passing hours.

The castle we see has stood since 1555. The crumbling moss-grown outer walls which shelter it have stood since the 12th century. The moat, still with water in it, is perhaps a survival of a Saxon settlement. No longer can we see the window through which Lady Jane Grey must have lifted her eyes from her books to gaze on the green restfulness of Astley churchyard. The window of what is called her room, which was reconstructed with the rest of the castle, is a new one, but a faithful copy of the old. The old castle had been the home of the Greys for more than a century, and here and at Bradgate in Leicestershire Jane spent much of her youth. In this rare place is enshrined the memory of another queen, for here a century earlier Sir John Grey brought Elizabeth Woodville as his bride. From her home by this churchyard Elizabeth went with her two sons when their father had perished in the Battle of St Albans. Her meeting in the forest at Grafton with Edward the Fourth, when she and her children waited beside a tree to speak with him, comes into the story of Northants; but we think of it here, where we are so near this simple scene these two queens must have loved before the cares of a kingdom brought sorrow to their lives.

Thrilling it is to look inside the church on things that would be known to them. We may even gather an idea of what Jane Grey looked like, for the lifesize figures of three of her ancestors are here. They lived practically a century before her: Sir Edward Grey, Cicely Bonneville, and Elizabeth Talbot. The three figures lie by the west door, protected by iron railings. That nearest the door is of Sir Edward, that by the wall is of Cicely Bonneville, wife of Sir Thomas Grey, and the centre one Elizabeth Talbot, Sir Edward's wife, is uncommonly beautiful. The high cheeks, the small delicate mouth, the calm and lofty brow, impress us by their loveliness. Her flowing hair falls over her shoulders, she wears two necklaces and a long and simple gown, and her hands are clasped in prayer.

Sir Edward's head rests on a helmet, and is cropped round. He wears a shirt of chain mail and armour minutely finished, and his feet rest on a lion. His lady rests her head on a cushion supported by angels; the hem of her long robe is held by a little dog, but the features are defaced and the arms broken.

Another striking feature of the church is the series of high oak stalls adorning the nave, nine on each side. For more than 400 years they have been Astley's pride, and are almost unique. They have lofty canopied tops and heads of delicate roses, cornices painted with vine leaves and grapes, and mouldings enriched with flowers. On the back of each is a painted figure, those on the north representing apostles and those on the south prophets. All the seats have their original misereres, carved with quaint animals and birds. There are very few choir stalls to match these, and they have survived in a marvellous way, for the church was in a ruinous condition when the spire fell in the 16th century, destroying the greater part of the nave. Originally they would be used by the priests and canons in Thomas Astley's church, and would be placed at the entrance to the choir. They were probably moved to their present position in the 17th century.

The old church ended at what is now the chancel arch, and above the arch we see the old east window, its elegant tracery filled, alas, with plaster, and the elaborate canopied niches on each side empty. A few fragments of the beautiful 14th-century glass which once filled it are now in the east window of the 17th-century chancel, and there are more fragments in the nave windows, including a perfect picture of a bear, four small faces, and bits of strange animals and birds.

Almost everywhere in this much-altered church are signs of its old glory. In the north wall is a doorway filled up, with a fine old arch and a worn face at the top. On the south wall is a headless brass, one of the oldest in Warwickshire, for its date is about 1400. Probably it represented a lady of the Astleys, and very graceful she must have looked, in kirtle and mantle and tasselled cord. There is a collection of 14th-century tiles which are continually being added to by discoveries in the churchyard. There is a 17th-century stone tablet to Lettice Bolton, who lived very handsomely on her narrow fortune, her life being without trouble and her death without pain; and the epitaph of a babe of the 16th century begins pathetically:

> *Here in the lap of Death lies, hushed and still,*
> *Sweet Innocence.*

A triptych over the communion table is an old Flemish painting of the Descent from the Cross, with a richly clad and jewelled figure in each side-panel, one bearing an exquisite chalice.

But it is Jane Grey who is first and last in our thoughts at Astley. A stile near the church leads across a few fields to one more link with her day, a reminder of her father's tragic end. Henry Grey, Duke of

C   17

Suffolk, fled to Astley Park when Sir Thomas Wyatt's rebellion failed, and here he hid in a great oak for three days and nights until he was betrayed. Here still is the withered trunk of a tree in which it is said he hid himself, and beside it is a conical shaped stone monument with an inscription to him.

A Great and Solemn Company

ASTON. A turn, and we are at the heart of things, says Browning. A turn here, and we have a great transformation. After a few miles of much dreariness from Birmingham it comes as a great surprise. In a moment the scene changes: the mean streets of the city are forgotten as we see the Jacobean turrets and chimneys of Aston Hall rise grandly from the park. Near it the spire of Aston church soars magnificently from its 16th-century tower. The two make Aston an unforgettable place, where ancient dignity triumphs over modern ugliness, where the past seems to live more vividly than the present, and history speaks in a hundred voices.

The towers of Aston and its groups of clustered chimneys are an impressive sight. This precious gem of architecture comes to us from the years just after Shakespeare, and the builders were busy on it for half a generation. Its wings and bays are now crammed with many treasures, for it is a great museum of the city.

The glory of the Hall is in its long gallery and its great staircase. The staircase rises the full height of the building, richly carved in massive oak. One of the newels was shattered by a cannon ball in the Civil War, and on the landing are two cannon balls still near the spot where they fell on that stirring day. The long gallery is 136 feet, and has 13 bays filled with carved panels divided by Ionic columns. It has five windows in the west wall, an oriel at the north end, and a richly ornamented stone mantelpiece. The floor is of huge oak beams. In one of the rooms is a children's museum of dolls and dolls' houses, with miniature furniture and table services. The long garret served as guardroom for 40 Royalist soldiers who vainly endeavoured to defend the Hall against a Parliamentary force of 1200 men. With 12 of its defenders dead, they were driven to surrender, and imprisonment and fines of £20,000 followed for Sir Thomas Holte, a man of grim and fiery temper.

We may climb to the roof to see the wide prospect of Birmingham's dismal roofs and chimneys, though more attractive are the reconstructed Elizabethan gardens which make this place a charming oasis in an industrial wilderness. Among the terraced lawns is a fine fountain with a figure of Pan by William Bloye, a Birmingham sculptor.

In the church of Aston sleep its famous folk, the Holtes and the Erdingtons, the Ardens and the Devereux. It is a noble place made new, with a magnificent timber roof over a nave of 14 arches, each arch with a rich capital of grape vines. A great and solemn company it is that is lying here, of knights and ladies known and unknown, giving to this place such a wealth of interest as few other parish churches possess. There are 12 figures, a fascinating group with a pageant of costume from the early Middle Ages to Jacobean times.

On a high tomb are the stone figures of William Holte and his wife, he clothed as in the 15th century, with his hair short and his head on a helmet; his wife in a peaked headdress, a close bodice, and long skirt and gloves. Around them are six angels. On another high tomb are the figures of a knight and lady, the knight (probably Sir Thomas Arden) in alabaster, the lady in grey stone. He wears a 14th-century helmet, and plate armour over a coat of chain mail, at his feet the trunk of a lion or a boar. The lady is probably later by a century; she wears a close bodice and necklace, a high peaked headdress, and a long robe to her feet. If the knight should be Sir Thomas Arden he would be an ancestor of Shakespeare's mother.

An unknown and much-mutilated figure of a knight is at least 400 years old, and close by it is the great tomb of Sir Thomas Erdington, whose son founded a chantry here during the 15th century. His finely sculptured head is bare and rests on a helmet, and at his feet crouches a lion. His wife has a peaked headdress with a cloak thrown open at the neck and fastened with a brooch. Her dress is carved with great delicacy. An alabaster figure facing these is probably her kinsman, Sir William Harcourt; with him are ten angels. In yet another tomb, of immense proportions, lies Sir Edward Devereux, builder of Castle Bromwich Hall, with his wife; they are here in Jacobean dress, with five sons and four daughters, all looking very prim.

In the nave is a monument to Sir Edward Holte of 1592 and his wife, both painted, kneeling at prayer under an arch on Corinthian columns. He wears armour and she has a ruff. Leaning against the west wall when we called was a huge stone from the tomb of the Sir

Thomas Holte who died in 1545. It has a fine group of brasses. The head is missing from that of Sir Thomas, who wears flowing robes, but his wife's portrait, in a very elaborate dress, is complete. Below them are three children, and there are engraved angels in the corner pieces.

A noble monument of white and grey marble to John Frederick Feeney, whose son built the nave and chancel of this fine church, was designed by Sir George Frampton. It has on each side a dainty marble figure of a girl, each holding an ornamental ball adorned with gilded bronze. In gilt, on small heart-shaped tablets below, are the names of nine children. A wonderful piece of ancient sculpture stands near the Devereux tomb, a quaintly carved head of a cross in white stone. It is about three feet high, mounted on a base so that it revolves, showing that each of its four sides has a carving under a trefoil arch. One side shows the Crucifixion, another Mary with the Child in her arms, and the others Peter and Paul.

An interesting window hidden behind the organ is a good example of the painted glass work of Francis Eginton, an 18th-century artist whose story belongs to Handsworth; it is a memorial to Letitia Dearden, showing her borne to heaven by angels.

We cannot leave this engrossing church without pausing to admire the wealth of stone carving in the chancel, the imposing modern pulpit, and the reredos with a moving Ascension scene in deeply carved alabaster. Figures of 32 angels and many saints keep company in the chancel arches; the pulpit rests on marble columns and has figures of saints and patriarchs. Arresting, too, are the east windows filled with singing angels, angels playing harps and pipes, figures of kings and queens, beasts of the jungle and the plain, with men and women toiling in the field, the workshop, and on the sea. We see the giving of the law to Moses, the printing of books, and the painting of pictures, and at the centre of all is Christ enthroned.

The World's Interest in a Village Wedding

ASTON CANTLOW. Here came Shakespeare's father and mother in their happiest hour: it is believed that they were married in this church among the trees overshadowing the small school.

There is a fine old street, a river, traces of a moat and ancient earthworks, a few relics of a castle, and an old Guild House now cottages; but it is not these that we come to see. There is a fine inn with low-raftered rooms and tiny windows, some black-and-white cottages, an old smithy, and an ancient mill; but it is not these we come to see. We come to see this fine church to which one day Mary Arden came from Wilmcote and John Shakespeare from Snitterfield for that union which was to give the world its greatest Englishman.

There are many things here that they would see. They would see the curious stone over the north door on which a figure of the Madonna is crumbling away. They would see the old clock in the tower, one of the oldest in England, the work of a 14th-century blacksmith in this place, and still striking the hour. They would see the fine 15th-century font standing on a stone pillar with carved heads of children. They would see, no doubt, the three chests in the tower, and the ladder that leads to the bells. Perhaps they would see this very pulpit, one of the quaintest in the county, its panels carved with foliage. Some of the country folk who came to see this simple wedding now so famous would sit on these ancient benches, where their eyes would fall, we doubt not, on the wooden candelabra hanging here. The chancel in which they were married has an old barrel roof, the sanctuary being roofed in with blue, picked out with gold stars. There are two tiny chancel gates.

The Eve of Bosworth Field

ATHERSTONE. The Roman legions passed this way, for Atherstone stands on Watling Street, 100 miles from London, Lincoln, or Liverpool, its milestone tells us. Sixty years ago there were found here Roman paving-stones on which marks of chariot wheels were plainly to be seen.

One of the inns here is prouder than its fellows because on the eve of Bosworth Field Henry of Lancaster stayed in it, while Richard of York slept uneasily in Maxstoke Castle not so far away. Before the battle was fought the champion of the White Rose received the sacrament in this church. We may guess where he knelt, for the lofty 14th-century chancel has been restored to its ancient aspect, though much of the church is modern. It experienced many vicissitudes after the reign of Henry the Seventh, and its chancel was converted to a grammar school. Here Obadiah Grew was headmaster. He was a famous man in his day, and father of a famous son, Nehemiah, the founder of English Botany. Obadiah was a man of great versatility and courage. He helped to found the science of vegetable physiology, but is remembered chiefly for the sacrifice he made for his faith. Though an ardent Puritan, he pleaded with Cromwell for the king's life. As vicar of St Michael's at Coventry he was much beloved. When he was 75, blind and decrepit, he was thrown into prison, but in his cell he dictated sermons to shorthand writers so that they were delivered every week to many congregations.

The arches of the central tower make a splendid frame for the beautiful glass in the 15th-century east window, showing the Crucifixion, Peter and Paul, the Annunciation, the Madonna, and Simeon in the Temple. Two other richly coloured windows in the chancel have the women at the tomb, Christ walking to Emmaus, and appearing to his startled Disciples. The west window shows Christ with a great company of angels, saints, martyrs, and bishops; seen from the altar steps, its light gleaming through the dim and spacious nave, the effect is charming.

The milestone which says To London 100 miles, Liverpool 100 miles, Lincoln 100 miles, is more interesting than accurate.

A Weather-Beaten Company

AUSTREY. We think its spire a graceful thing long before we reach the village which hides itself among the trees. The church and the thatched inn share a pretty corner with a 15th-century cross. The church was old when the cross was new, its oldest parts taking us back seven centuries. The clustered pillars of the nave are 13th century, and all this time the tower has stood bearing up its spire, while 40 weather-beaten faces have looked out from its heights. Some exquisite stone fragments from the arch of the old sedilia were lying in a stone coffin when we called. One of the windows has a few bits of 14th-century glass. There is an age-worn font, and an Elizabethan chest with four locks. In the choir are two old bench-ends with oak leaves and acorns. There is an inscription on the organ to a man who every Sunday for 45 years made the church resound with its music.

The Shepherd of His Flock

AVON DASSETT. On a pleasant slope of the Dassett Hills, it has fine old houses and cottages and a view of far horizons. We come up a broad flight of steps to its church, with a tower and spire impressively soaring to the skies. Nearly everything here is new, for the present church is less than a century old, but the tower still has a 14th-century window with ancient glass showing a bishop raising his hand in benediction. Two modern heads of bishops look toward him from the chancel arch.

But older than any bishop here is the priest on his tomb—Hugo, shepherd of this little flock 700 years ago. He lies as his people saw him then, in all his rich robes, one of the finest figures of an early rector in Warwickshire. A hundred years after his funeral they placed over him a canopied recess ornamented with the ballflower of the 14th century, and here he lies for all to see, a scroll in his hand and a bird in the foliage at his feet. Hugo, like St Francis, must have loved the birds.

The Lovely Home of the Ferrers

BADDESLEY CLINTON. It lies hidden in the very heart of Warwickshire, like a jewel. The church has a 15th-century chancel with old timbers in its black-and-white roof, a 15th-century nave with its original roof and clerestory, and a tower with a turret stairway and eight gargoyles.

The tower was built 400 years ago by Nicholas Brome in remorse for having killed a priest; all who come walk over his dust, and we see him as he was in the 16th-century glass of the east window, the greatest treasure in the church. In the middle of this window, glowing with red and blue and gold, are members of the great families here, with scenes of the Crucifixion, St George and the dragon, and St Catherine with her wheel. Kneeling below them is the armoured figure of Nicholas Brome the tower builder, and facing him is Sir Edward Ferrers with his wife Bridget. In the top corner of the window kneels another Edward Ferrers with three sons facing his wife and five daughters. There is a 17th-century screen and an ancient chest, and in the chancel a big canopied altar tomb, richly carved and brightly painted. Here in 1535 they laid Sir Edward Ferrers, the first of 12 generations who were carried from the manor house to this last resting-place.

Almost hidden by trees is the house, with a wide moat that may have been here since Norman times and is crossed by a bridge about 200 years old. As gracious a house as we could wish to find in Old England, it has venerable walls and an embattled gate-tower with all the charm the Tudor builders could give them, mullioned windows, timbered gables, and tall brick chimneys. There is a 15th-century tower and a magnificent oak door enriched with linenfold, studded with nails, still on the ponderous hinges on which it has been swinging to and fro 500 years. The hall has windows glowing with shields, and one of the possessions of the house is the 16th-century brass portrait of a lady (Elizabeth Brome) in a heraldic mantle.

It is said that in the days when the Roman Catholics were being persecuted by the Protestants many priests found a safe hiding-place in a little room below the level of the moat, for the Ferrers were staunch Catholics. The story is told that the priest-hunters arrived while a conference was meeting here and six priests were saved by rushing to hide. But of all the Ferrers who lived here the most notable was Henry, lord of the manor for threescore years and ten; he wrote verses much praised in Elizabeth's day. A man of great culture and a notable antiquarian, he was born in 1549 and was the friend of Sir William Dugdale and old William Camden, entertaining them in his beautiful home and helping them with their histories.

King Richard Stops the Fight

BAGINTON. It has been in our history for ages and it comes into Shakespeare, for here sleeps a friend of Bolingbroke, who set out from Baginton Castle on that day when he was to fight with Mowbray till King Richard stopped the fight and banished both.

It was in September 1398 that Henry Bolingbroke rode out to Coventry to meet the Duke of Norfolk in the lists, before their cousin Richard the Second, who had called them to combat for accusing each other of treason. Shakespeare describes the sequel in immortal language. Fearing and hating the rivals, Richard suspended the combat before either could strike, banishing Bolingbroke for six years and Norfolk for life, leaving old John of Gaunt to solace his fiery son with the thought that exile comes to an end. The lines in which Bolingbroke replies are rounded by the valiant declaration:

> *Then, England's ground, farewell; sweet soil, adieu:*
> *My mother, and my nurse, that bears me yet!*
> *Where'er I wander, boast of this I can,*
> *Though banished, yet a trueborn Englishman.*

The lament of Norfolk is no less moving; he must wander among strangers to whom his English speech will be a foreign tongue, incomprehensible:

> *I am too old to fawn upon a nurse,*
> *Too far in years to be a pupil now;*

What is thy sentence then but speechless death,
Which robs my tongue from breathing native breath?

These green and pleasant ways are but three miles from Coventry, under the sturdy oaks that line the glorious way to Kenilworth. It is full of the beauty of the centuries, and we may be sure that oaks like these were growing in Sir William Bagot's time. He has been lying here 500 years, with a splendid brass on the chancel wall and another of his wife. He has a helmet, long and short swords, three birds on his tunic, and a lion at his feet; she wears a robe and mantle held by red clasps, and has two dogs at her feet. There is rare red and black colour on this brass.

A tiny group of marble figures has a mother and two children with two fanciful companions, one holding a bird. It is in memory of Elen Campion, who was only 20 when she died in 1632; there is also a bust of her sister Elizabeth. They belonged to a family which gave us William Bromley, Speaker of Queen Anne's House of Commons. He sleeps here with his daughter, strikingly beautiful in her flowing robes, and his son is remembered by an appealing figure of a woman sculptured by Flaxman. Massive oak screens guard their tombs. There are heraldic panels of medieval glass, a stone angel on the wall, some crude oak beading, a two-decker pulpit, and a quaint gallery. The priest's doorway is 13th century.

Perhaps the impression we bring away is that of unusualness. It is all unusual as we enter: the deep square window in the chancel, the old pews all round, and the double arcade which divides the nave from the chancel. These arches support the tower, and are still adorned with the painted daisies and trailing stems put there over 500 years ago. Through them we get a delightful peep down the nave.

It is charming outside as well as in. We come to it down the path by the rectory, set on the crest of a gentle fold of land, with the quaint tower and spire rising between nave and chancel. We cannot but be moved by a little corner among the graves enclosed by chains and with a simple wooden cross. It is the village Field of Remembrance for those who did not come back.

We found an enthusiastic band of amateur archaeologists digging in the ruins of Baginton Castle. It was a great place on the edge of a plateau falling steeply down to a river valley and making a natural rampart, a deep moat protecting the other sides. The founda-

Balsall E.P., Meriden R.D., pop. 1691

tions which remain are firmly set on solid rock, and some of the remains have been uncovered, showing walls seven feet thick. Glazed tiles have been found with dragons and lions and the eagle emblem of Leofric, husband of Lady Godiva, on them, and keys and pottery and counters for gaming have been picked up, all these where only traces of a moat had been.

We found steps newly-revealed down which Henry Bolingbroke may have walked, for the castle was built some time in the 14th century, was still standing in the 16th, but in the 17th was a heap of rubbish.

The Leaning Tower of Barcheston

BARCHESTON. A green and tranquil place known to Shakespeare, it has an old mill at the point where the Stour divides Shakespeare's county from Worcestershire. It is linked with Art as well as with Literature, for here was the birth of tapestry weaving in England; it was at Barcheston that William Sheldon set up his looms.

For nearly 700 years its fine little panelled church of grey and gold has been here, and for 500 years the tower has been leaning till now it leans one foot in fifty and looks as if it will fall, though we understand it has not moved for 200 years. In the tower hangs an ancient door, and a solid oak step-ladder still leads up to the rooms above. The rooms are of remarkable interest, two, one above the other, for they are believed to have been the cells of anchorites. Most of the pillars of the nave are leaning like the tower; one of the arcades has a unique corbel of a hand which has been reaching out from the wall for 700 years. Older still is the fine priest's doorway in the chancel, for it was made by the Normans; there is another beautiful doorway in the lean-to porch with a head which has foliage issuing from the mouth.

The impressive possessions of the church are the alabaster figures of William Willington, a rich wool merchant, and his wife. They have lain here since the days before the Spanish Armada, calm and beautiful, seeming to be untouched by the hand of Time. Both have tiny ruffs round their neck and wrists, with hands at prayer. He is in chased armour with a long sword and dagger and a gauntlet by his side; she is in a very dainty dress with a necklet and cross, a girdle, and a pendant. Round the tomb are seven richly dressed daughters with shields, some carrying flowers and some gloves, and near one daughter are six children in swaddling-clothes.

26

There is a beautiful small brass to a man who would preach to the Willingtons, Hugh Humfray; he is shown in his academic robes, with very long hair. A 15th-century priest has his portrait engraved in stone but curiously inset with a diamond panel to a priest of 300 years later, Thomas Taylor. A third parson, Thomas Horton, has his name cut in one of the pillars. On a brass tablet with three bugle-horns is a tribute to a man with the queer name of Flammoch Colburn, who was, we are told, a man of fidelity like that of Theseus, and in military glory surpassed by none. He died in 1664 "to the intense regret of all."

The 14th-century font is richly carved with portraits of Edward the First and his Queen Eleanor, and it has ballflower round the stem and eight heads round the bowl. There are two old benches and an Elizabethan chalice. There is a remarkable curiosity by the path in the churchyard, a stone to Joannes Taylor, who died in 1781 on a day which never was, June 31.

Barcheston comes into Shakespeare with the fat man the poet must have known; and into industrial history with its tapestries.

Shakespeare's Fat Man

SHAKESPEARE lived 10 miles away and must often have been here, for all the experts believe that he gave the fat man of Barcheston a place in Henry the Fourth, where we read of Barson, the local pronunciation of this place. In that comical third scene of Act 5 in the second part of the play, where Falstaff, Justice Shallow, Silence, Bardolph, Davy, and the page are making merry, up comes Pistol, hot from London.

Falstaff: What wind blew you hither, Pistol?
Pistol: Not the ill wind which blows none to good. Sweet knight,
thou art now one of the greatest men in the realm.
Silence: By Our Lady, I think a'be but goodman Puff of Barson.

But in his mock heroics Pistol has news that does suggest greatness for the boasting Falstaff.

Sir John, thy tender lambkin now is king:
Harry the Fifth's the man.

It was the fat man of Barcheston who came into Shakespeare's mind as he was writing this, thinking of something of scorn worthy of the pompous Pistol.

William Sheldon and His Tapestries

WHEN William Sheldon began the making of tapestries in this quiet corner of Warwickshire his motives were such as we should warmly approve today. Great sums of money, said he, were going out of the realm for these commodities, and he saw the opportunity of providing much useful employment for the men of Warwickshire.

He had married the daughter of William Willington, the wealthy wool merchant, who lies in the church, and had acquired the manor with its fine house and mill. It seemed just the place for an industry which would go on for ever. Sheldon began well. He engaged Richard Hickes of Barcheston and sent him on a tour of the Low Countries to study weaving, and when Hickes returned, accompanied by several Flemish weavers, looms were set up at Barcheston and Weston.

Thus began, in the middle of the 16th century, the manufacture of tapestry in England. It was planned on ambitious lines. The looms were to produce "tapestry, arras, moccadoes, carolles, plonketts, grograynes, sayes, and sarges." Sheldon foresaw that the industry would be greatly beneficial to the commonwealth "to trade youth in."

Among his first productions were the quaintly amusing tapestry maps of the English counties which are now so highly treasured; we have seen fine examples in the museum at York and in the Bodleian Library. The tapestries were eagerly bought by people who desired to enrich their homes with them. Horace Walpole bought a number of the maps at a sale for 30 guineas, which he thought "very cheap indeed." He gave three of them to Earl Harcourt, who announced that he would build a Gothic tower at Nuneham to hang them in; but the tower was never built. So much admired were the maps that George the Third invited himself to breakfast with Harcourt "to enable me (he said) to pay due respect to the Venerable Tapestry."

Historically, as well as artistically, the Sheldon tapestry maps have become very valuable. They contained much geographical knowledge. In their tiny pictures of churches a distinction was made between those with spires and those with towers only. Beacons were shown, and so were parks and bridges, stone bridges being distinguished from wood. Pictorially they were the forerunners of our modern Ordnance maps, and as treasures of art they are priceless.

William Sheldon died, but his workshops continued to be hives of a very happy industry. Then, alas, they ceased to exist. The craft of tapestry weaving died out, and it was not until our time that the world was reminded of the Sheldon tapestries by a set of maps of the Midland counties collected from various places and hung at South Kensington. A search was made in old manor houses, and a tapestry of 1595 was unearthed in a servant's bedroom. The house had been altered since they were hung there, and someone had wantonly cut out the tapestry to allow a door to be set in the wall! Since then more tapestries woven at Barcheston have been found. They are particularly delightful because they show little pictures of the countryside, the houses and fields and animals, bear hunts and fox hunts, of those far-off days.

Cottage of Dreams

BARFORD. It is the home of Joseph Arch. Little it may mean to the great world in these days, but much indeed it meant when the old were young. For it was Joseph Arch who put a great hope into the life of those who live on the soil.

He stirred up the agricultural labourer to believe he was a man. He preached to him from the pulpit about his place in life, and he went to Parliament to get a better chance for him. The little cottage where his dreams began stands near the church; surely it is the smallest house in Barford. It has a stone tablet with his name on, and it is still as he left it; even the books he read we found still on the wall near the window where he would sit and read them. In this small house he was born; in it he lived through all his years of fame, even when the Prince of Wales called him his friend; and in its tiny bedroom he died at 93. He sleeps in the shadow of a fine line of yews, with a bronze plaque of a plough on his granite column and a farm just over the wall. The monument was put here by the National Union of Agricultural Workers in memory of the first agricultural labourer to go to Parliament.

Today Joseph Arch's village, in a loop of the Avon near Warwick, is a busy little place. It has a fine bridge of three arches, some timbered cottages, and on its 15th-century tower are marks of gunfire in the Civil War. The church has a fine old door to the belfry, and an ancient chest. Except for the tower the church was made new last century, but it has one very old possession at the foot of the tower

Barstan C. P., menden RD. pop. 322.

outside—the stone figure of a lady who has been here perhaps 600 years. At her feet spring the roots of the ivy which when we called was clothing the tower in a gorgeous green mantle.

The Ploughman Who Told All England

JOSEPH ARCH, like William Cobbett, was early put to work scaring birds in the fields, but he had a mother who encouraged him to read at nights, and a father who taught him to become a skilled farm labourer.

His work took him to various parts of the country, and his independent spirit was outraged by the poverty which seemed to be accepted everywhere as the lot of the agricultural labourer. He saw that the townspeople fared better because of their trade unions, and dreamed of such a thing for the peasants.

Knowing that the world would never listen to an ignorant plough-boy, he set about getting any book his pocket could afford. The good woman he married at 21 helped him in every way, encouraging him to study as his mother had done. Seven children were born to them, but still he managed to find time and a little money for more books, reading late into the night. He started preaching for the Methodists, going the round of the villages and proving a fluent speaker who compelled men to listen. And still about him he saw men toiling early and late for a miserable pittance of 8 or 10 shillings a week and a primitive life in a squalid cottage. He heard news of the organising of labourers in other parts of the country, and one evening in 1872 he called a meeting in the neighbouring village of Wellesbourne. From far and near the labourers came, a little fearful, but ready to follow a leader. Under an old chestnut tree, by the light of candles stuck in its branches, they listened to Joseph Arch.

In Parliament and throughout the country Joseph Arch strove by peaceful means to help the labourers. He was their voice. He transferred unemployed to less congested areas, and after a visit to Canada started emigration schemes to absorb the surplus rural population. His union secured for its members their first Parliamentary vote and became a sufficient power to obtain many improvements. In all grades of society the President was esteemed as an honourable man, sane and dependable. When he was 72 his autobiography was edited by the Countess of Warwick, his very great friend. As his own powers declined the union dwindled, and finally it disappeared, but not before it had achieved a lasting improvement in the status of our farm workers. Joseph Arch himself, for all his 93 years of life and all his energy, was almost as poor when he died in his Barford cottage as he was at the beginning, but he remains a noble figure in the history of social England. We leave him sleeping under the yews, remembering these words which summarise his social creed:

Make a man proud of and interested in his birthplace, make him feel he has a part in it, and you have started him on the road to good citizenship. The right development is from the home to neighbouring homes; then to the homes of the parish, the county, the country, the empire, and the world.

The Home of Shakespeare's Tinker

BARTON-ON-THE-HEATH. Famous indeed it should be, for it has a link with Merrie England and the games it used to play, it has a house built by Inigo Jones, it stands by the Four Shires Stone where Warwick, Worcester, Gloucester, and Oxford counties meet, and it was the home of Shakespeare's Christopher Sly, the tinker.

It was Captain Robert Dover who started the famous Cotswold games in the Cotswold Hills, on what is now called Dover's Hill above Chipping Campden. He was master of the revels, riding a fine horse arrayed in a suit of clothes belonging to the King himself. Ben Jonson was his friend and came to see the games, and it is said Shakespeare rode over from Stratford. There is nothing in the village now to remind us of Captain Dover, but here he died in 1641 and here they buried him.

The Inigo Jones house stands by the church of many gables, on the site of the house which had been here since Magna Carta; it is called Barton House, a splendid building in the Cotswold manor style. Here no doubt lived Edmund Bury. He died in the year the Armada came, and there is a small brass in memory of him with a portrait showing him in close-cropped hair and a pointed beard, with a shield on which three squirrels are cracking nuts.

The doorway of the church, and the chancel arch, are as the Normans left them, and the tower is 13th century. The roof is what we call a saddleback. There is a Jacobean chair, two charming old windows filled with medieval glass, and there is a curious carving of an animal running up the Norman chancel arch—nobody knows why: perhaps it was just the fancy of a mason 800 years ago.

If we were citizens of Barton we should be proudest of all that we came into Shakespeare, and that Shakespeare's cousins the Lamberts lived here. He used his local knowledge in The Taming of the Shrew, where in the mouth of the tinker Barton becomes Burtonheath:

Am not I Christopher Sly, old Sly's son of Burtonheath, by birth a pedlar, by education a cardmaker, by transmutation a bear-herd, and now by present profession a tinker? Ask Marian Hacket, the fat alewife of Wincot, if she know me not.

Marian was the alewife of Shakespeare's mother's village of Wilmcote, in whose alehouse Christopher Sly must have been well known.

The Thirty Men of Baxterley

BAXTERLEY. It lies among Warwickshire's collieries and it is of the perils of the pit that we are thinking in its lonely church among the fields. The gates through which we come to it were set up by a son in memory of his famous father; the father was Sir James Bacon, a judge still vigorous at 88 when he left the Bench after 64 years in the Law. The son Hugh, whose marble portrait is on the wall, preached here for 53 years. There is a Norman chancel arch, another little Norman arch only two feet wide leading into the vestry, and two deep lancet windows seven centuries old. The pinnacled tower speaks of a tragedy, for it was set up by Hugh Glover, son of that Robert Glover of Mancetter who was burned at Coventry in 1555 for being true to his faith.

This small place has the memory of as sad a day as any village can have lived through. It was in May about 50 years ago when an explosion at the pit entombed nine men. A brass plate on the wall tells us the names of two of those men belonging to Baxterley and of 10 who died trying to reach them.

This is the tragic tale of that most bitter day. Spring had come to Baxterley. Its woods were green, the birds were singing, and life seemed good, even to those who had to leave the sun and dive into the gloom of the mine. Then hurrying feet, hoarse shouts, and the news broke through the peace of a May morning like a thunderbolt. Stratford Pit was on fire. Smoke and fumes poured from the pithead, poisoning the air, while 1500 feet below were eight men and a boy with 11 pit ponies. Would they ever see a May morning again?

A rescue party was soon on its way down the shaft, headed by Mr W. S. Dugdale of Merevale Hall, the owner of the pit, and the

Bidford　　　　　　　　　　　　　The Avon and the Church

Rugby
School Chapel

King's Norton
Grammar School

Henley-in-Arden　　　　　　　　　　The Guildhall

Warwick
Guy's Cliffe Mill

Hartshill
The Castle

Chilvers Coton   George Eliot's Birthplace

Barford
Joseph Arch's Cottage

Bidford
The Falcon Inn

manager and his son. Those above waited with nerves taut. Was there a chance that he or he or he might be saved? To their horror they heard below a fearful explosion, then another, and another. All but three of the rescue party managed to get back to safety. Mr Dugdale was not one of them. Somewhere below he was lying dead or injured. In half an hour a second rescue party went down, making their way through dense volumes of smoke, knowing that any moment another explosion might blow them out of this world. A cry for help was heard, and they found Mr Dugdale so seriously injured that it was with the greatest difficulty that they managed to bring him to the top. Again they descended and the two others from the first rescue party were brought up only just alive.

Throughout the afternoon smoke poured from the pit and a heavy pall hung over the village. The men could not rest. They could not leave their comrades trapped while there was any chance of rescuing them. Time after time attempts were made. Time after time rescuers brought back other rescuers so badly burned or gassed that they died in a few minutes. Two men crawled 60 yards to reach another. Of the first victims nothing had been seen or heard, and the death-roll mounted hourly. All night the fire raged. Carbon dioxide poured out in deadly fumes. When day came again it was clear that no one could be alive in that inferno. The mine was sealed and made airtight to extinguish the flames, but it was like stopping a volcano, the rush of gas and smoke forced the seals away.

In Baxterley and the villages round the wealthiest home and the poorest were in mourning. Miners, engineers, members of the pit-head staff, one after the other died. Ten days after the fire began the death-roll was 27; a few days later it had reached 30.

"Have I the people's goodwill?" asked Mr Dugdale, as he lay dying after days of great pain, unable to forget his responsibility as owner of the mine. On being assured that all thought kindly of him he said: "Then I shall die happy, for I am dying for my people." Such was the horror and such the heroism of Baxterley's most tragic May.

A King Rides By

BEARLEY. It spreads itself about a wooded hillside, a little way off the busy Stratford road, and we imagine it must have looked very much like this on that exciting day when Charles the Second rode through the village with Mistress Lane on the pillion, escaping after the Battle of Worcester.

It has little for us to see; a few big farmhouses, thatched and timbered cottages, the manor house with its lovely gardens, and the church on the hill with a 15th-century font and fragments of two Norman doorways, saved when they rebuilt the church last century.

The Old Home Gone

BEAUDESERT. From the long street of Henley-in-Arden we come by a lane to the little river Alne and the great mound of Beaudesert. It was up here that Thurstan de Montfort built a strong castle to overawe the countryside. Its prosperity dwindled after the Battle of Evesham, and only a few ruins, a moat, and part of the courtyard are left of the magnificence of the old castle.

From the mound we can look across the river to the red roofs of Henley and see miles of Warwickshire where the Forest of Arden stood long centuries ago. Below is the church with mellow tiled roof and lovely grey tower and lychgate of ancient oak. The Normans built their church solidly on the foundations of a Saxon church, and much of their work is here today, including an impressive doorway with five mouldings and three shafts each side. But their most impressive work is in the charming chancel with its big finely moulded arch. Three of the windows, including the east window with a pillar on each side and chevron hood, are also Norman, and though the fine vaulted roof is new it rests on Norman pillars with carved capitals.

There is no chancel screen and, stranger still, no pulpit; only once or twice in our 10,000 churches have we missed a pulpit. Among the many saints and angels in glass is St George, sharing a window with St Nicholas, the children's Santa Claus, who quaintly shelters a tubful of children beneath his cloak. Not far off is the rectory where Richard Jago was born in 1715. One of Warwickshire's minor poets, he was the lifelong friend of that other minor poet William Shenstone, with whom he went to school at Solihull.

A Village Boy Wins Fame

BEDWORTH. A thousand years ago it was a hamlet, the 15th century gave it one of the fine churches that were rising then, but Coal has made it into a little town, and, alas, the tower is all that stands of the old church, with a bell that has been ringing since the days of Cromwell. Here there was born, about the time the 18th-century almshouses were built, a Bedworth boy who was to win fame all over Europe, William Hanbury. He was a parson, but it was as a botanist that he grew famous, in the days when botanists made physic gardens for use and study. He gathered seeds and plants from all over the world, and his garden at Church Langton in Leicestershire was one of his monuments. In the church there he lies.

BENTLEY. A high and lonely place, we remember it for its 600 acres of beautiful woods, with lovely ways winding through them. It is lovely at any time of the year, but entrancing when its bluebell carpet is spread. It has a new church as old as the Victorian Era, and one forlorn relic of its past—a wall of grey stone standing solitary in a field. It is all that remains of the old church and has stood more than five hundred years. Very odd it looks with cattle grazing where choirs once sang.

Manlike and Godlike

BERKSWELL. We should come here when spring is passing into summer if we would see a lovely sight, for then the rhododendrons in the park of Berkswell Hall are reflected in the lake, and it is like a dream. But always there is much to see.

There is a forge and a pump, charming white cottages with red roofs, and houses timbered with ancient beams. The stocks are curious for having five holes; it is said they were made to accommodate a perverse old pensioner with a wooden leg and his two boon companions.

We remember the churchyard for what is perhaps a unique remembrance of the men who never came back, a memorial on the lawn by the gate. A tiny chapel, it has an archway on three sides set in window tracery with a vaulted roof, an altar with a Crucifixion in relief on the wall, and in niches on each side the kneeling figures of St Nicholas and St George.

The sturdy medieval tower looking down on it all has a sundial bigger than its clock. It crowns a church with a beautiful exterior, a fine Norman chancel with pillars and arches framing its lancet windows, and a gallery of grotesque heads under the roofs. Most delightful is the porch, with its open tracery sides and a gabled room above a mass of timbering; it shelters a Norman doorway at the top of a small flight of steps.

35

This striking church has something rarely found in a place so small, a noble crypt replacing one the Saxons may have used, perhaps a shrine for sacred relics. It has a splendid Norman arch across the middle with a vaulted roof on both sides, the light filtering through seven lancets. It is possible that one part of the crypt may be Saxon and the other Norman. Along some of the walls are stone seats that have been here 800 years or more.

There are two fine Norman arches in the north arcade; the south arcade is 14th century and has a balcony. There are ancient oak screens in both aisles with hollow cornices finely carved with vines, a fine modern screen to a side chapel, and magnificent choir stalls with poppyheads and figures of four bishops in the ends, among them Wulfstan, Dunstan, and St Chad.

For generations the Eardley-Wilmots have been here. The Norman chancel was their vault and under it are their memorials. One of them brought home from the Crimea a Russian flag with a double-headed eagle on it. It was captured at Kertch and it hangs in the room above the south porch, a room with fine Jacobean timbering.

Here lies that John Eardley-Wilmot who was born under Queen Anne and went to school with Dr Johnson. He loved learning and was a great lawyer, and much has been written of his inflexible spirit and his high dignity. At a slight from Pitt he left the Law, but was recalled to become a Chief Justice. Three times he declined the office of Lord Chancellor. Some of his judgments are masterpieces still. We like him best for that story told of him by a gentleman who had been greatly wronged. "Would it be manly to resent it by a challenge to a duel?" the gentleman asked, and Sir John said, "Yes, certainly it would be manly to resent it, but it would be Godlike to forgive it."

The Treasure Hid in the Chest

BICKENHILL. A village of fine old farms, it has a church with a little treasure of glass almost as old as the Norman walls. It now has its place of honour in a window, but it lay for generations in the dug-out chest about eight feet long—rich and rare 13th-century fragments, one showing three birds pecking berries. The light streaming through the window falls on a greater treasure still, the remarkable stone screen, a piece of workmanship as rare as it is excellent, with sculptured niches and a lovely doorway adorned with heads of a king and queen. A fine timbered roof is a later discovery, found when the plaster was removed.

So this old place has seen discoveries one upon another in glass and wood and stone, all adding to its beauty. The Norman character of the church remains in its north arcade, massive and rude, and in its south doorway; but the tower and the spire, a graceful arch in the chancel, and the font are all 15th century. The arch has two weird grotesques; the font is a mass of carving with eight angels decorating the bowl above its traceried stem.

Our Master Englishman Goes Home to Die

BIDFORD. Its fame will never pass away, for it may be that here the last act of Shakespeare's life began. With the peace of many centuries about it, this small place of stone and timber cottages, an old bridge, bright gardens, and quiet byways that have hardly changed since Shakespeare's day, has drawn pilgrims to it for many generations.

On this bridge Shakespeare must have stood; into this church he must have been. It stands in a retreat of pure loveliness, with a tower rising above a small avenue of limes. The tower is 400 years old. From the top we look down on the bridge where the poet must have looked out to see the loveliness of the Avon and the fair prospect of the distant Cotswolds. The interior of the church is disappointing with the modern nave and aisles, but the chancel takes us back 500 years or more, and has a canopied piscina, a marble bust of Dorothy Skipwith who may have known Shakespeare, and silver plate given by the Duchess Dudley, the pathetic lady of Kenilworth.

It is one of Warwickshire's loveliest bridges that crosses the Avon here. Who does not love to hear the river swirling by these willow beds, under these eight arches, by Bidford's old houses and the grey walls of the churchyard? The parapet we lean against would be old when Shakespeare came this way. Here the charm of the river is almost at its best and it can have changed little since the poet saw it. All about us here is the countryside he knew, the placid flowing river, the bridges and the hamlets, the green meadows and pastures and still waters of his own homeland.

Only a little way off is a ford the Romans used, and about 100 yards away is a place where an ancient people buried their dead.

Over 200 of their graves have been found, and in them were men with shields and spears as if ready to fight again, women with their much-loved ornaments, the earthenware they used in their houses and the weapons they fought with, among them an iron boss for a shield with enrichments of bronze and gold. We have seen them all, these things older than Bidford, in the museum of Shakespeare's birthplace.

It is one of Bidford's corner houses which draws all eyes to it; no eye can pass it without looking, for it was once the Falcon Inn. It has known great changes, for after being an inn it became a workhouse, and then a group of cottages, always keeping its stone-ribbed front and the gables; and when we called the hand of Change was on it once more, for it was for sale again. Always these walls must be Bidford's chief possession, for nothing will ever dispel the legend that it was from the Falcon Inn that Shakespeare reeled home to Stratford to die. Two myths merge to form this incredible story.

The earlier one is that of John Ward, Vicar of Stratford in the reign of Charles the Second, who wrote in his chatterbox diary a bit of local gossip that in the spring of 1616 "Shakespeare, Drayton, and Ben Jonson had a merry meeting, and, it seems, drank too hard, for Shakespeare died of a fever there contracted." The quality of the vicar as a recorder of history may be estimated from the fact that in this same diary he gravely sets down the story that Milton was a Roman Catholic in disguise.

The other drinking story is centred here. It first became current nearly a century and a half after the death of the poet, and is to the effect that in the Falcon he engaged in a prolonged drinking bout with the local topers. In 1762 the innkeeper showed a visitor a crabtree not far off called Shakespeare's Canopy, and repeated a tradition that Shakespeare slept under it following a carousal. The legend gave the village a more than local fame until the crabtree, decayed and tottering, was cut down in 1824.

The blending of these gossipy stories has had the effect of creating a legend that the merry meeting of Shakespeare and his two friends took place here, and that he drank himself into the fever from which he died. There is not a shred of evidence to support this. Shakespeare died in the reign of James the First; the merry meeting was first mentioned two reigns later, and the Falcon revelry in the following century. The ardent spirits from which alcohol poisoning results were not in use in Shakespeare's day. Shakespeare was doubtless often here, but nothing we know from authentic sources hints that he was a heavy drinker. What is probably true is that he may have caught cold here and gone home to die, and that the story of the carousal has grown up round this simple fact.

Shakespeare's Way to His Mother's Cottage

BILLESLEY. A lovely corner of Warwickshire, it has a great house and a little church, and one of the biggest old barns we have seen. It is the great house that is the pride of the village. A splendid Tudor structure, it is near the barn and keeps faith with the centuries, for it has lost little of its graciousness, though added to in our own time. Here are beautiful gardens and a wonderful row of yews which have been clipped to look like windows and doorways. They were perhaps here in Shakespeare's day, and there are those who still believe the poet wrote As You Like It in the library of this manor house.

He must surely have known Billesley Manor, for it is only three miles from Shottery, at the end of a lane by which he would often walk to Mary Arden's cottage at Wilmcote. The house we see today has a fine round-arched doorway, a handsome tiled roof with gables, and charming windows with leaded casements, all said to have been rebuilt by a son of Sir Robert Lee, Lord Mayor of London in the 17th century. He encased the old timber house with stone and enriched the rooms with oak; and some of the locks on the old doors may have been made by one of the German armourers of his day who came to London to repair the armour in the Tower.

Billesley's tiny 17th-century church hides behind an avenue of limes. It was a beautiful place 100 years ago, when the vicar's family from Alveston drew up in their coach on Sundays and a footman served lunch in a pew. Much of the splendour has vanished from the church, but it has been carefully repaired.

The church it replaced has much interest for the Shakespeare pilgrim, for in it Elizabeth Nash, Shakespeare's granddaughter, was married to John Barnard. She was with her mother, Susanna Hall, at New Place when Henrietta Maria came to meet her husband at Kineton, and she would sit listening to Charles Stuart's queen talking of the Civil War and of the pitiful fortunes of the wandering king.

Addison's Only Child

BILTON. Here, in the fine hilltop church, is a pathetic memory of a poet's only child, who was born in this place and died in it after a long and lonely life. At Bilton Hall, so sedate and spacious, its Tudor gables uplifted above its terraced lawns and yew hedges, Addison lived as a country gentleman, the world forgetting, by the world forgot. Here he brought his wife, the Dowager Countess of Warwick, and their initials are on an iron gate in the garden. He planted these cedars. Here was born the child of his later years, his only daughter. She long outlived him, for Addison died while she was yet an infant, and her tablet in the church records that she was buried here in 1797 when she was 80, 78 years after her famous father had been laid to rest in the Poets Corner.

A gossipy contemporary of Addison's Spectator tells us that she inherited her father's memory but none of the discriminating powers of his understanding. With an astounding power of memory she could go on with any part of her father's work or repeat the whole, but was incapable of speaking or writing an intelligible sentence.

The church was old when Addison and his countess sat in the squire's pew, for it was built in the 14th century, and only the east window, the north arcade, and its aisle are modern. A 600-year-old chalice has been found in the churchyard, probably buried with a priest. The altar rails came from Great St Mary's, Cambridge. They are oddly close together, perhaps to prevent dogs from passing through. We have seen church doors with small doors in them for letting dogs out.

Quaint heads grace the doorways of chancel and vestry, and heads of men and a queen adorn the modern sedilia. The font, standing five feet high on its modern base, is finely framed by the tower arch. A window in the north aisle has a collection of old fragments of glass, and another in the sanctuary is filled with a 14th-century medley: heads of men and women, a Crucifixion, a man killing a boar, and shields. The Te Deum east window has the finest modern glass here.

There is a black-and-white house near the church and the fragment of an ancient stone cross on the green.

The Story of the Moated Abbey

BINLEY. It is only a step from its black pits to its green fields, with their view of Coventry's distant spires. Its church has an interior of simplicity and dignity we expect as soon as we know that it was built by the Adam brothers who made for themselves so great a reputation in the 18th century. The doors and the panelling are their work, and the festooning of the curved ceiling, the walls, and the marble pillars which give the church its rare and peculiar charm. There are lovely ovals in the white ceiling with great flower centres, garlands of leaves, and charming plaques. The walls are a delicate green with the same kind of decorating and plaques of romantic scenes standing out in white.

Binley has given England one man of some note, Thomas Wagstaffe, born here in the midst of the Civil War to live into the reign of Queen Anne and to suffer much for his loyalty to our last Stuart King.

This is the nearest village to the famous Combe Abbey, whose gables and mullioned windows and tall chimneys we see from the road. It is the moated Warwickshire home of the Earl of Craven, set in gardens no less lovely than itself, one of those houses which have grown up in England through the centuries, taking to themselves additions Time has moulded to a uniformity of beauty. If we approach it from one side we see the noble doorway flanked by deeply recessed and many-columned window openings which were the work of monks. Four centuries they dwelt here before their lands and abbey passed into the hands of John Dudley, Duke of Northumberland, at the Dissolution of the Monasteries.

After Northumberland had perished on the scaffold the abbey went to Sir John Harington, who built it as an Elizabethan house. So it remained till the days of the last Stuart, when an addition was made which left its appearance little changed. Another builder in the early 18th century gave it the delightful front now reflected in its moat.

The greatest days of the house were those of the Haringtons, when the Princess Elizabeth, who was to become Queen of Bohemia, was brought here entrusted by James the First to Lord Harington's care. She was the Elizabeth of Sir Henry Wotton's poem:

> You meaner beauties of the night,
> That poorly satisfy our eyes
> More by your number than your light,
> You common people of the skies:
> What are you when the moon shall rise?

So, when my mistress shall be seen
In form and beauty of her mind,
By virtue first, then choice, a Queen,
Tell me if she were not designed
The eclipse and glory of her kind.

In the great dining-room are the portraits of the King and Queen of Bohemia, their sons, Prince Rupert and Prince Maurice, Charles Stuart for whom they fought, and William Craven himself.

At Combe Abbey one night in 1605 was interrupted one of the most tense dramas of those days.

King George's Link With King Alfred

PRINCESS ELIZABETH, eldest daughter of James the First, was brought up at Combe Abbey under the affectionate care of Lord and Lady Harington, who made her a thorough little Protestant.

The Gunpowder Plot conspirators assembled at Dunchurch, ostensibly for a hunt but in reality to await news of the destruction of the King and Parliament, whereupon they were to seize Elizabeth and make her Queen. The Haringtons heard of the plot and hurried her to Coventry, where they placed her in the care of the citizens; in any case, the plot was exploded by the failure of Guy Fawkes.

Elizabeth did not become Queen but she did become the dramatic link which brought Stuart blood back to the throne of England. She became a central figure of the terrible Thirty Years War. One of her suitors was the immortal Gustavus Adolphus, but at 17 she married Frederick the Fifth, Elector Palatine, and in 1619 was called with him to the throne of Protestant Bohemia.

She was the Winter Queen of a year and was then driven forth to live in exile 40 years. Although not beautiful, she was a fascinating woman. During her distress 30 members of the Middle Temple swore on their drawn swords to live or die in her service.

Duke Christian of Brunswick loved her and did die for her, and Lord Craven not only helped to finance her abroad during her widowhood but offered her a home when she returned to England. He bought for her Combe Abbey, the scene of her childhood, and was so constant in his devotion that surprise has been caused that among her papers there is no proof that she married him.

Of her 13 children all but one of her daughters turned Roman Catholic, and the exception was remarkably interesting. She was Sophia, through whom the Stuart blood was in the end restored to the throne of England in the person of George the First. But for this the link of our monarchy with King Alfred would have been broken.

The famous Prince Rupert was Elizabeth's favourite son, and 20 years after her burial in Westminster Abbey in 1662 he was laid with her in our national shrine.

Captain Scott's Farewell to England

BINTON. We come to it through some of Warwickshire's stillest lanes, to find a rushing brook making music by the church's old grey walls. The village stands on a little wooded hill and looks far out across the valley of the Avon.

It is all a beautiful piece of England, and we feel that it must ever be, for by this stream there walked, and in this church there sat, a very gallant Englishman. It was one of the last English villages that knew Captain Scott. It was one of the places to which he came before he set out, when he was saying his farewell to England.

He loved the babbling of this little brook. He looked out from here across the Warwickshire Plain. He spent his last country days in England in the most charming house in Binton, the delightful parsonage snugly set among the trees below the church. His brother-in-law was vicar here, and he came to say goodbye before he sailed. Often as he lay in his tent the unspoiled beauty of this little place in the very heart of England must have come to his mind.

Binton remembers him in its west window, which will make its church a place of pilgrimage. As we mount the broad stone steps that bring us to it we walk where many generations have walked before, for the steps led to the ancient church, rebuilt when Scott was a little boy. The window in his memory tells a story boys will thrill to see and read as long as England lasts.

Very impressive it is, in its quiet glowing colours, with the scenes which bring all the gallantry and pity of those tragic days before our eyes. We see Captain Scott and his comrades filled with high spirits, as noble a band of companions as ever came together, saying farewell on their way South to carry the flag to the Pole. We see this little band again in the bitterest of all those bitter hours, when they saw they had been beaten, coming upon the Norwegian flag, realising after their 69 days of marching that Amundsen had been and gone. We see again that most touching of all stories of the annals of the Poles, the walking out into the blizzard of Captain Oates, that very gallant gentleman who gave his life to give a chance of life to Captain

Scott. We see in the last panel the last scene of all—the search party, having come upon the poignant scene of Scott and his comrades in their tent of death, setting up a cairn to mark the resting-place of Scott and Wilson and Little Bowers.

Above all these pathetic scenes is a picture of Christ, and the words, "Greater love hath no man than this," and there are two small panels, one showing the cairn with its wooden cross, the other showing the mast of Scott's last ship, the Terra Nova. Binton has nothing of which it is prouder than this proud and lovely window, paid for by the people of England in memory of England's immortal sons. Below the window is the roll of honour for the Great War Scott did not live to see; the first name on it is his nephew's. The neat oak chancel screen is in memory of Lloyd Bruce, the rector with whom Scott used to stay. There is an Elizabethan chalice exquisitely engraved, a dug-out chest 12 feet long with massive iron bands (one of the longest we have seen), and three stone coffin lids. Carefully treasured in the vestry we found three old coins dug up hereabouts.

An interesting modern window copied from one in the old church shows John Greville and his lady in the dress they wore 500 years ago, he in his heraldic coat and she with a kirtle brightly adorned. He was a knight of the time of Henry the Fifth, and sat in five Parliaments. One panel in the window shows his shield in its original glass; it is the only glass left from the vanished church, except for some fragments lying in the tower when we called.

Entrancing it is on a fine summer's day to linger by this porch with its view of the tree-clad slopes which make Binton like a piece of Wales. An arched yew tree frames our glimpse of the house in which Scott stayed; down the steps by the grave of Lloyd Bruce there is a sundial which may have been here in Greville's time, and a fragment of sculptured stone from the ancient walls.

How many artists have been here with their paints we cannot guess, but the barns and cottages of Binton are in many pictures. We go down the road that leads to the Avon and come to the splendid old bridge leading into Gloucestershire. It looks over one of the rarest stretches of Shakespeare's river, a scene which more than one of our heroes knew and loved, not only Captain Scott, for we may be sure that here many times stood Shakespeare himself, dreaming of this precious isle, this dear, dear land.

A Big Family Comes to Church

BIRDINGBURY. Here there walked about 200 years ago a remarkable rector with a remarkable family. Their Hall is still a gracious place among lovely gardens and fine yews. They came to worship in the church, the father to preach and his 17 children to listen to him: he could always be sure of a congregation. The church has been refashioned since his day, and has a carved chancel screen, a modern east window with the Crucifixion and the Ascension, and a chancel roof with painted angels and stars.

In the churchyard lies the wonderful rector Henry Homer. He sent seven sons to Rugby School, and though he must have been a busy man he found time to write about roads and canals and rivers and enclosed lands, and was far ahead of his time in his views about the development of our highways. He was an old man when he died in 1791, and among his children were three sons who made names for themselves.

Arthur, who died a year after Trafalgar, was a friend of Burke and Fox. Henry, who died in his father's last year and sleeps with him here, was a great scholar and was busy with a splendid edition of Horace when his life was cut short. Philip, the tenth son, a master at Rugby for 37 years, was a scholar and a poet. He was a close friend of Dr Samuel Parr, the famous scholar parson, about whom he wrote a poem with the lines:

> *So good, so bad, so foolish and so wise,*
> *By turns I love thee and by turns despise.*

The Wonderful Home of a Million People

BIRMINGHAM. Second city in the kingdom, home of 1200 trades, she is the cradle of England's industrial greatness, the birthplace of men whose genius changed the world for us.

Strangely varied is the great pageant of the city's story. There is no end to its industry, and we can trace no beginning. Birmingham makes the coins in our pockets and the cars in which we ride. It seems that half the little things we handle every day are from her workshops. She is the most inland city in the kingdom, yet she makes the turbines that drive our ships, our cabins when we sleep at sea are hers, the lighthouses that shine on many coasts are Birmingham-made. There is no corner of the globe in which her products are

45

unknown; do not travellers at the end of the earth pick up small "antiquities" and find that they are made in Birmingham?

Again and again she has seen the making of industrial history. She saw the early successes of the steam-engine, the spinning of cotton without the aid of human hand long before Manchester became the centre of that industry, and she saw a man walking in her streets at night with a flame from a pipe attached to a bag of gas under his arm, just to prove that he could make a light without a wick. As there was a man who used to walk about the streets of London sending wireless signals long before the Wireless Age, so there was a man who walked about the streets of Birmingham with a gas jet alight long before the Age of Gas.

And Birmingham has given us all more precious things than the resources of mechanical skill which flowed from the inventive minds of Watt and Boulton and Murdock.

A great pioneer city, she gave us our first secondary school, our first Children's Court, our first municipal bank, and the first municipal orchestra in any industrial city. Her university was founded by a man who began life by selling penny cakes. Birmingham has one of the finest art galleries in the country, and her people have more parks and open spaces than any other community in the provinces. It is Birmingham's misfortune that it cradled the industrial era at a time when the artistic genius of our people was at its lowest ebb, with the result that there is much that is ugly here; but all this is passing, slowly but surely, and Birmingham has set about the task of making itself a City Beautiful.

Let us run round this wonderful home of a million people, once a little station of the Romans on Icknield Street. The line of the Roman street survives, and keeps its ancient name; it runs through one of the densely populated parts of the city. The Bull Ring is another name from the distant past, and here, by the market hall and the open market, we are at the heart of what is left of Old Birmingham. Bright stalls and busy crowds, the voices of speakers of every creed and party (to whom the Bull Ring is Birmingham's Hyde Park), make this the most animated scene in Birmingham.

At the centre of it all the bronze figure of Nelson looks down, standing by a boat, his arm resting on a great anchor. It is by Westmacott, one of the fashionable sculptors of his day.

Above us soars the dark spire of St Martin's, Birmingham's

mother church. In two niches of the tower are Richard Coeur de Lion, looking over the market of this famous city; in another is St Martin dividing his cloak with the beggar. They are modern, but for six centuries the spire here has turned the thoughts of men to heavenly things. Its gilded weathercock is 200 feet high. Its 12 bells send their melody into some of the meanest streets of Birmingham. Once, from the top of this spire, only green fields met the eye; now we must look miles for the sight of one. Up Deritend, by the side of the church, walked old John Leland, Henry the Eighth's historian, listening as he passed to the clamour from the workshops of Birmingham's smiths and cutlers. Up the same hill one April day rode the troops of Prince Rupert, setting fire to the town which had made swords for the Parliamentary forces.

The church is a dignified and beautiful retreat from the turmoil of the marketplace. The nave, aisles, and chancel, all rebuilt last century, are lit with colour from fine modern windows. The open timber roof of the nave, its massive hammerbeams adorned with shields and angels, is a model of the famous roof of Westminster Hall. Near the entrance are modern screens exquisitely carved with oak leaves and Tudor roses, and here is a cenotaph-like memorial of white stone to the men of the first three Birmingham battalions of the Warwickshire Regiment who fell in the Great War. It is adorned with the regimental symbol, a little antelope gracefully modelled in bronze, and is inscribed with the simple words, To Our Fallen Comrades.

In the chancel lie the most interesting sculptures in Birmingham, three of lords of Birmingham in the 14th and 15th centuries and one of an unknown priest. A splendid figure is Sir William Bermyngham on an altar tomb. He is believed to have been the founder of the church, and wears the ringed mail he doubtless wore in the French wars of Edward the First. Near him lies a 14th-century knight greatly worn; it is said he was beaten down by the feet of window-cleaners when he lay neglected elsewhere in the church.

On the opposite side of the chancel is an imposing alabaster figure in plate armour, with nearly every detail complete. He is probably Sir John Bermyngham, who represented his county in the Parliament of Richard the Second. His head rests on a tilting helmet and his feet on a lion. Near him lies the unknown priest, beautifully carved in alabaster, wearing 15th-century choir habit, with his hands crossed in prayer. In front of the tomb, set between pinnacled buttresses, are seven angels.

The great east window, filled with modern glass, has Christ at its centre and angels above. In the upper part is a fine rose light showing the holy dove surrounded by the fruits of the spirit, and in other panels are six episodes from the parable of the Prodigal Son, the story of the Good Samaritan, the parables of the Sower, the lost piece of silver, the finding of the pearl of great price, the wise virgins, and the Good Shepherd.

In the south transept is a Burne-Jones window, filled with beautiful saints and prophets, a fine little Nativity scene, and 14 angelic children playing musical instruments, all in a harmony of browns, crimsons, and blues. The window was made by William Morris and is a memorial to Mary Ryland.

Glorious with a host of figures in delicate colours is the great west window, the finest in the church. It shows the Last Judgment, with Christ surrounded by seraphim and cherubim, and at the sides the Twelve Apostles. Four angels blow their trumpets to the four corners of the earth, and others hold crowns for the redeemed. In the smaller lights are ancient British saints, and in the tracery are prophets and patriarchs. In the windows of the nave are more fine figures of saints in modern glass; little gems of glowing colour are two small ones showing the Sower and the Good Shepherd.

The modern reredos is of great beauty. Deeply carved in alabaster, it was designed by Mr J. A. Chatwin, the Birmingham architect, and has under exquisite canopies the scene of the Last Supper. On either side are delicately modelled groups of the entry into Jerusalem, the driving-out from the Temple, Gethsemane, and the Betrayal. The beauty of this fine piece of work is greatly heightened by the light falling softly on it from hidden lamps.

Some of the oldest masonry in Birmingham still in its original place is in a window behind the organ, a bit of 13th-century wall which has escaped successive restorations; but the interest in this fragment is greatly lessened now that it has lost its 14th-century painting of St Martin dividing his cloak.

The modern pulpit has sculptured panels showing Christ with Moses and Elias, Peter and Paul; the font has groups of the Baptism, Cornelius the Centurion, Christ blessing children, and the Evangelists.

There is a tablet in the south transept to William Thompson,

The Last of England   By Ford Madox Brown
A Treasure of Birmingham Art Gallery showing the bitter pathos of two
Emigrants driven by hardship from their Homeland

Birmingham

first president of the Wesleyan Conference after the death of John Wesley; it was brought here from St Mary's when that church was demolished. Very grim is another memorial in this south transept, a plaster monument erected in 1612 by William Colmore to the memory of his parents, painted with a skeleton wielding a scythe.

Birmingham needs a new cathedral. It dreams of one which shall be among the architectural glories of our time. But it has in St Philip's a church with a tower and dome and far-seen cross which have been an inspiring sight for over 200 years. It stands on the highest land in the city, among acres of tree-shaded lawns and flower-beds. Very beautiful is this green heart of Birmingham. David Cox loved to paint the tower when the sun's warm light enriched the harmony of its stone; and in the minds of millions it is printed, a thing of beauty. The architect of St Philip's Church was a Warwick-shire man, Thomas Archer, a pupil of Sir John Vanbrugh.

Though much less imposing inside, the church has four great windows which are among the unforgettable possessions of Birming-ham. Here Sir Edward Burne-Jones was baptised, and it may be that in his father's house a few yards away he dreamed of one day enriching the church with these windows. They are among the finest stained glass art of modern times. William Morris bestowed all his skill in making them, and we think of them as a memorial to these two great friends in art.

The west window shows the Last Judgment, and the figures have a marvellous sense of movement. Christ is in a green robe with angels in crimson, and a magnificent figure is sounding the trumpet call of Judgment. In the background is tottering architecture, symbolical of the decay of all earthly things, and below is a group of figures answering the judgment call, in which is a warrior or a king wearing a crimson robe and jewelled headpiece. The middle of the three east windows shows the Ascension, with the Twelve Apostles gazing upward. The north-east window is a Nativity, with the infant Jesus lying on the pebble-strewn floor of a cave. Wonderfully expressed is the radiant face of Mary, and the shepherds and angels are aglow with colour. The south-east window, a masterpiece of design, depicts the Crucifixion, with the two Marys and the young St John, soldiers keeping back the crowd. The windows fill the church with a harmony of colour, though it is a great pity two of the

E

49

windows are half hidden by huge Corinthian columns which support the chancel roof.

The high oak pulpit, the choir stalls adorned with floral work, and the chancel rails and gate of wrought and gilded iron are all modern. The flags flown by H.M.S. Birmingham in the war hang on the walls, and in the churchyard is another dramatic reminder of warfare—an obelisk to Colonel Burnaby, who was killed in the unsuccessful attempt to rescue General Gordon in Khartoum in 1884. Near the porch is a bronze statue of Dr Gore, first Bishop of Birmingham, a grave figure with his pastoral staff.

St Chad's, the Roman Catholic Cathedral, has much fine modern glass and old carving. One of its windows has portraits of four workmen making the glass, one drawing the cartoons, one cutting glass, one painting it, the fourth firing it. A splendid array of small scenes is in a window to the memory of John Hardman, one of the cathedral's principal benefactors; it shows the Garden of Eden, the pillar of light on the Tabernacle, the raising of the Temple of Solomon, and many prophets, saints, and angels; while in one corner is a small portrait of John Hardman in a white cope, kneeling. Three good windows in the baptistry tell the story of St Patrick, and a memorial window to Bishop Walsh depicts the history of Thomas Becket.

In the bishop's throne is some rare 15th-century oak carving from Cologne showing Mary and Jesus and kneeling monks. It has a painted and gilded canopy designed by A. W. Pugin, 30 feet high and running up into finials with crockets and enclosing a carved figure of St Chad. The oak pulpit came from Louvain and is nearly 400 years old; it has on it sitting figures of St Jerome, St Gregory, St Augustine, and St Ambrose. The old oak choir stalls came from the same church and are a little older; they have fine misereres, and on the ends are groups of quaint figures. The rood screen, rich with fine tracery, painted panels, and kneeling angels, is the work of old carvers of Munich, and in the lady chapel is an ancient German oak statue of the Madonna, painted.

Lying on high tombs in the nave are beautifully sculptured figures Bishop Walsh and Bishop Ullathorne, both of white stone and in their robes, with croziers and mitres, under rich canopies.

At the Roman Catholic church of the Oratory Cardinal Newman is for ever remembered, for it was here he spent his last years. There is a white marble bust of him in the courtyard, but he lies under a simple stone cross in the private graveyard of Roman Catholic priests at Rednal, near the Lickey Hills. Most of this Birmingham church was built as a memorial to him, and it is rich with mosaic pictures, in the dome and over the altar, made by Italian craftsmen and showing the coronation of Mary, John the Baptist and John the Evangelist, and other saints and prophets.

A striking feature of this church is the group of marble pillars supporting the roof of the nave. They are 18 feet high and each pillar was made from a solid block of Italian marble; it is said they are the biggest columns in England to be cut from single blocks. The font is an impressive piece of modern work, carved with flowers and leaves in alabaster, with a massive top of wrought copper. On the walls of the nave are scenes from the New Testament in enamel.

Birmingham has over 30 churches near the centre of the city and many more in the suburbs, all built in the last two centuries. Thomas Rickman, the famous architect of the Gothic revival, built St George's in Tower Street, which has an embattled tower with eight pinnacles. St Agatha's, Sparkbrook, has a sculptured frieze by O. E. Collins, a Birmingham artist, of Christ surrounded by soldiers, sailors, and airmen, in memory of men of the district who did not come back. St Augustine's has one of the most graceful spires in Birmingham and a fine west window showing Christ surrounded by angels, prophets, and kings. Here Alfred Gaul, a musician notable in his day, is remembered with an inscription which tells us that he was master of music here from 1868 to 1913, when he joined the choir invisible. A tablet to two brothers who fell in the war tells us that they were the only children of their parents.

St Germain's, one of the newest churches in Birmingham, is one of the few in England begun and completed during the war. It contains some very beautiful enamelled metalwork by a Birmingham craftsman, Kedward Sheldon. The chalice is a copy of the Nettle-combe chalice, the earliest known specimen with an English hall-mark. Beautiful also is the altar in the side chapel of Norwegian green marble, pure tin, and fine wood. St Chrysostom's, Hockley, has a rare possession in a 300-year-old organ, its oak panels beautifully carved with violins, cherubs, and floral work by Grinling Gibbons. It is believed that Handel played on it.

The modern churches at Bournville, Erdington, and Water Orton, the Quaker colleges at Selly Oak, and the old churches at Yardley, Harborne, Handsworth, Moseley, King's Norton, Northfield, Castle Bromwich, and Aston come into the story of those places. The Central Hall in Corporation Street is the principal Wesleyan church, and its great tower, 200 feet high, is the most striking architecture in this part of the city.

Victoria Square, the hub of Birmingham, has much that is of interest. Here is the Council House, a 19th-century classical building, its pediments adorned with sculptured groups of art, science, literature, and commerce. In the centre group Britannia is rewarding figures which symbolise the city's manufactures. Above the entrance is a great mosaic panel with symbolical figures, in a corridor are oil paintings of Birmingham men, and the dome of the Council Chamber is painted with panels representing arts and sciences.

From an island in front of the Council House Edward the Seventh and his mother look down upon the city. The statue of the Queen, the biggest in Birmingham, stands on a huge granite pedestal and is by Sir Thomas Brock, who drew the Britannia on her pennies; the statue has a curious error, for the sculptor forgot to give the Queen her wedding ring. The figure of Edward, by Albert Toft, has under it small bronze groups of Peace, Education, and Progress.

Dominating the whole square is the town hall, now a centenarian. It is in part a copy of the Temple of Jupiter Stator in Rome. The lofty pediment is supported by 42 columns 36 feet high, and the great hall inside is 150 feet long and 65 wide. Here is one of the finest organs in England, and here in 1846 Mendelssohn came to conduct his first performance of Elijah.

From Victoria Square we walk into Chamberlain Square, a little retreat made beautiful by its trees, running water, and white sculptures, the great face of the Art Gallery clock looking down on them. In the centre is a fountain and a monument to Joseph Chamberlain, the famous Empire statesman and one of the creators of modern Birmingham. The monument is of white stone and has four main shafts surmounted by pointed arches, each with a pinnacled gable above it. The spire rises 65 feet and the spaces between the arches are filled with stone panelling and mosaics, one panel being a marble medallion portrait of Mr Chamberlain.

Near the fountain are four statues in white stone, a group of famous Birmingham men. One shows the sitting figure of George

Dawson, a preacher of last century; on the canopy above him are marble portraits of Shakespeare, Bunyan, Cromwell, and Carlyle. Another figure is Joseph Priestley, shown standing, with a sun-glass in his hand. The third is Josiah Mason, who sits benignly within the shadow of the college he endowed, the forerunner of the University. The fourth figure is John Skirrow Wright, the Liberal leader who stepped aside for Chamberlain's first election to Parliament. He died while attending a committee meeting in the Council House.

Two other statues of famous Midland men are in Calthorpe Park, one of Sir Robert Peel and one of Thomas Attwood, founder of the Birmingham Political Union. At Five Ways, in a park near Harborne Road, is a statue of Joseph Sturge, a notable Quaker and a founder of the Anti-Slavery Crusade. His is an imposing statue; he stands with one hand on a Bible, the other raised in an eloquent gesture, and a bronze tablet tells us that

> *He lived to bring freedom to the negro slave,*
> *the vote to British working-men,*
> *and the promise of peace to a war-worn world.*

There are women's figures on either side, one with laurels in her hand and a lamb and a dove symbolising peace; the other with a white child in her arms and a black child with broken fetters at his feet. In the Post Office, which faces Victoria Square, is a lifesize statue of Rowland Hill, introducer of the penny post, who was the son of a Birmingham man; a panel on the pedestal shows a postman delivering a letter to a child.

But perhaps the most interesting statue in the city is James Watt's. The great engineer stands between the town hall and the library, dignified on a high pedestal, with one hand holding compasses and the other on the cylinder of an engine. It is fitting that we need take only a few steps from this monument to the library, where the Boulton and Watt Collection is kept.

To see the relics of James Watt's workroom from his old Birmingham home (destroyed to make room for improvements) we must go to the South Kensington Museum, but here in the library are many fascinating things to reveal to us the inventive genius of Watt, Boulton, Murdock, and other brilliant men of their time. We see many of their drawings and manuscripts. The industrial age is here on paper. Here is a copy of the letters patent granted to Watt for his improvements in the steam engine, with the Great Seal attached. We see the leather basket in which he used to take his lunch to the Soho factory. In a little case is William Murdock's model locomotive of 1784. It is 19 inches long and 14 high, has a steering-wheel of lead, and looks very crude; but it was from this small thing that Murdock built his engines. There are enough exhibits to keep a curious visitor engrossed for a week.

The library itself is one of the best in the provinces. Birmingham spends £70,000 a year on it, and it has a magnificent collection of about a million books. The Shakespeare Library is its special pride and has been called the finest in the world. It contains 25,000 books on Shakespeare in 52 languages. It is constantly being added to, and British consuls and ambassadors everywhere cooperate with the Birmingham Librarian and the Foreign Office in keeping this collection up-to-date with new foreign books on Warwickshire's greatest son. In the room where they are kept are many portraits of Shakespeare. The library has also one of the finest collections of books printed by William Morris at the Kelmscott Press; and there is the Benjamin Stone collection of 30,000 photographs of old customs and buildings. In Margaret Street is another fine library containing 200,000 books, greatly enlarged by the efforts of Joseph Priestley.

Next to the Central Reference Library is the Midland Institute, a centre of musical, scientific, literary, and cultural life for nearly a century. Its older parts were designed by Sir Charles Barry, architect of the Houses of Parliament; and Charles Dickens helped to found it by giving three readings in the town hall in aid of its building fund. Facing the Institute is Queen's College, one of the most dignified buildings in Birmingham, founded in 1828 but made new in our own century. With Mason College it formed the nucleus of the University, the main buildings of which are now at Bournbrook. One of the finest schools in the Midlands is King Edward's Grammar School, founded by Edward the Sixth in 1552; its main building in New Street, with a frontage of 174 feet, was designed by Sir Charles Barry.

A thousand people visit Birmingham's Art Gallery every day. It is the best answer we can give to those who think Birmingham is concerned with only utilitarian things. A magnificent tradition has brought it from almost nothing a few generations ago to the front rank of our great provincial galleries. When the British Art Exhibition was held at Burlington House in 1934 Birmingham lent more pictures than any other gallery outside London, yet its superb collections have been built up without the aid of a penny from the rates. Everything, including the building, has been given or bought by voluntary subscribers. We could spend many days looking at its treasures, and simply to catalogue them would fill a book. On the staircase as we enter is a fresco by Joseph Southall, a Birmingham artist, which has been described by Sir William Rothenstein as the finest work of its kind done in our time. It shows a scene in Corporation Street, Birmingham, and among the figures is John Drinkwater, the poet who began his career in the city.

In the corridor are the famous tapestries of the Holy Grail designed by Burne-Jones and made by William Morris. They are perhaps the finest specimens from the Morris looms. In the extensive jewellery collection is an English medieval ring regarded as probably the most delicate example of 14th-century craftsmanship that has yet come to light. There are splendid collections of sculpture, porcelain, enamels, illustrated books, Venetian glass, old furniture, and costumes, and the museum of firearms is probably the most comprehensive in the world. Among the English sculpture is a 14th-century panel of the Madonna by the alabaster craftsmen of Notts and bronze busts of Joseph Conrad and Rabindranath Tagore by Jacob Epstein.

Admirably displayed in magnificent galleries built from a bequest by Mr John Feeney, the pictures of Birmingham are truly representative of our national art, and the collection has been proudly built up by the citizens themselves.

Here in the native city of Sir Edward Burne-Jones (whom they inspired) is a splendid series by the Pre-Raphaelite Brotherhood, while another native, David Cox, reigns over our finest collection of watercolour paintings outside London. Proserpine and Sir Galahad by Rossetti; the Blind Girl and The Enemy Sowing Tares by Millais; the Two Gentlemen of Verona and the exquisite Finding of the Saviour in the Temple by Holman Hunt, are typical paintings of the Brotherhood, while their mentor, Ford Madox Brown, is represented by The Last of England, the Death of Sir Tristram, and other great works.

A whole room is devoted to Burne-Jones, whose Star of Bethlehem stands out against his series illustrating the Story of Cupid and Pysche in ten pictures and Pygmalion and the Image in another set, as well as a hundred of his designs for stained-glass windows.

Among their great contemporaries are Arthur Hughes, with his Annunciation and Nativity, Sir Lawrence Alma-Tadema with Autumn, J. F. Lewis with Lilium Auratum, Lord Leighton with his bold Condottiere, and G. F. Watts with a portrait tribute to his great friend Burne-Jones.

Portraits and landscapes by the great Masters of the 18th century are Sir Charles Holte by Gainsborough and Lady Holte by Romney, Dr John Thomas by Reynolds and Mrs Hargreaves by Francis Cotes, The Distressed Poet by Hogarth and The Blunt Children by Zoffany, A Study of Clouds by Constable and Lake Nemi by Richard Wilson; while Old Crome, the weaver's son, is represented by the Walnut Tree Walk at Earlham.

Under the inspiration of two enthusiastic Keepers, Sir Whitworth Wallis and Mr Kaines Smith, his successor, the Art Committee have not lagged behind in acquiring modern works. Outstanding examples are: The Watcher by Sir George Clausen, King Feisal and a study of a Canadian Soldier by Augustus John, In Cornwall by A. J. Munnings, The Brown Veil by William Nicholson, The Bridge at Subbiano by Frank Brangwyn, and Blue and Silver by David Muirhead; while Dame Laura Knight, Russell Flint, Lamorna Birch, and Sir John Lavery are represented by characteristic works.

The Watercolour Galleries illustrate the complete development of this essentially English Art from its rise in the 18th century. The collection draws visitors to Birmingham from all over the world, for not only is David Cox here in his infinity variety, but every great artist in this medium is represented by his best works. Girtin and Turner, Copley Fielding and the Cotmans, the Varleys and De Wint are among the earlier colourists, and there is a fine group of drawings by William Blake and his followers Samuel Palmer and Edward Calvert. The later 19th century is represented by Albert Goodwin, Claude Hayes, Frederick Walker, Cecil Lawson, and Edmund Wimperis.

An exquisite study of St Privé by the Frenchman Henri Harpignies brings us to our own century with works by Sargent, James McBey, Charles Sims, Muirhead Bone, Henry Rushbury, C. M. Gere, and Martin Hardie. It is a fine collection, from which we may gather that watercolour painting is not declining in this country.

One of the most impressive corners of the city is what is beautifully called the Hall of Memory, Birmingham's peace memorial. It was built to the memory of nearly 14,000 men who went out to the war

Birmingham   The University

Birmingham   Aston Hall

Birmingham   Town Hall

Birmingham   The Cathedral

The Domed Exterior

The Book on the Altar

Birmingham's Hall of Memory

Birmingham   Joseph Priestley, Joseph Mason, and James Watt

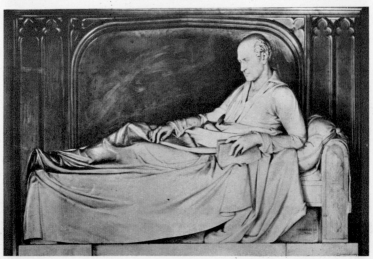

Alcester   Lord Hertford by Chantrey

and did not come back, many of them killed by guns or bullets made in Birmingham. The city spent £24,000 in clearing a few acres of ugliness to build this tribute to her dead. Their names are written on parchment in the Book of Memory, in ink that will not fade. The Book, enshrined in a casket of bronze and glass, took nearly four years to compile. The names are written alphabetically and a page is turned three times a week. It takes just over eight months for this record of Birmingham's sacrifice to be turned. The building is of white stone in Roman Doric style, was planned, built, and adorned by Birmingham men, and contains British stone, French and Italian marble, and Belgian glass. A beam of light shines from the dome every night. At the corners four bronze statues symbolise the Army, the Navy, the Air Force, and the Women's Services; and we do not forget that nine women's names are in the Book.

We enter through fine bronze doors. In an alcove the French tricolour hangs from a bronze branch of a tree, and the flag bears an inscription recording the gratitude of the town of Albert to Birmingham, this being the French town Birmingham adopted during the war. A bronze tablet records the opening of the hall, and round the base of the dome are carvings in stone representing the Call, the Front Line, and the Return.

In Broad Street is the fine home of the Municipal Bank, with a story that is an example to the world. It grew out of the war. The first bank of its kind in the kingdom, it flourished in spite of opposition. It began in a small office; now it has a splendid headquarters and 57 branches. In four years 40,000 people had put savings into it amounting to £747,000, and the Bank has approaching 400,000 accounts with savings amounting to over £15,000,000. The head office is a magnificent building in Portland stone, with imposing loggia, fine doors, lamps, and grilles of bronze, glass panels in the windows symbolising labour, perseverance, commerce, integrity, industry, progress, and finance. In front of the building are wide lawns, and we see in this a step toward the spaciousness and dignity of the new civic centre which is planned for Birmingham. Next to the Bank is the Masonic Hall, with a sculptured frieze telling the story of Freemasonry.

We must take a quick look at the Victoria Law Courts, in Corporation Street, designed by Sir Aston Webb. The great hall, 80 feet long and 40 wide, has a lofty timber-framed roof, and stained windows filled with historic scenes and portraits of famous men. In the great west window of 15 lights are typical Birmingham figures, a screw-maker, brass-founder, goldsmith, armourer, stamper, penmaker, iron-worker, electro-plater, ironfounder, glass-cutter, glass-blower, gun-maker, wiredrawer, watchmaker, and medallist. In the east window are portraits of Shakespeare, William Hutton, William de Bermyng-ham, Edward the Fourth, James Watt, Samuel Johnson, Matthew Boulton, David Cox, Joseph Priestley, John Baskerville, John Ash (a founder of Birmingham Hospital), Josiah Mason, and William Murdock. Inscribed beneath the west window in gold letters are the famous words of Magna Carta :

To none shall Justice be denied,

and under the east window is this line from Chaucer:

Truth is the hiest thing that man may kepe.

In the hospital are many memorials to men of Birmingham who have helped forward the progress of medicine. There is a portrait by Reynolds of Dr Ash, and a bronze tablet by Albert Toft to John Roderick, who gave the hospital £100,000. It shows his portrait flanked by bronze panels symbolising ministration to the sick.

Birmingham's truly old buildings are few. Deritend has one precious symbol of the past standing out above the streets and shops, a timbered house with gables leaning crazily over the pavement, and a quaint little porch. Old John Leland wrote to Henry the Eighth that this was a goodly piece of timber then, and so it is still. Across the road is Deritend's 18th-century church, unlovely successor of a much earlier one which was among the first results of the teaching of John Wycliffe. In a corner of this church is a 19th-century bust of John Rogers, who was born here about 1500, the inscription telling us that he was the first of the noble army of martyrs. He was the friend of William Tyndale.

Deritend lost one of its fine houses of the 15th or 16th century when the Golden Lion Inn was moved to the centre of Cannon Hill Park. There it stands in its new dignity, among trees as it was of old, complete with its 18th-century sign. It has three timbered gables and grouped brick chimneys.

Perhaps the most important suburb of Birmingham is Edgbaston, which has the University, fine Botanical Gardens, a Hall set in the midst of a beautiful estate, and a splendid old church. The Botanical Gardens in Edgbaston are among the most precious of Birmingham's possessions. Over 100 years old, they have perhaps the finest collection of trees and plants outside Kew. The rhododendrons and azaleas make a thrilling sight in early summer, there is a lovely Alpine garden, hothouses with rare orchids, aviaries and lily ponds, an excellent palm-house, and a zoo.

The park of the 18th-century Edgbaston Hall is one of the surprises of Birmingham. Here is forest scenery of the grandest kind, less than two miles from the centre of the city. In gentle slopes adorned with huge trees the land falls to a beautiful lake. Of a wonderful size are the trunks of some of the ancient oaks; they must have been sturdy trees when Birmingham was a hamlet.

The church is full of beautiful things. Here sleep the notable people of Edgbaston—Middlemores, Goughs, and Calthorpes. Two men to whom healing owes much are remembered in marble. A tablet tells of the services to mankind of William Withering, who nearly 200 years ago discovered the properties of digitalis, and was a founder of Birmingham's Hospital; and here is a sculpture of Gabriel Jean Marie de Lys. Exiled in early childhood by the civil troubles which then distracted France, he raised himself, his inscription tells us, to honourable distinction in his adopted country by his services to medicine and by founding the Institution for the Deaf and Dumb.

There are many beautiful windows, the most interesting showing Marjorie Middlemore building the tower of this church in 1486 and Humphrey Middlemore, one of the Roman Catholic martyrs, being led to execution. It was the Middlemores who built the modern timbered roof of the chancel, borne by angels. They look down on a lovely alabaster reredos, with the Last Supper, all its figures delicately carved. A modern window shows Christ receiving the children of the nations.

A peace memorial tablet with the names of the fallen has St George encircled in laurel and roses, with regimental emblems beautifully enamelled. In the lady chapel the screen and the reredos have some of the finest modern work in the county.

Under a white stone cross in the churchyard, a few yards from the tower, sleeps Joseph Henry Shorthouse, who wrote John Inglesant and was long a worshipper here, and close by his grave is a beautiful memorial of stone and bronze to Clorinda Haywood, wife of a Birmingham architect of our time; we remember it for these lines, which few will read unmoved:

Warm summer sun shine kindly here:
Warm summer wind blow softly here:
Green sod above lie light, lie light:
Good-night, Dear Heart: good-night, good-night.

Birmingham University stands on a magnificent site at Edgbaston. Joseph Chamberlain was its first Chancellor and he collected half a million pounds toward its cost. The great clock tower, 325 feet high and seen for miles, is a memorial to him. The buildings, not completed when we called, were designed by Sir Aston Webb. In the vestibule is a marble statue of Edward the Seventh, and in sculptured panels over the north entrance are Plato, Shakespeare, Newton, Beethoven, Virgil, Michael Angelo, Watt, Faraday, and Darwin.

At Ward End, close by the church, is a house in a garden like an oasis in a desert of industrialism. The house, a little over 200 years old, has on the roofs of the wings two queer statues, said to represent two soldiers who were gibbeted for robbery and murder. The church is modern and uninteresting except for the memorial to William Hutton, the Birmingham historian. He wrote poetry and history for half a century and died in 1812 at 93, when they buried him in this churchyard. The memorial has his portrait in white marble, showing us well what manner of man he was, sagacious, firm, and dignified. Below are sculptured books, a quill pen, and a bottle of ink; it is just as if the learned Hutton has paused from his labours to regard us with his penetrating gaze.

The city has 32 parks, 57 recreation grounds, and 19 small open spaces, totalling 3000 acres. It also owns 482 acres of the beautiful Lickey Hills, much of which was given to the city by the Cadburys. From Beacon Hill there it is possible to see into 10 counties on a fine day. From Frankley Beeches, a beautiful hilltop a few miles from the town, given to the National Trust by Mr Barrow Cadbury, we may look to the far horizons of the Wrekin, the Malverns, Clent Hills, Charnwood Forest, the Daventry Hills, the Bredons, and the Cotswolds. So generously equipped is this great city with open spaces; and most of its government is on the same scale of spaciousness.

When we looked round Birmingham on our tour of England we were told that in 13 years the city had built 30,000 houses and many new residential estates, and was planning for the construction of miles of wooded boulevards along two rivers, with boating pools and still more parks. Millions of pounds were being spent on a new civic centre, and Birmingham was dreaming of becoming the best-designed city in the kingdom. It should not be forgotten that the British Industries Fair had its origin in the city and is held every year in Birmingham as well as in London. The heavy industries at Castle Bromwich attract buyers from all over the world, and the frontages of exhibition stands there extend for nearly 12 miles.

The Poet and His Brother

BISHOP'S TACHBROOK. A poet's brother and a poet's wife are remembered in its 13th-century church. It has a Norman doorway now filled in and a Norman font recovered from a farm. There are graceful 13th-century arches, a roof with ancient beams, and two chairs with 15th-century tracery. Monuments of the Wagstaffes go back to Jacobean days, one telling us of a John Wagstaffe who left the memory of a jovial life, for "his religion did not make him unsociable, nor his mirth irreligious." Combe Wagstaffe has a 17th-century marble monument soaring to the chancel roof, and Thomas has an 18th-century sculpture with four weeping cherubs and two others with trumpets. A tablet of 1670 tells us that old John Rous, lying under the chancel, was one of the burgesses of Warwick in the Convention which restored the Stuarts.

In this charming place lived Walter Savage Landor as a boy, and the church has an inscription to him. In the nave are the engraved stones of the family vaults. It was of his brother Robert who lies in one of them that the "unsubduable old Roman," as Carlyle called him, wrote this epitaph:

> There are who guide the erring, tend the sick,
> Nor frown the starving from a half-closed door;
> But none beside my brother, none beside,
> In stall thick-littered or on mitred throne
> Gives the more needy all the church gives him.

There is a gallery of pictures in modern glass, among them charming figures of Ruth and Boaz in the cornfield, doubting Thomas in rich red robes, angels and shepherds, Christ appearing to Mary in the garden, and the Good Samaritan. The east window, in gem-like lustre, shows the Resurrection with the Roman soldiers waking startled. It is in memory of Charles Kingsley's wife. She loved this church when she lived at a house called The Grove, the old home of the Wagstaffes, where she died, being taken to rest with her husband by their old Hampshire home at Eversley.

Bevton C.P., Stratford R.D., pop. 182

One of the Happiest Places in the World

BOURNVILLE. It has surely the most contented community in England, nearly 8000 people living and working in conditions which make it one of the most visited and most remembered places in England.

The streets of Birmingham have crept up to its borders, but in Bournville are the love and beauty of green ways, gardens and banks where bulbs are like the stars for multitude in spring, and bright houses half-lost among leafy boughs, where all may hear the carillon ringing on the hill. Set amid wide lawns and trees the factory rises, good to look upon and without a trace of smoke.

In the heart of it all is the cottage garden with the pear tree George and Richard Cadbury knew when they brought their workers here from the grime of Birmingham a generation since; and marvellous changes this pear tree has seen! It was blossoming when Bournville Lane knew only the ringing feet of horses; now the road is lined every summer day with motor-coaches from all parts of England. From this garden, in the early days, flowers were sent to Manchester market to convince the doubting merchants of the North that Cadbury's was indeed a factory in a garden. It is one of the most treasured spots in this most treasured place.

As we look round this factory with its great modern organisation, we think of John Cadbury who about 100 years ago made his cocoa and chocolate with pestle and mortar in his Birmingham warehouse. We think of the days when women workers were escorted home at night by men with lanterns.

It is a happy place, from which all who come take pleasant memories home with them. Well may we wonder if it can be true that old John Cadbury's sons almost starved themselves, and went without their morning papers, to put their pennies into this bold venture. They lost thousands of pounds before they succeeded; today their success is measured in thousands of happy lives, in the spreading of culture in a hundred ways.

Fascinating are the many processes we see at work here, yet more fascinating is the thought of the vision that has gone to the making of Bournville. Everyone under 18 spends a day a week at a continuation school, and for older workers there are classes in schools and colleges. There is a splendid group of buildings with a gymnasium and swimming-baths, fine rest rooms, a spacious concert hall, one of the best equipped theatres in Birmingham, and 200 acres of playing-fields and parks. There are social clubs of many kinds. There is a profit-sharing scheme which gives back to the workers a share of the harvest of good years. Representatives of the workers sit on the Works Council, and all are encouraged to promote the well-being of this vast organisation which they serve. For noticing a loose brick in the building a boy will get half-a-crown; for suggesting some device to make work easier and more efficient a man may receive £100.

George Cadbury lived to see his years crowned with this great success; we remember his pride as he took us round in the olden days. Here he came dreaming dreams and seeing visions, but no more practical-minded dreamer ever lived. In 1895 he began to build this Bournville village, his "small contribution to the solution of a great problem," the problem of housing large industrial communities. He bought a few hundred acres, built a few hundred houses, and handed over the whole of the property to the Bournville Trust on behalf of the nation. He laid it down that the houses were not to be crowded together, that each was to occupy not more than a quarter of its own site, that new parts of the factory were not to occupy more than a fifteenth of any developed area, that a tenth of the land should be devoted to recreation grounds, and that roads should be planted with trees. That was his dream.

Today there are 2000 houses and Bournville remains a shining example to the world. There is not a dull spot in the whole of it. Every bit of land has been made to yield its contribution of beauty: corners, banks, and sloping sites have been dotted with flowers and trees. The gain in health has been remarkable. When measurements of Bournville children and those from a crowded Birmingham area were taken it was shown that Bournville children were from four to nine pounds heavier and from two to four inches taller.

At the centre of the village green is the resthouse given by the Cadbury workpeople to mark the silver wedding of the founder. Opposite are the elementary schools and Ruskin Hall, the school of arts and crafts, and it would be hard to find a more charming group of buildings. In the tower is the carillon, one of the finest in the country, containing 42 bells, the largest weighing two tons and the smallest 15 pounds. Recitals are given all through the summer. On the opposite side is Bournville Church, charming and with a wonderful simplicity, the most striking features being the great capitals of the columns, elaborately carved with flowers and birds. The chancel and the baptistry are paved with marble.

Facing the green is the delightful Meeting House of the Society of Friends, with a bronze bust of George Cadbury looking out over the green he loved so well. His spirit lives in all that is around us here. The very flowers should bloom more brightly near him.

There are two rare old manor houses, both brought from other places and rebuilt. One is a 14th-century building from Selly Oak, a graceful place to look on with its harmony of mellow gables and black-and-white walls, containing old furniture and pewter and a fine open hearth with all the fittings as they were in olden days. The other came from Minworth Greaves, and its heavy timbers are probably 700 years old. The huge uprights are in one piece from ground to roof, and the whole building is a most interesting example of early timber work. Inside is an oak table 22 feet long.

Nor must we forget the fine fountain before the terrace of the dining-rooms. It was given to the firm by their workpeople to celebrate 100 years of happiness and goodwill. The work of a Birmingham sculptor, William Bloye, the fountain has a classical figure of Youth in bronze, with a lyre and a coronal of palms, supported by a bowl from which water pours through four heads into a lily-pool. An inscription round the outer rim records the occasion of the gift, and another reminds youth of the passing of the years with the line:

One Hundred Times the Swallows to the Eaves.

Thus we may think how each year of progress in this famous firm has come like a flight of summer birds. The area round the pool is paved with blue and brown stone, and a hedge of yew trees encloses the whole, stone seats and all.

Those who see Bournville in spring will bring away a precious memory of millions of flowers; those who come at any time will remember it as one of the happiest places in the world.

The Little Traveller

BOURTON-ON-DUNSMORE. Many travellers have trod the road across Dunsmore Heath which passes the mellow thatched houses here, and one small traveller is remembered in its church little Amelia Venour, who was born in the East Indies but passed this way and has a memorial which tells us that she was an intelligent and amiable child, who had seen eight summers when her short life journey ended.

The 13th-century church in which this little traveller lies has been made new but preserves much that is old. The stone figure of a lady in a gown and wimple has been here about 600 years, the massive arcaded font is 15th century, and the roof has ancient beams. The pulpit with a desk below is of Shakespeare's day, one of those which fits both parson and clerk, a kind of accommodation brought in by the Reformation.

Bourton Hall, handsome and modern, has from its noble park a wide view of the countryside, and has its own chapel.

Thirty-Seven Dear Children

BRAILES. Upper Brailes has old stone cottages with thatched roofs and an earthwork from the Long Ago; Lower Brailes has a 14th-century church which the people like to think of as a small cathedral. Its splendid tower, with an embattled parapet and pinnacles, rises 120 feet, one of the finest in Shakespeare's county.

One of the oldest relics in this ancient place is a stone figure brought indoors from a churchyard tomb. The winds and rains of centuries have worn it away, and it has lost all recognition, but at its feet is still the figure of an animal they set there, perhaps five centuries ago. Poor indeed are now the proud man and his lion.

The porch has beautiful windows, old stone seats, a heavily timbered roof, and a sundial on the imposing arch. A gallery of sculpture graces the outside walls, the parapet of the south aisle being a mass of carving. There are flowers, great gargoyles, animals and strange men, one with three faces, one blowing a horn, others as solemn as a judge. Inside the nave are 18 corbel heads, among them curly-haired women and grinning faces.

The church treasures two ancient chests, one a remarkable piece of 15th-century work. It reminds us of the fine Flemish chests of that day and has magnificent tracery and roses, among which we noticed a two-headed eagle, a dragon, and two faces with their tongues out. The 14th-century font is very beautiful with eight panels of tracery and ballflowers trailing round it. The chancel is paved with 17th-century tombstones, some over the graves of a family from which came the first Roman Catholic bishop in England

F

after the Reformation. He was William Bishop, who was born at the house now on the farm, next to the Roman Catholic chapel. The house is interesting for its ingenious hiding-place in the attic floors. It must have been well used, for the house of the Bishops was constantly raided. In the chapel are 16th and 17th-century vestments given by the Sheldons of tapestry-weaving fame. Here lived Edward Sheldon, and it is recorded that as late as 1834 a man was hanged for setting fire to 13 of his hayricks.

An Elizabethan scholar is remembered in a monument above a tomb of black marble, with a small shelf holding a heap of books; he was Richard Davies, and we read these quaint lines of him:

> *Though dead he be yet lives his fame,*
> *Like rose in June so smells his name;*
> *Rejoice we at his change, not faint;*
> *Death killed a man but made a saint.*

The 15th-century clerestory has 12 windows on each side and there are many other splendid windows, some with good modern glass; notable among them is a sower with a red cloak flying in the breeze. There is a window by the magnificent arch of the tower showing Christ receiving children, and it must bring tears to the eyes of the old folk of Brailes when they see it. For this window is here in memory of "37 dear children" who died in this village about 60 years ago during an epidemic of diphtheria. It was in the days before science had conquered diphtheria, when doctors dreaded it like the plague, and these 37 little ones sickened and died with appalling suddenness.

This village was probably the home of a man whose portrait peers out at us from the pages of two 13th-century manuscripts.

A Man Well Pleased With His Work

HIS name was William de Brailes, one of the only two names known today of the many English artists responsible for our exquisite 13th-century illuminated manuscripts. The other is Matthew Paris.

Only a few years ago six pictures drawn on six leaves by this craftsman from Brailes were bought for £3500 by the National Art Collections Fund and presented to the Fitzwilliam Museum at Cambridge, whose Director was the first to discover the artist's signature and portrait tucked away in a corner of the picture of the

Last Judgment. Here we may see him as a tiny figure with shaven head being pulled out of the flames of Hell by Michael.

The other illustrations show the Fall of the Angels, the story of Adam and Eve, the Tree of Jesse, and the tale of Theophilus, who sold his soul to the Devil, repented, and was saved. All of them are carried out in that dramatic lively style which makes experts feel they would recognise a William de Brailes drawing anywhere. It is thought that besides illustrating books he made designs for rich embroideries, and there is in existence a fine cope of this period with embroidery suggesting that he must have had a hand in the design.

The other portrait we have of him is in a Book of Hours, now in a private collection. Here he not only painted himself but wrote proudly underneath that it was *W. de Brail qui me depeint*. Certainly he was proud of his work, and he had a right to be, for it is brilliant and spirited and the centuries have scarcely dimmed its colours. He must have been one of the most famous artists of Medieval England.

Thomas the Woodcutter

BRINKLOW. The Mowbrays had a castle here, but nothing of it remains except the mound crowned with elms. From the top of it we see Edgehill, and it is said the Ancient Britons had a camp here before the Romans made their road close by.

Among the gravestones in the churchyard is one to Thomas Bolton, a deaf and dumb woodcutter who was felling trees when George the Third was king, who never heard a sound and never spoke a word, and of him we read:

> He chiefly got his livelihood
> By faggoting and felling wood,
> Till Death, the conqueror of all,
> Gave the feller himself a fall.

On his gravestone is an axe, a tree trunk, and a glove.

The church has come from the 13th, 14th, and 15th centuries. From Tudor days came the good west doorway of the tower and the carved oak front of the north porch. Indoors is a great surprise, for the floor climbs uphill 12 feet from west to east, the graceful arcades growing gradually shorter. The old rood stairway is here with a tiny window and three doorways. Tucked away in the aisle windows are fragments of glass in which we noticed a proud peacock, two small birds, two chalices, and a man's head in black and gold. But it is the modern west window which draws us to it, with over 100 figures in glowing colours. The window shows Christ in glory with a host of saints and angels, and below is the Last Judgment, a scene often found in medieval wall paintings but rarely in glass. Here St Michael is weighing a soul and the dead are rising from their graves.

Two miles from Brinklow is the stately house of Newbold Revel, made new 250 years ago, but two centuries before that the home of one who was for centuries the mystery man of literature. It was at Newbold Revel that Sir Thomas Malory translated the Morte d'Arthur into noble English prose.

The Mystery Man of Literature

FOR centuries scholars sought to track down the Thomas Malory who translated the Morte d'Arthur into English 450 years ago. All they knew about him was that Caxton said this book which he printed was "reduced into englysshe by Syr Thomas Malory Knight" in the ninth year of the reign of Edward the Fourth, and was printed 16 years later in 1486.

It seemed as if we could never know anything more definite about the author, for three families of Malory flourished in the 15th century, and all had a liking for the name of Thomas. The author of one of the most famous books in the English language might have been any one of these Thomas Malorys. But one scholar, Professor Kittredge, felt sure that the writer of the Morte had been in prison, because of a vivid passage on the horrors of imprisonment which fitted very well into the story but was not to be found in the original French, and because of a footnote to Book 7:

I pray you all that redyth this tale to pray for hym that this wrote that God send hym good deliverance sone and hastely. Amen.

Deliverance from sickness or from the cares of mortal life might have been Malory's desire, but we know now that Professor Kittredge was right in guessing that it was deliverance from prison. The mystery has been solved.

In the summer of 1934 someone found by chance a manuscript of the Morte d'Arthur in the Fellows Library in Winchester College. How it came to be overlooked before is another mystery. There is no other manuscript of the work known. By the watermark and other indications its date is fixed between 1470 and 1480. It is believed to be, not Malory's manuscript, but a copy of it made before Caxton printed the story, and it *contains things Caxton left out.* The most important of them comes at the end of the part which Caxton calls Book 4, and it runs:

And this booke endyth where as Sir Launcelot and Sir Tristrams com to courte. Who that woll make any more lette him seke other bookis of Kyng Arthure or of Sir Launcelot or Sir Tristrams. For this was drawyn by a knight presoner Sir Thomas Malleore that God sende hym good recover. Amen.

That is how we know Malory was a prisoner, and that the Morte, like Pilgrim's Progress, was made in prison; and, knowing this, we also know which Thomas Malory was the author.

He was Brinklow's neighbour, the lord of Newbold Revel, who succeeded his father about 1433, after serving for some time in the retinue of the Earl of Warwick. He became M.P. for Warwickshire, but was arrested in 1451 and again the next year because of the part he took in the Wars of the Roses. It seemed as though his prayer remained unanswered and he was still in prison when he died, for in 1470 he was buried in Grey Friars near Newgate. That is all we know of him, save that his grandson inherited Newbold Revel; but at least the author of the Morte is no longer a splendid shadow, but a real man, who saw service with the Earl of Warwick, who loved his country and his home and strove to serve them in Parliament and in battle, bravely enduring long imprisonment and turning the solitary hours into a noble book for English literature.

The Grocer Who Founded Rugby

BROWNSOVER. It stands high above where the Avon and the Swift join streams, and has a church with neither tower nor spire. We come to it because Lawrence Sheriff lived here, owning some fruitful acres of the hamlet. He grew up to be rich and famous as a grocer in London in the days when noblemen were not ashamed of being grocers, and he lived and died in Newgate, where he is buried, but first of all he founded Rugby School and left the rent of his parsonage and farm at Brownsover to help to keep it going.

BUBBENHALL. It lies in a quiet bend on the Avon, with some good old houses, a mill, and a simple 13th-century church all keeping company. The timbered porch of the church was new in Shakespeare's last days, but the doorway within it and the simple font are 700 years old.

The church is remarkable for having a triple chancel arch, the side arches having been added in our own time. It faces the ancient arch under the tower, on which are two carved faces among the foliage. There is a modern stone reredos of the Last Supper, with Judas clasping his purse and spilling the salt in his anxiety; and in the windows are St George with his dragon and St Equidius as a blue-robed bishop with an ass at his feet.

BUDBROOKE. The busy railway and the busy road have left its ancient peace unspoiled, and nothing could spoil its grand view of Warwick, with the tower of St Mary's and the castle in the trees. Lofty elms shelter the pleasant church, which has a filled-in Norman doorway with a shaft each side, an embattled tower of the 17th century, and a richly studded old oak door. There are two stone heads by the 13th-century chancel arch, one wearing a mitre and the other a crown, companions in a long vigil.

A 17th-century marble monument to Rowland Dormer has two high columns, with a winged angel head on each side and two long trumpets above the canopy. His old home, which Queen Elizabeth gave to Robert Dudley, is in a wooded park not far away.

Artists of the Village

BULKINGTON. It is a rambling place with winding roads, groups of bright new houses, and old cottages. The church, with a fine tower, has an old friend growing up beside it, a perfectly shaped yew perhaps 500 years old.

There are 10 arches in the spacious nave, with 12 stone faces. There is a very old recess, perhaps a founder's tomb, and near it an aumbry with sculptured ivy leaves. The east window has modern glass with Evangelists and fine figures of Abraham, Moses, David, and Elijah, all rich in colour.

The nave has box pews about 200 years old, and there is much work by an amateur sculptor of the 18th century, Richard Hayward, who lived at the hall and loved this place. The memorial he made to his father and mother is here, showing a woman sitting by a temple overthrown, and fixed to the chancel wall is the top of an altar table he made, inset with a carving of the Last Supper. But his masterpiece is the marble font, something like a Grecian vase, standing on a base said to have been brought from a temple at Rome. On it are women in flowing draperies, one at a well with her dog, and children

Burmington C.P., Shipston R.D., pop. 69.

with flowers. Other local artists have enriched this church. The fine head of a young man on the arcade near the pulpit was carved by a 19th-century rector, and the rich carving of flowers and foliage on the reading desk was the work of a village girl.

Queer Things in a Wild Country

BURTON DASSET. We came to this wild country, with bare hills like a bit of Derbyshire's Peak astray, when a long drought was breaking with a raging storm, the heaviest rain for 100 days falling like drum-beats on these great roofs, the lightning playing on some of the most captivating medieval sculptures we have seen.

One of them is tucked away in the corner of the roof, looking like the Big Bad Wolf watching for the old parson to come out of the roodloft doorway below. Others are set as little heads between the arches of the north arcade, one a charming little lady with a dainty wimple, who seems to be weeping, another a man with his lips pouting, and another like a soul in trouble. But most of them are running round the great piers of these Norman arches, three of which are as interesting as any stone columns in the country.

Above their capitals, at the spring of the arches, are curious creatures like horses walking round. Below them are bands of moulding, and under the moulding are all kinds of wild imaginings turned to stone. Sometimes it is the pursuit of one creature by another; sometimes two animals upside down, one with a rope round it; sometimes a strange beast eating, or a sort of tiger fighting a winged animal, both showing their teeth. One of the columns has a most captivating body of a bird with the head of a man and the long tail of a dragon, ending in something grotesque. It is all wonderful.

The church was set by the Normans on the slope of a hill, with the curious result that it climbs up from west to east, and from the tower to the altar are seven groups of steps. Some of the old tiles are still in the floor, both Norman doorways are still here, and the chancel arch comes from the days when the Norman style was passing away and the English style was beginning. There are 10 very simple clerestory windows, an old altar stone in a chapel with five consecration crosses still plain to see, two medieval altar tombs in the chapels, and an elegant sculptured wall monument to John Temple, who died in the same year as Queen Elizabeth and has on his tomb, with a little array of painted shields, a row of Tudor roses.

Bushwood C.P., Warwick R.D. ph. 14

Burton Dasset has a long history, having been a big and prosperous town until the Black Death overwhelmed it. The church has a history, too, for its tower looks out over the battlefield of Edgehill. Keeping company with its windmill is a 16th-century beacon tower from which news was given by fire of the battle, and it is believed locally that during the battle Cromwell climbed to the top of the tower to watch the fighting.

But that is almost news of yesterday compared with the oldest bit of news from Burton Dasset, which is of the burial of 35 skeletons in two long trenches here. They came from some great fight long before the medieval sculptors came this way, before the Normans built these doorways, for they were Saxon warriors.

Close to Burton Dasset, near the Oxfordshire border, is the delightful village of Farnborough, with attractive stone cottages, a winding High Street, a 19th century church with a spire, and a hall in a park of 100 acres. Near the park gates are some venerable walnut trees.

BUTLERS MARSTON. A spacious village with ancient mounds near by, it has a church by an old manor house set in pleasant lawns and gardens. The church has a 15th-century tower with a narrow lofty arch, but the most impressive things are its massive Norman pillars, still bearing the marks of the workmen's tools. The roof is rich in old timber embossed with flowers, the beams held up by four small angels. There is a tiny peephole, a richly panelled Jacobean pulpit and a Jacobean lectern, and a small triptych showing Our Lord talking with the Elders, the Entombment, and the Stoning of Stephen. The neat oak chancel screen, its tracery tipped with roses, is in memory of a recent rector; the cover of the old font, with a dove alighting on top, is in memory of his wife; and an almsbox with an open hand on top is in memory of his daughter.

A Gallant Little Host

CALDECOTE. It is one of the shy villages, for it hides among trees and is a little hard to come by; but how well worth while the journey is! Caldecote has gathered much beauty to itself.

The lane leads to cottages where the world seems to end, but the reward is along the drive through beautiful grounds where the great house and the little church keep company on the lawns. An imposing house it is, its terraced gardens approached from a noble gateway. The house we see belongs to the eve of our own time, but there was a house here when the fair fields of Warwickshire were in the bitter strife of the Civil War. Here came Prince Rupert at the head of his troops to capture Colonel Purefoy. We may well wonder how the course of the war might have differed had he succeeded, but the colonel was elsewhere, and he lived to sign the death warrant of the King. Only George Abbott, his son-in-law, eight men, Mrs Purefoy, and her maids were in the house, and stubbornly they resisted the Royalists. So desperately indeed did the little garrison fight that it is said the pewter was melted down for bullets, but at the last unhappy moment the house was set on fire and its gallant defenders were defeated.

One splendid relic of the house the flames spared to come down to us, the oak door of the hall. We may see it now in the church porch, an eloquent witness of tragic days, for it is pitted with bullet-marks. Happily the bullets did little to mar the remarkable feature of this fine door, its massive hinges, which are believed to have been fashioned by craftsmen of the 13th century. We have not seen in all Warwickshire another example like this. The bottom hinge is long and straight, but the top one, a fine piece of work, has a long central shaft with six scrolls ending in fleur-de-lys. The striking feature about the ironwork is that the scrolls are moulded instead of being flat, with a narrow fillet running along the centre and the sides hollowed out. Such a section could only be obtained by forcing the hot iron into chilled dies, in the way the roses and leaves of the Eleanor grille in Westminster Abbey were made.

In this beautifully cared-for church are the memorials of the Purefoys of Shakespeare's time. In the nave is a monument with a heraldic shield between two columns to the 16th-century Michael Purefoy. In the chancel are three other Purefoys in Elizabethan dress. Francis and William are kneeling together at prayer. Both have short swords and kneel on crimson cushions with gold tassels, their gauntlets behind them, while above them is a raised canopy with two ornamental arches, one large shield, and a row of 14 small ones. It is all very impressive. On the opposite wall is another Michael Purefoy in his armour, he "who lived a bachelor 65 years and so died" in 1627. George Abbott has an alabaster wall monument, with an inscription telling us how "in memorable and unparalleled manner" he defended the house against Rupert's onslaught.

The choir seats have carved heads and panels, and there are three old chairs, a fragment of an ancient screen, and an old painting on wood showing the Descent from the Cross. Twelve angels with books and shields and emblems look down from the modern roofs, and eight more angels keep St Michael and St George company on the reredos. The windows have modern pictures of saints, among them Etheldreda holding Ely Cathedral, and Hilda with her beloved abbey of Whitby. A vestry window has a small figure in 15th-century glass, and in the west window are four charming 15th-century saints, gems of antiquity.

The Old Lady on the King's Balcony

CASTLE BROMWICH. Its mound has lost its Norman castle, and the old church on the hill was made new in the 18th century, built round a 15th-century timber-framed structure much fairer to look upon. For this Queen Anne church is truly not handsome in or out, though ivy softens its formal air. It has tablets and windows to the Bridgemans and the Bradfords, high pews for the people and a higher one for the squire, with panels and shields and Jacobean chairs in it. But most striking is the very fine three-decker pulpit, canopied and enclosed by an oak screen. The outlines of the alabaster Ascension on the reredos are touched with gold.

Almost too high for us to see the horror they portray are little scenes in old foreign glass in a nave window; they show the torture of St Lawrence. Other fragments have sprays of flowers and fruit.

Through fine iron gates in the churchyard we catch a glimpse of the great house, the Jacobean home of the Dowager Countess of Bradford when we called. Here Disraeli loved to come: was he not in love with the two beautiful sisters, Lady Chesterfield and Lady Bradford? Here he came before the last General Election he fought; here he made one of the last appearances of his dazzling career, being at the christening of the son of Lady Newport, the girl friend who was to live to remember him 50 years after his death, and to think of his great days, no doubt, as she stood on the balcony of Buckingham Palace completing three generations of great ladies, herself the Dowager Countess of Bradford, her daughter Dowager Countess of Buccleuch, her granddaughter Lady Alice Scott, Duchess of Gloucester, bride of the King's son.

Disraeli in those happy days walked in these spacious gardens. He would admire the painted ceiling in the house and the magnificent staircase by Louis Laguerre. The red-brick walls of the house have won a myriad tints from the centuries. Over the fine porch are Sir

John Bridgeman's arms with two figures in niches, Peace and Plenty. On the west side of the house are twelve windows for the Twelve Apostles and four gables for the Four Evangelists the door being in the centre of an ancient vine which is cut as a cross.

Here is still the garden house in which Sir John Bridgeman dared a great thing 200 years ago, for he made in it a cold bath, and next to it a room with a fireplace, not only for his grandchildren, but for any grown-up person, and he recommended the friend to whom he wrote of it to ask the doctor and the surgeon their advice about taking a bath in it when it pleased God they might use it in safety! His bath is still here, unused today.

In the valley, where run the two rivers Cole and Tame, are the long low buildings of the British Industries Fair. For two weeks every year Castle Bromwich is one of the most visited spots in the world, with miles of things to look at made in British workshops. The fine old Hall and the younger church stand apart on the hill, and only those who love a gracious scene climb up to their weather-beaten walls.

But perhaps the thought we brought away from Castle Bromwich was of the proud old lady loving her great house and her gardens, defying Time itself in spite of her years, interesting herself in local matters with an earnestness that must shame our younger generation. Who that remembers it can ever forget the glimpse of the Countess on the balcony of Buckingham Palace on the day of the Silver Jubilee, standing there with her granddaughter the Duchess of Gloucester, and with King George, looking on that amazing multitude of people, yet thinking of the days of another England far away, with her friend Disraeli at her side?

A Golden Patch from Italy

CHADSHUNT. We leave the well-wooded road and climb a path to the church, passing the massive base of an ancient cross. There are two simple Norman doorways, and the chancel, although but 200 years old, keeps its plain Norman arch. The font with its border of crude flowers and arcading below is also Norman; and the roof still has some of its ancient beams with a holy lamb and a crowned head among their carvings. A brass shows William Askell in the ruff and gown of Shakespeare's time, kneeling at prayer, and near him is a fragment of stone with an elaborate cross, perhaps the lid of a

13th-century child's coffin. A chapel oddly set in a large bay, and forming one roomy pew for the squire and his family, has 12 panels of 16th-century glass, a golden patch of Biblical scenes brought from an Italian convent.

Mr Justice Shallow in His Armour

CHARLECOTE. We may never know the truth of the tale that all people think of here, for it is not certain that Shakespeare was pillorying Sir Thomas Lucy when he invented Mr Justice Shallow.

The story is that Sir Thomas punished Shakespeare for stealing a deer, and that Shakespeare remembered it all long after and made the lord of Charlecote the butt of the world's laughter for all time. How inimitable is the scene when Justice Shallow, trembling with age, calls on Falstaff to witness to his tales of a boisterous youth, while Falstaff listens half-wearily, yet delighted that here is a goose he will presently pluck.

There is little of Justice Shallow or of the boisterous youth in the alabaster figure in the Lucy Chapel of Charlecote church. He is clad in armour, his bare head resting on a cushion, his hands clasped in prayer, and he looks lovingly at his wife, who is in a gown and cap, with a chain, a locket, and a lace collar.

In the panels in front of them are a boy and a girl, Thomas and Alice Lucy, and facing them on a splendid canopied tomb we see the boy himself in armour, now the second Sir Thomas, kneeling with seven pairs of children all in mourning, their mother kneeling on a cushion apart, wearing a black mantle.

Close by lies the third Sir Thomas with his wife, under a great canopy resting on pillars of black marble. He is in armour, his head excellently modelled, and in truth they are magnificent figures in shining white marble. He has a grave and learned air, and behind him, reminding us that he loved books and had a great library, is a marble panel carved as a bookshelf containing volumes of the classics. He was a friend of the poet Lord Herbert of Cherbury, who was with him when he fought two duels and in a shipwreck on the voyage home. A panel at his feet shows him riding his horse, as if to remind us that he died after a fall from it.

Exquisite is the figure of the third Lady Lucy, her long dress falling in graceful folds about her feet. A chain, marvellous for its intricate carving, rests on her breast, and the lace round her neck, on her sleeves, and in her headdress is superbly wrought. It is good to know that this figure is the work of an English craftsman, an assistant of our famous Nicholas Stone; his name was Schurman.

Leaving the gloom of the Lucy Chapel with its rich treasure, we come upon the first Sir Thomas and his wife again, both richly robed, in a modern window of the nave; he has one arm held protectingly round a deer, and St Leonard is with him.

It was the first Sir Thomas, Shakespeare's Justice Shallow if we are to believe the old tradition, who died in the first summer of the 17th century and was buried with great pomp, the funeral being organised with heraldic ritual by old William Camden, who happened to be in the neighbourhood and bore the dead knight's coat-of-arms to the church.

One of the windows of the nave has figures of St Michael and St George and St Cecilia with her pipes, and the great circular east window has Jesus in the midst with the Apostles about Him; it is delicately beautiful in mauve. There are two fonts, ancient and modern. The old one is from the earlier church of Charlecote, cut by the Normans from a solid stone, severely plain and round. The other is 19th century, carved by John Gibson of Westminster, who is said to have been paid £1000 for this rich arcading with four figures of angels bearing crowns and shields. There is more wonderful carving in the gargoyles and corbels outside and in the richly carved buttresses; some of the gargoyles are extraordinary wild boars.

The village is delightful with red-brick cottages and farm buildings, most of them with jet-black timbers. Not far from the church is one of the few tumbledown gates still left, a gate that falls almost at a touch, so that we can step over it before it leaps back. It is near the gates of the great Charlecote Park, a magnificent setting for a magnificent Tudor House. The park has two gateways, one on the Alveston road with high pillars of ornamental stone and iron gates framing a splendid avenue of limes; the other framing an avenue nearer the village, where the house itself is seen.

We look with a thrill at the great house where lived the man who may have put Shakespeare on his road to fame.

Here Shakespeare Set Out on the Road to Fame

UNLESS tradition lies, Charlecote is the scene of Shakespeare's deer-stealing. Sir Thomas Lucy had rebuilt the house with the detached gatehouse we still see.

The story runs that one night, when he was 21, Shakespeare crept into the park and carried off a deer, being arrested for his offence and imprisoned. Stung by his imprisonment, he avenged himself by writing a scathing poem on Sir Thomas, the first poem he wrote, and he pinned a verse of it on the gatehouse. This further provoked Lucy, and to escape the consequences Shakespeare fled to London, where he held horses outside the theatres in which he was later to gain immortal fame. The deer-stealing story is drawn from four sources during the century in which Shakespeare died, and the poet's biographers believe it to be credible. Deer-stealing once involved the torture and death of the culprit, but the days of frightfulness had passed, and to take a buck was an adventure attracting a high-spirited young fellow.

Until 1931 there existed no doubt that Sir Thomas Lucy unconsciously sat to Shakespeare for his portrait as Justice Shallow, but a brilliant piece of research among State records has brought to light quite a different man who may also be part of Shakespeare's conception of the shallow justice. The new discovery does not challenge the truth of the adventure in the deer-park, and does not destroy the belief that something of Sir Thomas is left in the play.

There is a story that when Shakespeare became famous and returned to Stratford to buy an estate he was welcomed at Charlecote by the new owner, and if so he would know these rooms and many of their treasures. It is a noble house, half hidden from the road by a parapeted gateway with an oriel window above the arch. The gateway brings us to formal gardens surrounded by old walls, and beyond is the magnificent front of the great house with two-storeyed oriels, towers with copper domes, gable after gable, and charming stacks of Tudor chimneys. In front of it is a lake crossed by a charming bridge.

It is said that Elizabeth was flattered that Sir Thomas Lucy built Charlecote in the form of an E, and even in those spacious days she must have been impressed by the character of the great hall, on which Sir Thomas Lucy dressed in black is still looking down from the wall. He has rosettes on his shoes, and about him are his wife and their children, a quaint-looking company.

William Lucy's Canopy

CHERINGTON. It has much that is quaint and much that is lovely in its prim grey church, with a 15th-century tower looking over the valley of the Stour. Under the roof beams are sculptures of long-eared men and strange beasts with human arms, and in many of the windows are birds and heads and shields, foreign Bible pictures, a tiny rural scene, and a saint in green, a charming coloured medley of 16th and 17th-century glass.

The elaborately carved altar table and the reredos with cherubs and texts on the panels are both Jacobean; the chest is 18th century. But the most striking possession is the monument under a lovely canopy, a splendid altar tomb with 10 richly moulded arches, one of the arches having a piscina under it. On the tomb lies a man in a 14th-century tunic and a hood, battered angels at his head, his feet on a vigorous lion. There is no name on this impressive monument, but it is believed to be that of William Lucy, who walked Warwickshire's leafy lanes more than 600 years ago.

Creators of Beautiful Things

CHESTERTON. A rare beauty has this lonely place, little disturbed by the march of time, and it has a thrilling discovery for the artist, for here we meet two men whose names stand for ever among English creators of beautiful things.

Its story begins far back with the Romans, for their earthworks stand on the Fosse Way, and even to this day it all seems as remote as when the Roman invaders trod these hills; the church has one lonely cottage for company among the fields. It is much as it was six centuries ago, with a low tower and an embattled parapet along the nave. The sundial over the porch has an inscription oddly out of keeping with so quiet a place, for where we wish to stay the sundial says, See and be gone about your business.

We stay in spite of it, for there are treasures here. There is a piece of sculptured tabernacle work with three figures under small arches, all facing one way; they may be older than the church itself and are thought to represent the Three Wise Men, whom we see in ancient glass in the chancel. There is a Norman font, and a canopied piscina with its vaulted ceiling meeting in a rose. The roof has sturdy old timbers, and there is a fine screen of Warwickshire oak.

But it is the impressive Peyto tombs that we come to see; a fine Tudor group in which the lords of the manor for generations lie. Under an arch in the nave is Sir William Peyto as Nicholas Stone himself chiselled him in Shakespeare's day. His wife is with him, clothed in a single garment sweeping down from her head, round her shoulders, and ending in a knot.

On another great tomb Humphrey Peyto lies in Elizabethan armour with his head on a helmet and a great lion at his feet, his wife in a long robe and a ruff, with a purse at the end of a long chain, a book in her hand, and at her feet a dog with a red collar. Their 10 small children are at prayer in flowing gowns or in armour, and all with shields; one child is wrapped in a shroud. The base of the tomb is rich with painted shields.

There are big classic monuments with busts of Sir Edward Peyto and his wife; he was lord of the manor in Charles Stuart's day, and he it was who brought to this place one of the greatest architects of his day, the famous Inigo Jones. Inigo must have come into this church to look at Nicholas Stone's monument of Sir William Peyto, for he knew Stone well, having employed him as a master mason for the banqueting-room in Whitehall.

It is the pride of this village today that it has a monument fashioned by Nicholas Stone and a windmill designed by Inigo Jones, though the great architect can little have imagined that the tower he built for Sir Edward Peyto would come to such a use. It was to give Sir Edward a noble view of the countryside, and so it did. It is a landmark for miles around, a round stone building on six arches with a revolving dome roof and four sails.

Past the windmill the road dips to a valley with a watermill, and a charming stone house of Stuart days. The only remnant of the great house Inigo Jones built for the Peytos is a noble red-brick gateway standing alone.

The Birthplace of George Eliot

CHILVERS COTON. George Eliot's sprawling manufacturing village has sprawled still more, till Chilvers Coton is almost one with Nuneaton; yet it has still some of its ancient charm, and especially it has the beautiful Arbury estate where George Eliot was born.

We may think of the church as the last sentinel that refuses to yield, a proud grey witness of the centuries, graciously touched by the hand of Time. The vicarage, small and quaint with its old red walls, had succumbed when we called, holding out till 1936. It was the home of Mr Gilfil of the Love Story, who was vicar here 42 years. One thing we feel, amid so much change that must sadden us, is that even

Bournville   In the Grounds

Maxstoke   The Castle Gateway

Radway

Warwick Castle

Ladbroke

Little Packington

Brailes

Coventry Cathedral

Astley

Towers and Spires of Old Warwickshire

George Eliot would approve the fine new school by the church, a model of what a school should be, with windows down to the ground and bright lawns round it.

The church has been here 600 years and our own time has added to its beauty. One of the chancel windows has rich fragments of glass 500 years old, mixed with modern glass to make up a fine mosaic of patches of colour with pinnacles and fleur-de-lys and small yellow flowers. The old glass came from the east window, which has now modern pictures of two saints and the Crucifixion. The light falls through this rich window on a mosaic reredos with Our Lord against a background of gold, and in front is a fine modern altar table. The pulpit has modern panels of linenfold. There are splendid modern windows in the aisle with a picture of the Sower, a Resurrection scene, and a portrait of Peter, and other pieces of modern crafts-manship are the ironwork of the screen in the tower and of the gates between green marble pillars, guarding the font.

Arbury Hall was the Cheverel Manor of George Eliot's love story of Mr Gilfil, and the grey stone house is still as fine an example of domestic architecture as this part of Warwickshire has to show. Within the outer walls is the Elizabethan house built by Sir Edmund Anderson, a judge. There is an air of magnificence about its battle-mented walls, its tall traceried windows, and its cloistered garden walks. The great porch was built by Christopher Wren, who also designed the stables, above which he put a sundial with the words, Life's but a walking shadow.

The house is full of rare and beautiful things, with portraits by Romney and Lely, and one of the rooms has a fan tracery roof. Its greatest treasure is the oak carving in the chapel, for it is the work of our master carver Grinling Gibbons. Everywhere are cherubim and drapery and strings of fruit in abundance. Here Gibbons must have spent much time, for he made the pulpit too; it is on record that he was paid five pounds for it, ten shillings for a cherubim's head, ten shillings for a string of fruit, and for other things so much a yard. It all seems very cheap for something that has come with so much beauty down the centuries.

It was in the midst of this beautiful Arbury estate, where her father was steward, that Mary Ann Evans was born. Here she learned to love the rural scene which figures in the George Eliot books; these woods and fields were her school before the sterner school of life began. The place where she was born is called South Farm, and a blue granite obelisk has been erected in her memory.

Out of the Jungle

CHURCH LAWFORD. The Avon valley here has grown from a jungle swamp where the elephant, the rhinoceros, and the hyena used to roam. Out of the jungle has come all the loveliness we see.

The treasures of the village are sheltered in its little ivyclad church, standing proudly in a lovely garden churchyard looking across the valley, flowers round its walls and a picture-gallery in its windows. It has been made new in modern times, but the nave arches with their quaint faces have seen the centuries go by.

Much of the oak is fine 17th-century work, the pulpit carved with sea-serpents, the altar rails, the panelled sedilia, and a solid screen. There is a tablet to Thomas Evans, who died four years before Shakespeare, after being for a generation a messenger "attending the Great Seal of England." The ancient font has a charming modern cover carved with a cluster of lilies floating on rippling water, indeed a thing of beauty.

Other lovely things of our own day are the windows. The east window has a host of attractive small figures, showing Christ in glory with 24 richly apparelled saints and patriarchs. Here are Noah and Moses, Isaiah and David, Peter and Paul, and the two Johns; Elizabeth, the two Marys, and Catherine; Lawrence, Stephen, and a beautiful figure of Ambrose. Alban our first English martyr is with his sword, Aidan with his mitre, the Confessor with his ring, Colomba with his staff in one hand and a small church in the other, Jerome in a hat and a red cloak, Augustine carrying a banner, St George, St Chad, and St Benedict in a rich blue robe. Other splendid windows show the child Jesus in the arms of Simeon, the Good Shepherd, golden-tinted Resurrection scenes, a fine figure of St Barnabas, and the Sower with birds flying in his wake.

Pass, Friend

CHURCHOVER. It stands near the Leicestershire border, with many treasures in its ancient church. Much of the building is new, but the tower is 15th century, and the stern faces on the south arcade have watched the generations come and go for 700 years.

There is a Norman font with a 17th-century cover, and part of an ancient stone with a cross set in a wall. The east window has 19th-century glass with Christ enthroned and figures of Justice and Mercy in glowing colours, and another shows Our Lord with Mary Magdalene. Two monuments have come from the 16th century, with fine sculptures of Elizabethan families. One has kneeling figures of two armoured men and their wives and 11 children, all in Elizabethan costume and framed in a great array of shields and rich carving; the other shows a kinsman, Charles Dixwell, with his curly hair, and his wife in flowing gown and long headdress, kneeling at a desk above their five children, a prim and proper family indeed.

On the tragic cross in the churchyard, to the memory of 11 men who never came back to this village, are the words, poignant yet full of comfort, "Pass, friend, all's well."

A Man Who Loved His Fellow Men

CLAVERDON. Winding lanes bring us uphill to sudden views of miles of Warwickshire with the Cotswolds far off. Enshrined in trees, Claverdon has an old forge and a few timbered cottages gently touched by the hand of Time.

Along a charming lane a mile away is what is known as the Stone Building. A stone building it is, a giant house of three storeys, all that is left of one that may have had a touch of grandeur long ago. Built in Shakespeare's day by Thomas Spencer, it is stern to look at, but it was comfortable enough when Thomas lived in it and became renowned for his hospitality. He loved nothing better than entertaining guests in this grand place and showing them round his terraced gardens and his tilting ground.

Thomas Spencer sleeps as grandly as he lived, for though the glory of his home has vanished, his astonishing tomb has a rich canopy with stately columns reaching to the roof. His resting-place has been much restored, although it still has its 15th-century tower, in which is a modern screen with canopied figures of St George and two archangels. The east window has richly coloured modern glass with angels surrounding Christ in glory. Another window has red-winged figures of Justice and Sacrifice, in memory of those who did not come back.

A more modest man than Thomas Spencer shares the shelter of this church, Sir Francis Galton, almost 90 when they brought him here in 1911. He was a pioneer of science who devoted most of his life to thinking out a method whereby human beings could enjoy a fuller and happier life. He was the man who gave the name of Eugenics to the study which has been taken up by social reformers intent on raising human beings to a higher plane. A cousin of Charles Darwin, he was a devoted disciple who applied that master's teaching.

Born near Birmingham in 1822, of Quaker stock, and possessed of ample means, it was not necessary for him to earn his living, but he had an alert and tireless mind and the study of medicine fascinated him. His energy and curiosity made him a traveller, too, and after tours in Europe and the Near East he decided to make a journey of exploration. He chose unknown Damaraland, and won for himself the Gold Medal of the Royal Geographical Society, but his travels exhausted his physique, though they stimulated his mind, and he settled down to devote his life to science.

His first enthusiasm was the science of the weather; he was the originator of the word Anti-Cyclone of which the B.B.C. Announcer is so fond. He worked at Kew, charting the weather, standardised the sextant and added to the value of the chronometer, and was a master of statistics. He measured hundreds of people and tested their strength, sight, taste, smell, and hearing. He invented the Galton Whistle, an instrument used in testing the range of the ear; and he discovered that impressions made by an individual's finger gave the same variations from youth to old age and were distinctive for each individual. He was one of the founders of the finger-print system.

Treasures of the Altar

CLIFFORD CHAMBERS. It would like to have us believe that Shakespeare was born here. Here, it is said, his mother came to live for a while because the plague had come to Stratford; having lost two little ones, it was not likely that the father would risk another, and so he came (they say) to this small place, fine today with a street bordered with grass and planted with trees leading us to its 17th-century manor house.

It is a village Shakespeare would know, and there is much that he would see. He would see the lovely timbered rectory with its two gables, for it was old even then. He must have passed it coming into the church, where he would use the doorway the Normans made soon after the Conqueror came; it has round pillars with scalloped capitals. He would be interested in the dial roughly scratched over the door, with half a dozen rays to show the villagers the time of mass. He might even have touched this font, which the Normans made first and some medieval mason took in later days and, not liking its tub shape, gave it eight sides to be in keeping with the fashion.

There were on the chancel walls in those days the brass portraits of a man in armour and his wife, with their three children; he is Hercules Rainsford, and he died young when Shakespeare was young. Elizabeth's dress is tied tightly at the waist with a bow, and open in front to show her richly embroidered petticoat. Their daughter holds in her arms an infant in swaddling clothes: a rare thing among brasses it is to find a mother holding a baby.

There are three wild birds sitting on the top of a monument on the sanctuary wall, and kneeling below them on a tasseled cushion is a man who may be one of the boys on the Rainsford brass. He is life-size in armour, carved in alabaster with his wife beside him in a ruff and flowing gown. In a panel stand two sons and by them a baby in swaddling clothes with a bib and cap, a quaint little thing.

The pulpit is Jacobean, panelled and beautiful, and the altar has two rare treasures. The chalice of 1494 is one of the oldest we have come upon. It is adorned with a crucifix, tiny crescents, and a sprig of foliage, and has a face of Christ in the centre. In the hall-marks are a tiny leopard's head and the head of a bird. It is the second hall-marked English chalice known, the earliest being at Nettlecombe in Somerset. The second treasure of the altar is a frontal made from the pall used at the funeral of Catherine of Aragon. It has a rich border of gold and silver lace four inches wide.

Back to the Past and Into the Future

CLIFTON-ON-DUNSMORE. A village near the heart of the English-speaking world, it takes us back to the past and leads us into the future. It is near an old and a new thing, the Watling Street along which the Roman legions marched and the great wireless masts of Hillmorton. And here the main stream of the Avon comes into Shakespeare's county.

A bear looks down from the low tower of the 13th-century church, which has lofty arches in the nave and a roof resting on quaint stone heads and still keeping a few ancient beams with bosses of roses and grapes. The fine oak porch with elaborate bargeboard shelters a 13th-century doorway, and the chancel, although its arch is new, keeps some of its original lancets. There is a plain 17th-century chest, a modern pulpit with linenfold, and a striking font which has a cover like the top of a tower and spire. In the chancel is a round lead casket found in a vault not long ago, one of those rare survivals of a heart burial.

Two men Clifton remembers, a historian and a poet. The poet was a friend of Izaak Walton, Christopher Harvey, who has been sleeping in the churchyard since 1663; the historian was Thomas Carte, who spent the first half of the 18th century promising to write a history of England, but seems to have been so busy getting in and out of prison and quarrelling with all sorts of people that he had no time to finish the great thing he meant to do.

A Rich and Impressive Interior

COLESHILL. A matchless bit of Warwickshire; we may come to it a hundred times and find some new thing. The way from Coventry by Stonebridge brings us between delightful woods and past Coleshill Pool, as lovely a stretch of water as one may wish to see. Soon the first old red cottages and the great spire of the church appear, and we are in the town itself, broad, spacious, and dignified. It has a fine medieval bridge with five arches.

In the long main street we pass Father Hudson's Homes, with their handsome modern buildings, and many are the fascinating turnings to explore. One turning has a great surprise, for at the top of the hill. where we turn for the church, a grim relic of the past confronts us—the village stocks, pillory, and whipping-post. Gaunt and black they stand, looking sound enough to receive another victim, and in great contrast with the dignity of the fine Georgian houses looking towards the church. The tower, which has come from the 14th and 15th centuries, has small canopied openings and stone heads; its spire soars to a great height and is conspicuous for miles.

The interior is impressive with the perfect symmetry of its long and lofty nave, windows rich in colour, the clerestory above it all, and two aisles. It seems that nothing has happened here to mar the serenity of the centuries.

The magnificent Norman font is the oldest thing Coleshill has. Nearly five feet high, it is one of the biggest and best pieces of Norman work in England; it has rude sculptures of a Crucifixion scene and figures of saints, all set in Norman arches and little touched by the hand of Time. Each aisle has a sleeping figure of a 14th-century knight, both Clintons. Their legs are crossed and they wear surcoats and chain mail. Hard it is to believe that they have been lying as we see them more than 600 years; one might almost have been done in our time, so neat is his figure, with fleur-de-lys on his shield, a sword at his belt and a dog at his feet.

Very rich is this place in monuments like these. On a high tomb in the chancel lies Simon Digby, who knew the Tower of London in Tudor days, when he was Deputy-Constable there. He wears his armour and has a lion at his feet; his wife is with him dressed like a fashionable lady, with a headdress down to her waist and a lapdog keeping vigil with her down the centuries. It was this Simon Digby who conducted another famous Simon, Sir Simon Mountford, to the Bar to stand his trial as a traitor for supporting Perkin Warbeck in his rebellion after Bosworth Field.

John Digby has been resting his head on a fine helmet since 1558, his wife and their four little ones with him. Sir George Digby lies in armour, with his wife in the stiff gown and ruff of the 16th century, both painted figures, with five children below. On a fourth Digby tomb, with painted shields round the base, are the portraits engraved in alabaster of Reginald Digby and his wife, richly drawn with great detail in 16th-century costume, eight boys and four girls at their feet. On the chancel floor are brasses, one showing Simon Digby's daughter Alice, and one a 16th-century priest in a plain cassock and with a Bible; he is John Fenton. His predecessor, William Abell, who died in 1500, wears mass vestments and holds a chalice.

In the chancel wall is a perfect gem of art—two small canopied recesses with faces no bigger than a baby's hand, very old but looking new. There is fine carving also on the choir stalls, and a carved oak screen in the tower, where we found two old chests. In the north aisle is an old doorway adorned with stags. The great east window has seven lights with the Crucifixion. It is in beautiful colours and adds greatly to the charm of a lovely chancel into which the light streams through the tracery of six 15th-century windows.

COMBROOK. It is worth seeing, if only for its delightful setting. It lies deep in a hollow close by Compton Verney, and a lonely gated road runs steeply from it to the Fosse Way, which seems lonelier still and runs for miles through some of the best of Warwickshire's scenery. There are good thatched cottages, and a little modern church with gabled aisles, an angel at each corner guarding its bell tower. The ancient treasure of the church is the simple bowl of a Norman font, but it uses a modern one.

The Splendour of the Verneys

COMPTON VERNEY. It lies in a quiet valley by the Fosse Way, with a fine house in scenery of unforgettable beauty. Two splendid lakes mirror the trees in its grounds, which have some of the noblest cedars in England. The grounds were laid out by Capability Brown.

Very imposing it is, with an 18th-century facade of grey stone in Italian style. On its site stood the ancient home of the Comptons and Verneys which was given to Alice Perrers, the shame of Edward the Third's last days; she robbed the dying king even of the rings on his fingers.

Till the 18th century a church stood by the edge of the lake nearest the house, and there under the trees sleep some of the Verneys, their memorial stones overgrown by grass. The church was replaced by one nearer the house, set in lovely surroundings, but rather a saddening place to see. Its walls and its roof, with roses in its 21 panels, were designed by the brothers Adam; but they no longer echo with gladsome song and heartfelt prayer. It is not now used. The rare old glass it possessed has been sold to America. It is full of memorials to the Verneys, who were eminent in their day and are now almost forgotten. In the loneliness of this small place they sleep in a silence rarely broken. On a fine tomb lie Sir Richard Verney and his wife, who died on the eve of the Civil War. He is in armour and she in ruff and gown, mantle and veil, both resting on richly embroidered cushions.

There is a 17th-century bust of Sir Greville Verney with hair flowing over his shoulders, under a canopy on Corinthian columns; 18th-century medallions of John Verney, Master of the Rolls, and his wife, and a 19th-century portrait of Henry Peyto.

On the floor are brasses large and small. One of Richard Verney who died in 1527 shows him in armour, another is of his wife in hood and gown, and at their feet are nine sons and five daughters. A beautiful brass shows Anne Oddyngsdale, Richard's sister, in a veil, gown, and petticoat, her hands at prayer. A brass of George Verney shows him in armour with flowing hair, moustache, and tiny beard, as he was in the days before the Armada.

Compton Wynyates   The Wonderful Clipped Yews

The House and Gardens

Oriel Window

Banqueting Hall

The Famous House of Compton Wynyates

Charlecote   **The Gateway**

Charlecote   **From the Deer Park**

Monks Kirby Panel of Basil Feilding's Tomb

Charlecote Sir Thomas Lucy's Son's Monument

Coventry Julian Nethermyll and Family

On the floor of the sanctuary are four great slates engraved with skulls and adorned with heraldic brasses of Verneys long ago.

One of Nature's Secret Places

COMPTON WYNYATES. It lies like a dream in a hollow; to those who can find it in these winding lanes, who catch the first glimpse of it high up among the trees, it is a vision that will never pass away. It is a corner of Tudor England that must be now as it was then, sandwiched between the Stratford roads to Banbury and Oxford, lost in the deep silence of one of Nature's secret places.

There is no other place like it if we think of the house; there is no setting quite like it if we think of the country round this gabled and turreted mansion, with Tudor battlements and twisted chimney-stacks, oriels and dormers, a house by itself, known to every architect, to every antiquary, to every historian. There is no more interesting Tudor house in England, no structure more serenely blended in wood and brick and stone. It is, of course, the Warwickshire home of the Marquis of Northampton.

It stands amid its spacious lawns and all the glory of trimmed yews, with roses, roses everywhere, and the spirit of Father Time walking its many ways. It has known Henry Bluebeard and Queen Elizabeth and James Stuart. It knew the Comptons centuries before they had earldoms and marquisates to keep company with this noble place. Before Magna Carta the Comptons were lords of the manor; before the 15th century was out Edmund Compton built the oldest corner of this house. William Compton was with the King at the Field of the Cloth of Gold, and it is of this William's great-grandson, another William, Earl of Northampton, that the story of the bread-basket elopement is told.

On the porch are the arms of Henry the Eighth and Catherine of Aragon—we see Catherine's castle of Castile, the pomegranate of Granada, and the sheaf of arrows of her mother Isabella. The big doors were there when Henry came, and have curious locks. We see two notches worn in the stone by the chains of the old drawbridge, and two holes in the brickwork on either side into which a great beam of wood was placed in times of emergency.

The porch leads us into a 57-feet square, the heart of peace in this very peaceful place. We pass into the great hall, which rises loftily to the wooden roof. Its treasures are the minstrel galleries and the screens with quaintly carved old panels. One shows the French and English knights at the Battle of Tournay. The timbered ceiling was here in the time of Henry the Seventh, and there is a picture of John Talbot, first Earl of Shrewsbury, which takes us back farther still, for it was he who commanded the English army against Joan of Arc. He fell mortally wounded with his son, and his death is in Shakespeare:

> *Come, come, and lay him in his father's arms;*
> *My spirit can no longer bear these harms.*
> *Soldiers, adieu! I have what I would have,*
> *Now my old arms are young John Talbot's grave.*

The dining-room has a plaster ceiling by Elizabethan craftsmen and is full of pictures of the Comptons. Among them is Henry, who entertained Queen Elizabeth here; James, who fought for Charles at Edgehill; Henry, sixth son of the second Earl of Northampton, who as Bishop of London signed the invitation to William of Orange to assume the English crown; who, with the uniform of his old regiment partly covered by his bishop's robes, rode before William and Mary into Oxford, and afterwards crowned them. We see Sir William Compton whom Cromwell called "that sober young man and godly Cavalier."

The drawing-room has also its Elizabethan ceiling, a chimneypiece and panelling of similar age, and a picture by Giorgione. In the chapel drawing-room is more old panelling and ceiling, a stone fireplace of the 15th century, and a picture of Margaret Tudor, grandmother of Mary Queen of Scots. She is reading a book. In the room where Henry the Eighth slept are his coat-of-arms, and that of Catherine, in ancient glass. There is old Italian carving on the door of the priest's room.

The barracks are still here as when 400 Parliamentary troops slept in them, and the chapel has fragments of glass broken in the Civil War. It shows the Passion, and one of the Comptons with his wife and children at prayer. Most curiously carved are two panels in a screen, one with a row of kings wearing crowns and holding swords, the other showing the devil sitting in the mouth of hell, receiving seven queer figures in short frocks riding strange beasts, each with a little imp behind. It is said to represent the seven deadly sins. On the other side is an Ascension scene, and a stag with gigantic horns.

It is a house full of treasure, full of faces looking serenely and solemnly out of the past. There are hiding-holes, staircases everywhere, panelling with secret places, one room 130 feet long now made into many, a table 23 feet long cut out of one huge elm; and in all there are something like 80 rooms and 275 windows; it is not surprising to learn that many of the windows were bricked up to escape the window tax.

This melancholy chapter might have been worse, for the Lord Northampton of the time sold the contents to pay for a ruinously extravagant election in Northampton, and ordered the house to be pulled down; but good John Berrill, his steward, loved this noble place too well to let it go and did no more than fill the windows up. When the second marquis returned years later he had to explore with a lantern. He found the house dark and dismal, and rain pouring in through the roof, but he set about the restoration with such a will that soon the Comptons were living here again. The lovely gardens were designed and planted on the eve of our own time.

Hard it is to believe, as we walk among the marvellous yews or by the portion of the moat with flowers mirrored in it, that this rare place could ever have been regarded as a danger to the peace of England, but the Commonwealth Parliament issued orders to fill in the moat and destroy the battlements. Soldiers came and pillaged the gilt bed for their commander; they destroyed the church and threw the Compton monuments into the moat.

We walk past a charming dovecot to the church, built on the old site in the year of the Great Fire of London, to see the relics of that pitiful time. Three splendid yews are so old that compared with them the house seems young. They must have been old when the first brick was laid.

The natural wonder of the gardens is in the remarkable group of clipped yews. They are in strange and shapely shapes, one completely bordering a path, and the quaintest of all being in the form of an odd little man in a top hat and a lizard-like creature creeping over a great ball.

The church is plain, rather bare, a little forbidding, yet has much interest in its memorials. Under the north aisle lies the Compton who was Cromwell's godly Cavalier. A marble tablet above tells us that he was major-general of Charles's army at Colchester. On the walls, frayed and dusty, hang the banners that floated in his battles; all their glory is gone, and the pieces of armour that hang beside them are mouldering away.

Five alabaster figures lie here as they were when rescued from the moat: some of the heads and some of the limbs have gone. On one side is what remains of the figure of the William Compton who was Bluebeard's friend, who, in the company of Henry before he became King, challenged all comers at the tilt and at the tourney. He wears round his neck the SS collar with a rose badge of the Tudors. Close by him is Henry, first Lord Compton, in Elizabethan trunk and hose, and Dame Werburger, wife of Sir William Compton, who was with him at the Field of the Cloth of Gold. The two wives of the first Lord Compton have their heads on pillows decorated with fine lace.

A bronze plate near the door tells us that under the nave the good John Berrill lies, he who saved Compton Wynyates from destruction. On the wall above are two framed relics of the ancient church, fragments of fresco painting, one with the sun and clouds for Day, another with the moon for Night, both almost worn away.

We leave Compton Wynyates with a sigh. None comes away without a lingering look. On a grey day it is beautiful, on a bright day it rejoices in the sun: it is passing fair at any time.

Here lies a gallant Cavalier, second Earl of Northampton, whose body was exchanged for cannon he had captured.

A Life for King Charles

NO one seemed less likely to draw sword against his fellow-countrymen than Spencer Compton, second Earl of Northampton, during the first 40 years of his life. In public life he was a sound constitutionalist, and urged Charles to summon a Parliament, declaring that that one word of four syllables was like the dew of heaven. When armed strife became inevitable, however, he felt that his duty called him to the side of the anointed King. With four of his sons as officers and a troop of horse raised at his own cost, he was one of the little army standing by Charles when the standard was raised at Nottingham in 1642.

Compton had only a year to live, but in that time he made gallant history. He was a chivalrous spirit, full of fiery courage, now attempting a surprise attack on Warwick Castle, now defeated by Hampden at Southam, but a shining figure at Edgehill, in the defence of Banbury, and in raising the siege of Stafford. He made his headquarters at Stafford until the approach of a Parliamentary force under Gell and Brereton challenged him. He sallied out with his little troop and met his enemy at Hopton Heath. In the battle his sons, James the third Earl, and Charles (whose capture of Beeston Castle, Cheshire, with only six followers, is like a page from Froissart), charged side by side with their father.

They crashed through the Commonwealth cavalry and captured eight guns, but the sturdy Puritan infantry stood like a rock. Northampton continued his charge too far from his supports and was surrounded, and, refusing to yield, was killed.

After the battle James and Charles sought the body of their father. For once the Puritans were unchivalrous, and refused to surrender it unless the eight guns he had captured were first delivered to them. So the guns were given up, and a very knightly gentleman's remains were bought with the spoil of war, and sadly brought here for burial.

Within a generation a junior brother of the two young heroes, Henry Compton, the famous Bishop of London, was thankful to vote for the expulsion of the dynasty for which his father had died and his brothers had ventured all.

The Lonely Sleeper Near the Heart of England

COPSTON MAGNA. It is one of the places which believe they are at the core of the very heart of England; Copston Magna and Leamington have both claimed this distinction which seems rightly to belong to Minworth. But certainly we may feel here very near the heart of England, even though we only stand and stare at the vast expanse of wooded countryside. If we stand at High Cross the land falls east for many miles and we see into Leicestershire, while westward lie the lovely hills of Warwickshire.

But something even more stirring than this we come upon at Copston Magna, for here two of our most ancient highways meet, the Fosse Way and Watling Street. A remarkable point it is, with six roads radiating from it like the spokes of a wheel. Fosse Way is quiet and green, losing itself among the trees; Watling Street is busy with unceasing traffic between London and the Midlands and the North. Both were great highways in ancient times, but one is forgotten while the other thrives. Briton and Roman, Saxon, Dane, and Norman, all have tramped these roads, and we may think there can be few spots in England where so many races have trod and so many centuries passed with so little change of scene.

There is little to see and we are glad it is a quiet place. A monument in a garden is still where it was put, where Fosse Way crosses Watling Street, about 200 years ago, set up as a "perpetual remembrance of peace at last restored by Queen Anne." It had then a great base with heraldic shields from which rose columns supporting a sundial with four faces. It stood for 80 years, and was struck by lightning. The columns and the dials were destroyed, and the base was left broken and forlorn. So it remains, pathetic in ruin, with a bit of a Latin inscription telling the traveller that here the Romans trod and here their roads crossed to the utmost boundaries of Britain. The inscription told in other days how the Roman quarters were near this spot and how Claudius, commander of a cohort, had a camp towards Watling Street, and towards the Fosse Way a tomb. It is believed that Claudius was buried at a place called Cloudesley Bush, a mile away, and there no doubt he lies, the lonely sleeper of the centuries in this sleepy countryside.

Home of Ancient Britons

CORLEY. It stands high where we can see the smoke-clouds of the Midlands and a fair prospect of beautiful Warwickshire. Not far away is Corley Rock, a home of Britons in prehistoric times. We see traces of its walls, and there are terraces on the hills. A mile from the village is a Jacobean hall sometimes said to be the original of Hall Farm in Adam Bede.

We come to Corley along lanes with sandstone rocks on one side, and pass through one of the biggest lychgates we have seen, the peace memorial. In the churchyard we are greeted by a gaunt skeleton of an enormous elm. The church has fortress-like walls and much Norman work : two arches in the arcade with spearhead ornament on the capitals, a chancel arch, two windows, and a pillar with two of their queer sculptures. One is a strange animal, the other may be a man's face, though we have seen it described as many different things.

High in the wall is an oak doorway with two oak steps; something unusual in our experience of roodlofts. In the north aisle are traces of wall paintings in blue, red, and green; we can see quite well a crude tree and a man. The font is 17th century, and the two lamps in the 13th-century chancel are a thanksgiving for a soldier's safe return.

The Blacksmith's Clock

COUGHTON. The great house and the little church among the trees are both linked with its famous family. A handsome place is Coughton Court, at the end of a fine avenue of elms, and it is said that in 1605 many friends of the Gunpowder Plotters were gathered here when Robert Catesby's servant brought the ill news that Guy Fawkes and his fellow conspirators had been arrested. Here lived the Throckmortons, who had a hand in the first Fifth of November and were relatives of a conspirator who made a stir in England 20 years before Guy Fawkes. More than one priest was hidden in these walls; only 60 years ago a secret room was revealed in one of the turrets, its ladder, bed, and folding altar just as a priest had left them in escaping.

From the house many of the Throckmortons came to their last resting-place in the church, one of three very old things in Coughton. The second is a magnificent oak about 30 feet round, its branches spreading over a quarter of an acre; and the third is the broken shaft of a cross, still on the ancient steps where travellers in the lost Forest of Arden knelt to pray.

The spacious 16th-century church, in a lovely setting, has a sundial on an ancient cross among the gravestones, and inside is an old chest with iron clasps of fleur-de-lys and much old glass of the 16th century with saints, apostles, and figures from mythology. There are choir stalls with 16th-century carving, two with priests at their devotions. There is a 16th-century screen in a chapel and a pulpit and reredos with panelling from the old chancel screen. The surprising thing for Coughton to show with pride is the gift of a village blacksmith who must have loved to come to church to see the wonderful thing he had made, a clock he put together in 1690. It has no face, but its wheels and levers, although crude, still do their work and vigorously strike the hours on the great bell.

A gracious resting-place for the Throckmortons it is. Here are the figures of Sir John and his wife on an altar tomb, her hand still in his after nearly four centuries, their children with them. Elizabeth, the last abbess of Denney, has a fine tomb with a big cross in brass and enamel; and in the nave is a magnficent marble tomb Sir Robert built for himself in the early Tudor days. He had hoped to lie here when his day was done, but he died on a pilgrimage to Palestine and sleeps in some distant spot, while an 18th-century descendant sleeps in his English grave. Splendid brass portraits on another tomb show his son Sir George Throckmorton in armour with his wife in a beautiful gown and kirtle; below is his huge family of 19 sons and daughters, who added 112 grandchildren to his blessings.

The Friend of Mary Stuart

THE most distinguished member of the old Throckmorton family of Coughton, Sir Nicholas, born in 1515, is remembered in Throgmorton Street in London. He grew up a page in the house of Queen Catherine Parr, whom he called cousin by marriage. A strong Protestant, he was high in favour under Edward the Sixth, who knighted and enriched him.

He signed the document which gave the throne to Lady Jane Grey, but when the hour came he declared for Mary, while endeavouring to secure merciful treatment for Jane. Mary found him an early ally, but sent him to the Tower over Wyatt's Rebellion; and when a brave jury acquitted him they were imprisoned for months and heavily fined.

Keeping in touch with the captive Princess Elizabeth, he was the first to notify her, prematurely as it proved, of the death of Mary. Fearing that any incautious act might involve her in a charge of treason, she bade him ride to the palace and obtain as proof from one of the ladies of the bedchamber who was in her confidence "the black enamelled ring her Majesty wore night and day." On his way he passed the messenger bringing news of the actual death.

Elizabeth used Throckmorton for many delicate missions, one to Mary Stuart, by whose beauty he was fascinated. He remained to the end her devoted friend, although always in opposition to her policy. He prepared the way for the widowed bride's return to Scotland. While in France he fought on the side of the Protestants in Normandy, where he was taken prisoner but released. He strove to enlist English aid for the oppressed Huguenots.

With Mary in Scotland Throckmorton had difficult missions to her court, and after the murder of Darnley he did his best to secure her release from Lochleven Castle. Always friendly to Mary, he favoured her suggested marriage to the Duke of Norfolk and so became suspect again and was imprisoned in Windsor Castle. He was soon released, but two years later he died in London, in 1570. His daughter was the wife of Sir Walter Raleigh.

Coughton   Front of Coughton Court

Wilmcote   Mary Arden's Cottage

Bearley   Village in Forest of Arden

Coventry   **A Cathedral Corner**

The Town of Fortune's Wheel

COVENTRY. In the middle of England like the hub of a wheel stands Coventry, and it is the happy town of Fortune's Wheel, for the wheel has made its fortune. It is its delight to call itself the centre of England and the centre of progress. All those things that have contributed so much to the changed life of the world have their manufacturing home in this fine town. It is England's birthplace of the age of speed and swift communications.

Coventry gives us the means to span continents in the aeroplane. It has made all England our parish if we own a car. Probably most of our ten million cyclists ride machines from a Coventry factory. The city puts a girdle round the whole earth with its telephones. If we turned back the pages of this town's history as a manufacturing centre, we should see how one great industry and then another has risen and often declined, but above all we should see how the long view, and faith in the future, have made Coventry what it is, an industrial city with a marvellous vision of prosperity before it. In a single generation it has nearly trebled its population. Its area today is five times as big as at the beginning of our century. Its rateable value doubled in seven years, and in King George's reign over 700 new factories or extensions of factories were built.

And the marvel of it all is that Coventry, with an industrial life so varied and progressive, is a city of clear skies which have sometimes turned the thoughts of a visitor to the Mediterranean. Its buildings are almost free from dust. The stained glass of its churches, though so near to the factories, is not obscured by smoke. There is pure air in the centre of the city. Its factories are clean and well-lighted, and all because Coventry saw the future in electricity, and insisted on using it where it could instead of burning coal. It has become a great industrial city without blotting out the sun or destroying its beauty, and it stands a high example to cities everywhere.

If it is proud of its industrial history and achievements, Coventry is also proud of its place in our country's story. It loves the tale of Godiva's Ride and the legend of Peeping Tom, the memory of the miracle plays and pageants, and of the many kings and queens who have been this way. It is proud also of its adaptability to change, the quality that has made it the capital of the motor-car world. Again and again it has seen its prosperity threatened and has adapted itself to something new. As today it builds up new trades in place of old ones, so in early times it raised new churches on the ruins of the old. Coventry had four great monasteries and all are gone; but it has three famous spires, inspiring witnesses to the story of a city which enshrines as much of our English spirit as we find anywhere within so short a compass.

Hardly can we set foot in this fine town without following steps illustrious in history. We walk to Gosford Green (a little greensward Coventry has kept throughout the centuries) and we are at the spot where, on a September day in 1397, the lists were set for the trial by combat between Henry Bolingbroke and Thomas Mowbray. At Mount Pleasant we stand where Richard pitched his tent before the fight and stopped it.

With music of harp and dulcimer and lute Coventry greeted its kings and queens in ancient times; with the roar of motors it receives us now. From the city walls the trumpet would sound; now it is the hooter at the factory gate. Arrayed in scarlet were the brethren of the guilds, and the commonalty in gowns of green and hoods of red, when kings came to this city of brave processions and fine attire; today it goes about its business sombrely clad, but with a rich store of memories, and with as much of Tudor England to show as we shall find perhaps in any of our working towns.

Great beauty it has, but one bitter memory, for we cannot forget the shame of Coventry's burnings in the days of Mary Tudor. A little more than 400 years ago, in this city of pageants and spires, 11 men and women went to the stake for their faith, among them a mother whose crime was that she had taught her little ones to say the Lord's Prayer and the Commandments in their mother tongue.

But let us look at the heart of Coventry, where the old city mingles with the new. The cathedral and St Mary's Hall, Holy Trinity Church a few yards away, and near it the ruins of the old cathedral of St Mary, the ancient timbered dwellings for neighbours to the church and the cathedral—what a rare group it is! In a radius of 200 yards is packed a world of beauty and wonder to fill a book.

We come to St Mary's Hall (the old Guildhall), its walls eloquent with age. Nature has sculptured the soft red sandstone, rounding every edge, leaving many a groove and furrow. It is as though great waves had surged over the building, almost washing the walls away. Beautiful it must have looked when new, nearly 600 years ago, and we may be sure the men of Coventry's guilds who used it then were proud of it. In it, as in so much of Coventry, we feel the spirit of these medieval guilds, the piety and the pageantry that stirred men then. The archway from the street leads to a porch with vaulted roof, from which looks down a quaint carving of the Coronation of the Madonna, sheltered under two tiny canopies. On another stone is carved the Annunciation, and on a third is carving so worn by Time that we may only guess its meaning. South of the courtyard is the 14th-century kitchen, still partly used for its original purpose, with a statue of Henry the Sixth looking very odd in a windowsill; it once adorned the medieval cross, one of the lost glories of Coventry. A few feet away the knave's whipping-post, a grotesque human likeness in wood, grins from the wall to which it is fixed. West of the courtyard is the crypt, a great vaulted chamber for all sorts of ancient things. Coventry has so many that it has to put them here; we noticed a 13th-century stone coffin, remains of old stone fireplaces, some early bicycles.

In the Treasury, opposite one of the most fascinating rooms in Coventry, are the old guild records and many precious letters. There is one from Ann Boleyn to the Mayor of Coventry announcing the birth of her daughter, the baby who was to be Queen Elizabeth; and one from Elizabeth herself ordering the safe keeping in the town of Mary Queen of Scots. To see these rare documents it is necessary to find the town clerk, but the other treasures of St Mary's Hall are here for all to see. Most of them are in the great hall, a room associated in many ways with Coventry's long story. Here is much splendour of ancient glass, a wealth of carving, a superb old tapestry, and a fine minstrel's gallery. Remarkable is the nine-light window of 15th-century glass, each light with a portrait of a king. Henry the Sixth is here in armour, and with him the Emperor Constantine, King Arthur, the Conqueror, Richard the First, Edward the Third, Henry the Third, Fourth, and Fifth.

The great tapestry is one of the finest of its kind in England. It has been here about 400 years and is 36 feet long and 10 feet wide, divided into six compartments. Though of Flemish design, it is believed to have been woven in England, perhaps in Coventry. The colours are faded, the outlines are often blurred, yet it is astonishing how much detail we can trace, and when the floodlights are switched on it is revealed as a glorious array of colour and design. In the top left compartment are 11 saints, John Baptist with a lamb and a book,

Peter with a key, Andrew with a cross, Paul with a sword, Simon with a saw, George with a banner, Thaddeus with a halberd, Adrian standing on a lion, Bartholomew with a knife—so they go. In the top sits Justice with the scales among angels carrying the instruments of the Passion.

On the right are 10 women saints, all in Tudor dresses: Catherine with her wheel, Margaret with a queer animal entwined round her, Dorothy with a basket of roses, Mary Magdalene with a box of ointment, Anne with a staff, Gertrude with three white mice, and so on. At the bottom is Henry VI in a jewelled cap, kneeling at a prayer-desk with his crown and book; near him kneels Cardinal Beaufort with 17 standing courtiers. The middle compartment at the bottom has the Assumption of the Madonna, whose feet rest on a crescent moon held by angels, while grouped about her are kneeling apostles. On the right is Queen Margaret in yellow, with crimson-lined sleeves and a richly embroidered headdress. She kneels with a child and a group of ladies, with whom are two little dogs in collars. The tapestry contains altogether about 80 heads, all intricately worked; it must have taken many years to make.

Near it is an alcove lit by a beautiful oriel with medallions of 16th-century life in fragments of old glass; and in more fragments we noticed a little picture of a church and a graceful head of a girl. In a niche are two tiny figures from the lost 16th-century cross, and on the floor are medieval tiles. In the alcove is a white stone figure of Godiva, nearly lifesize, a modern addition to this hall of ancient treasure.

Modern also are the windows in the east and west sides, a magnificent series in brilliant colours. They were the gift to Coventry of William Coker Iliffe, who was made a Freeman of the City in 1930, and were designed by Mr Reginald Bell. The figures are all nearly lifesize. One side shows kings and queens and brethren of the guilds; the other side has a fine array of 14th and 15th-century mayors. They are a noble collection of portraits. Among the kings, queens, and nobles are Richard Beauchamp and Isabella his wife; the queen of Edward the Second in a blue gown adorned with fleur-de-lys; the Black Prince; Richard the Second in a richly embroidered coat; Sir William Babington in the crimson robes of a judge; Humphrey, Earl of Stafford, in a crimson robe; John, Duke of Bedford, son of Henry the Fourth, and his brother Humphrey, Duke of Gloucester.

Nor are these all the interesting portraits the hall has to show, for round the walls are paintings, some by Lely and Lawrence, of kings and queens from Mary onwards. Hanging by the minstrel's gallery is a collection of Stuart armour used in the Godiva pageants of Charles the Second's time.

The hall has still its original panelled roof. The tie-beams are carved with musical angels, and there are six stone corbels richly carved. In the Mayoress's Parlour, with a fine stone fireplace, and more portraits of kings and queens and benefactors, is a chair which is among Coventry's most precious possessions. It was the chair of the medieval guilds, and is of superbly carved oak with the Madonna, the elephant and castle, and two lions holding up a crown. Big enough for two, it used to accommodate the Master of the Guild and the Mayor of the City, and with its finely carved scenes and its rich tracery, it is one of the most beautiful guild chairs in existence.

Under the minstrel's gallery, in a room known as the Prince's Chamber, with Jacobean panelling, Elizabethan furniture, and medieval stone carvings, is a fascinating group of small wood sculptures from the roof of the hall, where they would first be seen 500 years ago. They represent St Sophia, the Good Shepherd, St Michael slaying the dragon, St Catherine with her wheel, and a Madonna.

Above St Mary's Hall, above everything in Coventry, soars the spire of the cathedral, one of the architectural glories of England. It rises 303 feet sheer from the ground at the west end, yet it is only 30 feet square at the base. Only two other English cathedral spires exceed it in height, Salisbury and Norwich. The erection of it in the 14th century occupied 21 years. William and Adam Botoner, brothers and both mayors, paid £100 for the tower, their sisters paying for the spire; the spire has statues of all four of them, each holding a model of some part of the church.

The walls of the tower are six feet thick. Exquisitely wrought with a wealth of detail, they have 40 delicately carved niches sheltering modern stone figures of saints, kings, queens, bishops, and benefactors, among them Earl Leofric and Godiva. Some of the ancient figures which stood there have been taken into the crypt; one, of St Michael, stands on a finely carved corbel in the mercer's chapel. The octagon connecting the tower with the spire is supported by flying buttresses, and the slender spire has two beautifully panelled lower stages.

The spire leans a little to the north-west because for some technical reason it was found impossible to build the tower exactly in line with the nave, but the foundations were ill-laid, and the tower gradually sank into the ground which had been filled up. In 500 years the sinking near the ground level amounted to seven inches, and cracks had to be filled in to prevent it from falling. When it was examined last century it was moving a little every day, and £17,000 was spent in making it safe.

The south porch, built late in the 13th century, is the oldest part of the cathedral, and is still largely as it must have been when Henry the Sixth came with Margaret of Anjou. This way, doubtless, came the next Henry from his victory on Bosworth Field, and here he would come, an older man by 20 years, with his queen to see the miracle plays. The stout oak inner door is finely carved and panelled. For hundreds of years it has guarded this lovely place. All through the centuries people have paused as they opened this door, lost in admiration of the scene that awaits our gaze.

The nave, long, lofty, and wider than most cathedral naves, and the chancel of equally imposing proportions, stretch before us in a marvellous perspective of soaring stone and shining glass. The church is nearly 294 feet long and 127 wide, the 12 arches of the nave being 20 feet wide, rising from slender clustered columns. From where we stand by the south door the distance to the east window is 240 feet, and we have an uninterrupted view of the chancel and its great windows, in which hundreds of colours and tints melt into a glorious harmony. The clerestory windows form an impressive series. There are 24, all uniform, some with fragments of ancient glass, others with heraldic shields. The splendidly vaulted roof is nearly 100 feet above us.

Many glimpses of elegant architecture we have from the nave, looking through its great bays to the chapels. Each chapel in medieval times belonged to one of the guilds; today one chapel is for men, another for women, a third for children, and all contain something of interest for the traveller. We come to them one by one, and this is something of what we see in them.

In the children's chapel

Delightful modern oak screenwork, a beautifully carved Jacobean chair, and a modern oak crucifix with an exquisite figure of a child at the foot.

In the lady chapel

Roof-beams about 600 years old, with groups of angels holding shields and a pelican feeding her young.

Twelve misereres nearly as old as the roof, with fascinating carvings of a death-bed scene, a kneeling man whose shirt is being taken off and given to a cripple, a man threshing wheat, and Death leading several figures, including Satan in chains.

Elegant poppyheads and fragments of an old screen.

A 17th-century altar table.

A Chantrey monument to one of Wellington's colonels, with a white marble medallion of a fallen soldier.

The tomb of Julian Nethermyll, mayor, one of the most beautiful things in the cathedral, with kneeling figures of Julian and his five sons facing his wife and five daughters. Looking closely, we see variations in the dress of all the figures, all skilfully carved. At the centre of the tomb is a small Crucifixion scene, and at the ends are cherubs holding aside curtains.

A magnificent modern bronze by Sir Hamo Thornycroft of Bishop Yeatman-Biggs, first Bishop of the revived See of Coventry, who died in 1922. It is the most impressive work of our time that the cathedral has, a life-size figure sleeping, sculptured with remarkable detail and great feeling. The bishop holds a model of the cathedral.

In the capper's chapel

A wall monument of coloured marble, 15 feet high, with three busts and much floral adornment, to Richard Hopkins, who served Coventry in seven Parliaments from 1660 to 1701, and to other members of his family. His house still stands in Palace Yard, a short distance from St Mary's Hall, and we see it in our journey through the town.

A precious piece of medieval embroidery, the capper's pall, complete but greatly faded, though we still see the scissors and teasel, ancient badges of the company, on shields in the corners. It was used at funerals of members of the company.

In the men's chapel

Much elegant screenwork in oak, a carved oak table several centuries old, a pair of pewter candlesticks of 1668; the tomb of Sir Thomas Berkeley, who lived in Shakespeare's time; and the high tomb, in carved alabaster, of William Stanley, benefactor to Coventry in the 17th century.

A 16th-century brass showing Mary Hinton, a vicar's wife, a small figure in a high-crowned, broad-rimmed hat, ruff, and long dress, kneeling at a prayer desk, with four babies in swaddling clothes lying before her.

In the dyer's chapel

An ornate marble monument with medallion portrait and inscription to Dame Mary Bridgeman, widow of the son of Sir Orlando Bridgeman who conducted the trial of the men who tried Charles Stuart.

A stately Tudor lady meets us in the south choir aisle. She lies on a fine altar tomb, Elizabeth Swillington, in a Tudor headdress, with her two husbands beside her, one in armour, the other in his chain and robes as Recorder. Another 16th-century altar tomb here has on the sides nine beautifully carved figures in quaint costumes; it is probably the tomb of John Wade, a wealthy mercer, one of many tombs in the cathedral which repay close study.

Two sanctuary windows have hundreds of fragments of old glass, much of it 15th century, and probably from the workshop of John Thornton, who painted the famous east window of York Minster. Among the fairly complete subjects are cherubim on wheels and Judas giving the kiss of betrayal. The three great east windows are filled with modern glass, richly varied in colour, with 36 panels of scenes in the life of Christ and hosts of angels. A window behind the organ contains glass to the memory of Thomas Sharp, the Coventry antiquary and writer who died in 1841. It contains a coat-of-arms, the Parable of the Talents, the Good Samaritan, and the Pharisee and the Publican.

On two modern doors in the sanctuary are iron knockers, gems of medieval art worth more than a glance; and we should pause, too, at the choir stalls, the richly carved ends of which are perfect after 400 years.

Near the Bishop's Throne, an elaborate piece of modern oak carving, two squirrels sit cracking nuts. They are carved on a choir stall, also modern. High up on a wall are ancient stone carvings of a monkey and a bear. The fine pulpit, of wrought iron and brass, was made by Frank Skidmore, a Coventry craftsman who fashioned the metalwork for the Albert Memorial at South Kensington and the choir screens in Hereford Cathedral.

Now we come to Coventry's grand old chest, one of the finest of its period in England. It stands near the tower, a beautiful example of the skill of some unknown 15th-century carver. It has a modern top, but the chest itself has survived with most of its intricate detail. The ends are framed up, each with 16 small panels, but it is the front that thrills us. It is covered with carvings. In the end panels are Tudor roses, thistles, and grotesque figures, one of an animal, another of a bird. The middle has 24 traceried panels, and in the small centre panel are two tiny figures quaintly carved, sitting on a bench and apparently conversing. In the spandrels below are two carved dragons with knots in their tails.

We turn from the chest to see on the wall the little picture of Anne Sewell, in a brass which shows her kneeling before a prayer desk, wearing a high-crowned hat, ruff, and tight-waisted Tudor dress.

Looking up the nave from the tower wall is the peace memorial, a

Coventry   Courtyard of Ford Hospital

Wolvey
Thomas and Alice Wolvey

Merevale
Knight and Lady

Coventry Cathedral   Elizabeth Swillington and two Husbands

A Smiling Dragon

A Musician

A Grotesque

Saint Michael

The Good Shepherd

Old Wooden Figures in Coventry Guildhall

Coventry   Our Patron Saint in the Guildhall lifesize carving of St Michael in wood, with sword and wings outstretched, all painted and gilded. It is the work of Alec Miller, of Chipping Campden, the town famed for its craftsmen.

Two quaint memorials we noticed here. One is a brass inscription of 1705 near the south porch to Gervase Scrope, who died "in the agony and dolorous pains of the gout." It has some crude lines by himself, beginning:

> *Here lies a poor tossed tennis ball,*
> *Was racketed from spring to fall.*

The other is on the stone of a gladiator buried here, a surprising discovery to come upon in the churchyard, where we are told that John Parkes, dying in 1733, was "a man of mild disposition, a gladiator by profession, who, after having fought 360 battles in the principal parts of Europe, with honour and applause, at length quitted the stage, sheathed his sword, and with Christian resignation submitted to the grand victor in the 62 year of his age." For a man of mild disposition he seems to have led an extraordinary life.

A few steps take us from the cathedral to Holy Trinity, the sight of which stirs us with wonder that Coventry should build these two churches side by side and that the glory of the one should not dim the glory of the other. For Holy Trinity is a beautiful world of its own. The graceful central tower was rebuilt after being blown down in 1665; its spire is 70 feet shorter than St Michael's.

The north porch is the oldest part, chiefly 13th century, with a vaulted roof and a priest's room above. What impresses us as we enter is the finely painted roof. The arcades with pointed arches on stately clustered pillars have echoed hymns of praise for 600 years. The panelled walls and the square clerestory windows are still as in the 13th century. The carved and panelled roofs of the nave and chancel, newly painted last century, have still many of their original timbers, the ground in charming blue, the mouldings red and white, while gilded stars and leaves and painted angels contribute to a delightful effect. The north aisle roof, put up in Tudor times, has panels richly carved with grapes and leaves.

There are faint traces of a Last Judgment fresco, and a little ancient glass. The few fragments that have survived are all in one window, and include a small figure and part of a horse, which is said to have been a portrait of Godiva. A brass in an aisle shows a charming family group of Shakespeare's time in which we see John White-head, bearded and bareheaded, standing before a prayer-desk, his nine children and two wives kneeling, one in an enormously high-crowned hat, the second in a flowing headdress, both with ruffs.

A great scholar of the 17th century is remembered in a wall tablet to the memory of Philemon Holland, who was buried here in 1637. Fuller describes him as "the translator-general of his age," and Pope writes of groaning shelves sagging under the weight of Holland's translations.

One of the rare treasures of the church is the pulpit, a splendid piece of stonework 500 years old, though looking almost new. It is built on to a pier of the tower and is one of the finest examples in England of a 15th-century stone pulpit, one of about sixty surviving. Beautiful also is the lectern, as old as the pulpit, its magnificent brass eagle vigorously modelled and standing in a lifelike pose. It is said to have been used as a collecting box, people placing money in its beak. The font is from the same century and has traces of gilding and painting. An Elizabethan almsbox stands on a round shaft several feet high, its oak adorned all over with delicately carved arabesques. The stone reredos was designed by Sir Gilbert Scott.

The past lives on into the present in St Michael's and Holy Trinity, but just to the north of them are the pitiful ruins of a cathedral famous long before their time. No insubstantial pageant was the story of the old cathedral of St Mary which Leofric endowed, and it must have been of striking beauty. We know it was as big as Lich-field Cathedral and that it had three spires, but all we can see of it are small parts of the walls and pillars. On part of the base of the north-west tower a modern house stands. Somewhere beneath these ruins Earl Leofric was laid, and Godiva, perhaps, was laid beside him.

A short journey through the town brings us to Coventry's third old church, St John's, linking us with the days when Coventry was much in the esteem of kings and queens, for part of it was built on ground given by Queen Isabella and part on ground given by the Black Prince. What we see is mostly of the 14th and 15th centuries. Very imposing is the central tower, with battlements and three round overhanging turrets, a feature common in ancient forts but very un-usual in a church. It is as though the builders in that age of warfare thought they were building for a siege.

Of the interior of St John's Sir Gilbert Scott said he knew no church more beautiful, yet it is all so oddly constructed that there is no perfect rectangle in it, no corner is a perfect right angle, and no two walls are parallel. But its lighting effects are beautiful. The nave has an ancient timbered roof, and in the west window are fragments of 16th-century glass, in which we noticed quaint animals and a man carrying a cross. The peace window has our four national saints. The fine modern stone pulpit is a copy of one in Cambridge. On the pillars supporting the tower are queer carvings. On the wall is a brass inscription recalling a tragedy at sea in 1870. It is to the memory of Commander Sheepshanks and Lieutenant Castle, two members of the crew of the ship Captain, which capsized on its maiden voyage off Cape Finisterre, drowning 473 people, among them the designer of the ship, Cowper Phipps Coles.

As we stand in the churchyard here our gaze takes in a perfect little picture of Coventry as the guildsmen of old would know it, and as Shakespeare would see it.

Facing a quadrangle covered with a lawn are the almshouses founded by Thomas Bond in 1506 "for as long as the world shall endure." Coventry has treated them with careful regard for the thought of their founder, and they are excellently kept. They are half-timbered, 118 feet long, and their carved bargeboards and gables are a pleasant sight. On another side of the quadrangle stands Bablake Old School, founded by Thomas Wheatley in 1560, a building of two storeys. Its erection was the result of a curious error, for Wheatley, a steel merchant, sent an agent to Spain for some ingots of that metal. What he received turned out to be silver. He waited, it is said, for a long time expecting the precious metal to be reclaimed, but no message was received, and when the silver was sold Wheatley gave the money for the founding of the school. His timbered building has been replaced by a splendid modern one in Coundon Road, and it is odd to think, when we look at it, that it is due to a mistake somebody in Spain made nearly 400 years ago.

There is one more church the traveller will wish to see. It has the third of Coventry's famous tall spires, the elegant Christ Church spire of the 14th century, built by the Grey Friars with stone given by the Black Prince from his quarry near the town. It is all that remains of their church. The small church is modern, and round it, where the friars sang their chants, are shops. The monastery was famous for its pageants. The spire is faced with new stone. It rises from a slender octagonal tower to a height of 204 feet. For nearly two centuries it stood alone in an orchard, and at one time was tenanted by a gardener who kept his pigs at the foot of it and boasted that he had the tallest pigsty in Europe.

Coventry had its White Friars monastery also, and to this the centuries have brought a change no less profound than that seen at Christ Church. The cloisters and the vaulted room where Queen Elizabeth was entertained now shelter the vagrant and destitute poor. Was ever so strange a turn of history as this? Then came the highest in the land, now come the humblest.

Our pilgrimage through Coventry will take us through many parts where the town still wears the face of medieval days. Timbered gables look down over modern shop fronts, ancient walls with dormer windows appear wedged between modern walls. In all but the sound of traffic that penetrates almost every corner of Coventry we may live with the spirit of the past. Near the cathedral is a timbered Tudor house with overhanging storey and a dovecot of nine holes under the gable. The Golden Cross, a half-timbered inn at the corner of Pepper Lane and Hay Lane, has three fine gables. Butcher Row has quaint old houses. Looking out from a perch by the top window of the King's Head inn in Hertford Street is a little wooden figure of Peeping Tom.

Old Palace Yard, near St Mary's Hall, is a rare spot in which to pause. Its Elizabethan house, the old home of the Hopkins family, is a picture of low gables topped by the cathedral spire. The house looks as it must have looked when James the Second held his court in it, or when Princess Elizabeth was brought to it for safety from Coombe Abbey on the night the Gunpowder Plot was discovered.

But in all Coventry there is no lovelier glimpse of Tudor England than Ford's Hospital in Greyfriars Lane. Founded by William Ford when the 16th century was young, it provides a home for old women, and is one of the most beautiful examples of timber framework of that period. It is of two storeys, with a front 40 feet long resting on a base of stone, and has at the centre a charming archway with richly carved spandrels. On either side is a long window of nine lights with diamond panes and exquisitely carved headings; in one of the other windows are bits of ancient glass. The overhanging storey has three gables with carved bargeboards ending in handsome pendants; the whole of the front is adorned with panels and pilasters all differently carved, and the main beams under the gables are also carved. The garden behind the house is a little world of ancient peace, with the old white spire of Christ Church making a perfect centre to the background.

Near Christ Church, amid the pleasant lawns of Greyfriars Green, the white marble figure of a Lord Mayor of London looks down. He is Sir Thomas White, founder of St John's College, Oxford, and a great benefactor to Coventry. Across the road is the memorial of a humbler man who in his way did just as much for Coventry, turning its thoughts to transport as the future means of prosperity. This granite monument shows us a sculptured portrait of James Starley, inventor of the safety bicycle. On the sides are engravings of his machines, a sign of the pride Coventry feels in being thus associated, only a little more than half a century ago, with this early method of democratic travel.

What is left of a Carthusian monastery in Coventry is at the Charterhouse, where is still to be seen a portion of the wall which enclosed the monastery in the 14th century. The house, built from the old materials, has fine panelling, carved beams, and an old staircase; but its greatest treasure is part of a medieval fresco, showing the Crucifixion.

Two other memorials in Coventry must claim the thoughts of every traveller here. One is a Celtic cross of grey granite 20 feet high, decorated with the laurel leaf and Coventry arms in gunmetal, erected near the spot where in five tragic years 11 martyrs suffered for conscience sake. The second monument is in memory of the 2587 men of Coventry who in four tragic years suffered death for our country's sake. Their memorial is an imposing buttressed tower, 100 feet high, with a chamber of silence in the base for those who pause to remember, and a beacon to shine at night in the top. The monument was unveiled by Earl Haig in 1927, and the ceremony was the last of the kind he performed. The beautiful park in which it stands is called War Memorial Park, but it stands for peace. Among the trees which grace the lawns and walks are 240 copper beeches radiating in avenues from the monument, planted by relatives, friends, and societies in memory of the fallen, and there is one oak grown from an acorn picked up at Verdun.

Coventry's Central Library, given to the city by a business man, reminds us in a graceful way of George Eliot's association with the city. Here she received part of her education, and she loved to hear the busy hum of the town's machinery. The house, at 29 Warwick Row, where she went to the school kept by the Misses Franklin, is now a grocer's shop and has a tablet telling us that the novelist attended school here. In the library is an oak-panelled alcove to her memory, the names of some of her books worked into the window design. Here stands the oak desk on which she wrote, a small carved oak table which belonged to her, her stationery cabinet, a small statue of Christ which stood in her study, a handworked tablecloth and a reading lamp she used, and a complete library of her works in a case made of oak from trees on the Newdigate Estate at Arbury, where she spent so much of her childhood.

The Council House is an uncommonly graceful building, modern, with a delightful tower and lifesize stone figures in niches of the Confessor, the Black Prince, Leofric, and Godiva. Over its charming porch are tall panels in the walls containing shields, and the windows of the council chamber are filled with heraldic glass.

At three more places in this rare city we must look before we leave: Priory Gate, Cook Street Gate, and Cheylesmore Manor House. It is thrilling to see a bit of the medieval city in these two gates. Priory Gate's huge walls of sandstone bear the marks of the wind and rain for about 600 years. It contains a blocked-up archway. Cook Street Gate is still a substantial relic, with a long run of the wall beside it; together they are all that remain of the embattled wall and 12 towers, on the erection of which the monks and people of Coventry spent 40 years of the 14th century. Near Cook Street Gate is a touch of grace of our own time: a memorial garden given to the city in memory of his wife by Sir Alfred Herbert, who was made a Freeman of Coventry in 1933. Cheylesmore Manor House, though mostly modern, has an ancient chimney-shaft, but is of interest largely because it is suggested that near this spot Lady Godiva set out on her ride.

We leave Coventry feeling that it has been an unforgettable pilgrimage. It has shown us much that is fine and noble and dignified. It has inclined our hearts to the pity and pathos and splendour that make up Old England's story. Change and decay it has seen through relentless years, but the solemn beauty of its churches and the memory of its guilds live on. The famous spires, soaring still to heaven, are like pointers to yet greater things.

He Shaped the Unity of a Continent

IN our own time Coventry has taken under its care a cottage at Canley, a mile from the heart of the town, which has a link with the Empire across the world, for in it was born a servant of the British Empire of whom we may say perhaps that he was more responsible than any other man for laying the foundations of the Australian Commonwealth. He was Sir Henry Parkes.

Born in Waterloo year, this boy went out across the world to found a State. No man in Australia was more talked of or more photographed in his day. He was the great Free Trade leader. He gave the movement for Australian Federation its practical shape and roused tremendous enthusiasm for it, summing up the whole matter in a famous phrase, "the crimson thread of kinship."

This moulder of the destinies of a continent was born in a cottage which may still be seen; it belongs to the people and is a place of pilgrimage. Here his father was a poor tenant farmer struggling to keep the wolf from the door. Henry found work in a brickfield before he was in his teens, and at 23 he was tramping London selling buttons. They brought him in next to nothing, and his wife and himself became one of those families whose setting-out for the colonies might have inspired Ford Madox Brown's picture in the Tate Gallery. Henry, with his wife and baby, landed in Sydney with three shillings in his pocket. Still hard times pursued him; employment was scarce, food was dear; but the family lived down its troubles, and the tide turned when Henry obtained a post in the Customs. He wrote to a sister in England that he had now time to write poetry!

It was like the man to find poetry in his hard life; but he soon showed that he could write something else. He became a journalist and an editor; he founded a newspaper, and then New South Wales found he was just the man for Parliament. Five times he was Premier of the State, and before he died Sir Henry Parkes was a household name in the land of his adoption.

I Mark Time

CUBBINGTON. The church stands high watching over the old village. It was first built by the Normans, and much rebuilding has left traces of their work, including one arcade. The south porch shelters a richly moulded 13th-century doorway. Within is an

Easter sepulchre, a triple sedilia, and a Norman font. On the slender columns of the 14th-century arcade are four heads, said to be those of a vicar, his wife, and two churchwardens of the time. The chancel has a fine brass screen. The windows are full of life and colour, their glowing tints reflected on the walls. The fine east window has Christ in glory and a company of saints and angels. An American family gave two windows in memory of ancestors here; they show Aaron and Peter, St Ambrose, and the Madonna in blue and white.

In the vicarage garden is a sundial with a motto commenting on the changes of the passing years: I mark Time; dost thou?

The Bullet Through the Window

CURDWORTH. We find timbered cottages, old inns, and lovely churches everywhere in Warwickshire, but Curdworth has something rare if not unique in Shakespeare's county. We see in this church the work of a Norman artist who turned his thoughts toward enriching his work with colour. He painted the deep splays of his windows, and, though most of his colour has faded with 800 years, fragments of it remain of marvellous interest. The best of it is in the splays of one of the nave windows; one side has the word Angelus above the figure of an angel, and the other has Assumptio and three figures, one with a golden halo probably being the Madonna. It is believed to be one of the oldest examples of wall painting in England. There are more of these relics of the past on two windows in the chancel, but only fragments of scrolls.

Next to the painted Norman window in the nave is another window with a captivating canopied niche which has also been painted. It is the work of a 15th-century craftsman, but what is striking about it is a tiny hole near the top which is said to have been made by a bullet fired through a window in the Civil War. Here it was, in Curdworth fields, that the first blood of those tragic years was spilt. The King had left the garrison at Kenilworth Castle, the strongest fort in the Midlands, but the Parliament men were stirring at Coventry and Warwick and it was feared that Kenilworth would be besieged, so the Royalists withdrew. They were hotly pursued, and in Curdworth fields were forced to make a stand. It is thought the hole in this small vaulted canopy was made by a bullet fired then.

Far older than the Civil War are the medieval tiles kept in a frame, one showing the head of a king and another with a curious alphabet which would puzzle any child, for it has only 23 letters and they read from right to left. They are probably as old as the 15th-century tower built by the last great Earl of Warwick, Richard Nevill; or perhaps as old as the huge dug-out chest in the tower, one of the biggest we have seen, 10 feet long and 13th century. Many centuries old are the three mass dials on the south wall of the nave; yet all these things are young compared with the flints, spearheads, and axeheads preserved in a case in the tower, shaped by the Stone Age men of Warwickshire.

There is an old font kept in the 18th-century porch, and another which has been in use for 800 years and is now resting on yet another font upturned as its support. It is a mass of Norman carving with evil symbolised by figures of Babylon, a dragon, and the mouth of hell, and the triumph of goodness by evangelists and angels. Near the steps of the old roodloft is a small figure of an angel, carved in stone and painted, but with its head gone. For centuries it was the guardian angel of the ancient bridge between Curdworth and Water Orton.

The fine Norman chancel arch has bold zigzag and a window on each side, the one on the south 15th century, the other modern, traceried but unglazed, this unusual effect being heightened by the elaborately carved loft and organ above. The sanctuary has an aumbry made of oak said to be from a tree which was growing when the Conqueror came There is an oak bench with poppyheads 500 years old, and in the east window are St Nicholas and St Peter with Gabriel taking the good news to the Madonna.

The Midnight Messengers

DUNCHURCH. In a long low gabled house here (then an inn) Sir Everard Digby and a company of squires gathered on a November night in 1605. They seemed a roystering hunting party, but at midnight other men burst in on their merriment. They were Catesby, Rokewood, and others who had arrived in panic from London with the news that Guy Fawkes had been arrested and the Gunpowder Plot exploded. The conspirators had hoped to seize Princess Elizabeth and raise a rebellion, and at Dunchurch they found no counsel but the wise counsel to continue their flight.

The town which this night made notorious has a placid oldfashioned air today in spite of the busy life streaming by its two elm-shaded

Dorsington C.P., Stratford R.D.
pop. 62.

greens with their old stocks and the steps of an ancient cross. The cross lost its shaft at the Reformation, and the one we see is little over 100 years old. On the opposite side of the cross-roads is a statue by Joseph Durham, R.A., of Lord John Scott, a great sportsman, son of the Duke of Buccleuch, and much interested in seafaring life. At the time of his death he had equipped a new vessel to test some of the problems of deep-sea fishing.

The 14th-century church has a fine tower, a Norman doorway, and a Norman font. Among the modern glass is a fine St Nicholas, a peace memorial window with Michael, Gabriel, and St George, another symbolising War and Peace, a fine scene at the tomb in memory of a vicar killed at Ypres, and two armoured knights in a window in memory of a boy who served all through the war and died on duty at 20 when it was over.

A curious monument with folding doors is to Thomas Newcombe, a 17th-century printer to three kings. He founded the almshouses near the church, which were rebuilt a few years after Waterloo.

The Legacy of a Merchant Prince

ERDINGTON. It has lost its antiquity, though it was in the Conqueror's Domesday Book, but it is known far and wide for one of the best institutions of its kind in England, its Orphanage.

In the heart of this great place lies one who should receive the gratitude of generations of children, Sir Josiah Mason, who from a humble beginning as a maker of steel pens amassed a fortune and with it built Mason College, forerunner of Birmingham's great University. He spent a quarter of a million pounds on the great Orphanage. We find two figures and portraits of him here, and windows reminding us of Sir Josiah and his wife. In one of the windows we read his charge to the trustees of the Orphanage who were to care for the children he loved. This is what he said to them:

They will be what you make them,
Make them wise, make them good,
Make them strong in time of trial,
Teach them temperance, patience, kindness, and fortitude.

Another window has the Good Shepherd, and another Jesus talking to children.

In the hall is a second small figure of the founder with children about him, and panels in relief below suggesting the spirit of charity that moulded his life. There is a bust of him in the chapel and a portrait in oils, and he looks what he was, a loving father of the poor and a friend of learning. He died at 86, a year after his college in Birmingham was opened. The Orphanage takes children from all parts of the country, and in this delightful piece of England 250 of them have their school and their home, all so generously endowed that they have never had to ask for help.

Erdington has no old church, but its modern church has much good work. Its best possession is a wonderful oak screen, a peace memorial, intricately enriched with fruit, corn, animals, fishes, and shells. On it are carved 22 bells and the last one is broken, a symbol of the broken life of those who did not come back. The windows have pictures from John Bunyan showing Christian in the Slough of Despond at the Wicket Gate, in the Castle of the Giant Despair, and reaching the Celestial City. The east window has scenes in the life of Our Lord, and below it is an elaborate reredos with a fine sculpture of the Last Supper. The nave has a splendid roof of open timber.

Erdington has near by the Roman Catholic training centre, Oscott College, which has a great library of books and many paintings and old masters. One of its famous sons was Alfred Austin, Poet Laureate.

The Shadow of a Great Glory at the Heart of England

ETTINGTON. To those who pass by it is almost nothing—a new church and an old tower standing with the shadow of its past; but for those who know where to look it has one of the wonders of our countryside. We found it on a lovely summer's day, far away in the wooded heart of Warwickshire, driving a lonely mile through a park before we came upon one of those moving spectacles which must stir the heart of any Englishman in these days. It is the sight of a great house of the 19th century with all its glory gone, and across the lawn something seven centuries older than itself, the walls of a church which rings with praise no more except for the songs of birds.

Lower Ettington House stands where the house before it was set up in 1641; the old church tower and one of its chapels stand haunted with their memories, and even yet still rich with ancient treasure. We may wonder if there are any more interesting ruins in Warwickshire than those of Ettington's lost church.

We found a Norman window set in a buttress of the tower, and in another buttress of the nave a remarkable piscina shaped with a

trefoil arch with a shelf at the back of it under another trefoil arch.
Looking down from the tower, peeping out from the mass of ivy
creeping over it when we called, is a tiny balcony, and looking down
from its oak-panelled roof are still four stone angels. On the walls
of the tower are still brasses on which the wind and rain of generations have left their mark; they are of Thomas Underhill and his
wife in their Tudor costume, with only four of their 20 children left.
It was an Underhill of an earlier date, Anthony of 1587, for whom
there was written a very beautiful epitaph still kept in the tower; it
ends with these beautiful lines:

> *As dreams do slide, as bubbles rise and fall,*
> *As flowers do fade and flourish in an hour,*
> *As smoke doth rise and vapours vanish all*
> *Beyond the wit or reach of human power,*
> *As summer's heat doth parch the withered grass,*
> *Such is our state, so life of man doth pass.*

In the modern chapel, built on the site of the south transept of
Ettington's ancient church, are three interesting sculptured groups and
much ancient glass. One of the sculptures is generally accepted as
being the work of Nicholas Stone; it is the sleeping figure of Dame
Frances Freckleton and she lies under a canopy borne on four pillars.
She has been here since 1633. Lying on an altar tomb much worn by
time are two Shirleys who lived and died in this lovely bit of Warwickshire 600 years ago, Sir Ralph still with his sword and shield, his
faithful Margaret at his side. It is said that the Shirleys have as long
a continuous history as any family in England, and this venerable
couple have been here since 1327. More imposing is the 18th-century
group with three marble figures of the first Earl Ferrers and his
countess, with their son George Shirley between them. The son is
sitting on a raised seat, the father has elegant buckles on his shoes
and at his knees, the mother wears a lovely pearl necklace, and both
the parents are holding their coronets.

The 15th-century glass in two of the chapel windows was brought
from Winchester College 100 years ago, when the chapel was made
into the burial-place of the Shirleys. The panels have bearded figures
from the Old Testament, including Absalom with a sceptre, and the
prophets Micah and Zechariah. We noticed a lovely Madonna, a
king kneeling at prayer, a charming figure of Nathan, and a head
believed to be that of William of Wykeham. On one of the walls,

hidden under the ivy, we found a scratch dial with 24 rays, and among the shrubs we were able to discover an old stone marking the boundary of the lost churchyard. Still within the consecrated ground is a great stone coffin, and still inside the tower is the iron chest covered with rust.

The 19th-century home of the Shirleys has sculptured panels on the outer walls showing incidents in the story of the Shirleys, among them the death of Hugh Shirley, a knight who dressed himself to look like Henry the Fourth in the battle of Shrewsbury, and another showing the Ralph Shirley whom Cromwell sent to the Tower. Carved on a stone are four lines telling us the proud story of this estate:

> *When good St Edward wore the crown*
> *Saswallo here was thane:*
> *His male stem still this manor own*
> *Now in Victoria's reign.*

It is thrilling to know that the Shirleys hold today the same land as they held 850 years ago when the Conqueror's Commissioners were on their travels for his Domesday Book. Alas, the house was empty when we called in 1934, and one inhabitant alone we came upon; he called himself Old Noah, for he had been in these gardens for more than half a century, having gone to them from—Bethnal Green! He remembered the days when Bethnal Green was a green indeed, and in all these years while time has been transforming it he has been in the country still, in this corner of the world where time brings little change.

And yet change comes, for here we stopped our car at the stables and stepped into a Victorian coach. We found it as it was in its great days, though not quite so smart; its silver fittings a little tarnished but its badges bright with paint, the head of Saswallo above them. We opened the door, unfolded its four little steps, climbed them, and sat down as if we had been Victorians riding through Shakespeare's Warwickshire before the motor car was born. So easy it was in Lower Ettington to run down the corridors of time.

When the old church fell into ruin they built the church of Thomas Becket in 1798, and it stood as the church until the 20th century. Now its tower is kept for funerals and we can read the names on the old gravestones round about it in living words of moss. When the second church came down they built a third one at the cross-roads.

It has a fine window of the Good Shepherd, an example of the splendid glass of our time from the workshops of Christopher Whall, and it has a curious little possession, a few olive leaves brought from the garden of Gethsemane. But still it is the old place that draws the pilgrim here to the ruined choir where only birds now sing, where we were not surprised to see an owl, where squirrels sit eating tamely as we pass by and rabbits scuttle at the sight of these strange things called human beings.

A Tuneful Voice from the Silent Walls

IT was in the seclusion of this great park, far from the noise of the world, that there was born one of our masters of music, for William Croft began life in the great home of the Shirleys in 1677. His anthems are sung in our churches and cathedrals and in Westminster Abbey where he sleeps, and, though they are sung no more in this church that he must have loved, it stands still as a sort of small cathedral for the birds whose anthems never cease.

As master of the children and composer to the Chapel Royal he wrote many splendid compositions in celebration of victory and peace in that troublous age. Composing, writing, and publishing, he was already one of the busiest men in the world of music when, in addition to teaching music and singing to the children of the Royal Chapel, he became their schoolmaster as well, and for an extra £80 a year instructed his choristers in the mysteries of reading, writing, and arithmetic.

Thirty of his finest anthems, with a grave and noble burial service, he lived to see published, and it was his proud boast that the two handsome volumes containing his work marked a new departure in the printing of music, the score being engraved direct on plates. He was able to break away at times from church music and for some years composed overtures and incidental music for the theatre, to accompany plays now forgotten except for the fact that he furnished music for them. Songs, sonatas, odes, and three of the most famous chants survive, and from time to time, "in quires and places where they sing," as the Prayer Book says, we entertain Croft unawares, a tuneful voice from Ettington's proud past.

EXHALL. Some of the stone and timber cottages of this hilly place near Alcester were here in Shakespeare's day, neighbours of a church which seems young still. Young as most of it is, it has a Norman doorway and some old windows, one with ball-flowers. There is a plain old font and among its other treasures is an ancient bowl, perhaps the old stoup, and a chair carved by an Elizabethan craftsman, but its best possessions are the brass portraits of John Walsingham and his wife, who lived in Elizabeth's day, both looking very serious, John in armour and his wife in a beautiful patterned gown.

EXHALL. A few miles from the busy streets of Coventry, the 20th century has robbed it of much of its peace but has left it with something of the beauty of a 13th-century church. The chancel is 600 years old, the tower is 15th century, and there is an old porch with a fine arch. Two beautiful bosses, appearing to be the work of a 13th-century craftsman, are on the vestry door. There are very old carved faces keeping watch near the windows, among them a horned animal looking very strange.

Little Elizabeth

FENNY COMPTON. A lonely spot among the Dassett Hills, this peaceful place has a handsome old inn, a house with a 14th-century window, and a signpost of the Warwickshire Bear set up in response to the King's appeal for signs illustrating local tradition.

A charming picture is the low spire of the church peeping above the cottages. The narrow nave has 10 impressive arches, attractive little clerestory windows, and a handsome roof. Right at the top of the chancel is a lonely head of a man with his tongue out. There is old oak panelling, a chest with three locks, a few fragments of medieval glass kept in a frame, the wreck of an old font, and an oak door in the north porch with what are said to be bullet-marks made when a company of soldiers took refuge here after the Battle of Edgehill. Very charming the chancel looks through its tiny arch, with the blue altar and the blue curtains.

It is said that the first known rector here was a man whose heart is in Winchester Cathedral, a half-brother of Henry the Third. Neither he nor any of his successors could have had a more model parishioner than little Elizabeth Croke, who has lain here since 1719, and of whom we read that she was

a dutiful child, careful to please and fearful to offend; of a modest, mild, and merciful temper; pure and unspotted from the world, she never had an enemy, lived beloved, and died lamented.

Not all Elizabeth's virtues were shared by Henry Bate Dudley, who was born here in 1745 and ended a fretful life in 1824. He seems to have quarrelled with most people, although he was fond of pleasure and won a little fame as editor of several papers and author of a few comic operas. He was a friend of Garrick and a magistrate of seven English and four Irish counties, but Dr Johnson disposed of him in a few words to Boswell: "Sir, I will not allow this man to have merit."

In this church is one of the daintiest royal arms that we have seen, delicately carved in oak.

The Broken Windows of the Civil War

FILLONGLEY. In a hollow where two streams flow, Fillongley has old timbered cottages and traces of a castle built by that John de Segrave who tracked down William Wallace and led him to the block.

Its 14th-century church is notable for its treasures in stone and medieval glass, and in the churchyard is a cross which must have been here over 500 years, although its slender shaft is modern. Perhaps as old as the cross is the great yew by the beautiful south doorway. The doorway has two stone faces almost worn away and the lofty chancel arch has two more. Lovely medieval windows and a modern roof with golden bosses in its panels give dignity to the spacious nave. The Norman font, which has come into its own after being used in a garden, has a massive bowl. Very handsome is the modern screen in a chapel, carved with thistles and roses. There is an 18th-century chest, and a pair of old candlesticks from Florence. Among the old glass treasured here is a small panel showing a man praying with his eight children, a rare bit of loveliness from the 15th century; and in the nave are other fragments of this ancient glass which were damaged last century. A relic of another war is something Fillongley must always cherish, a processional cross made from fragments of wood picked up in a shattered Belgian church on the battlefields of 1914.

FOLESHILL. Coventry has swallowed it up, and its church is hard to find among houses and factories. The pinnacled tower has stood about 400 years, and the font is thought to have been carved by a Norman sculptor, a very old thing in a very new world. There is a modern oak lectern with a figure of the Sower and his basket of grain, and in the new transept are two fine windows, one with St George and the dragon and St Lawrence with his grid, the other with St Elizabeth in blue and St Luke clad in green.

FRANKTON. A charming 13th-century church with ivied tower and a 17th-century manor house share the quiet of this place. The church has two queer stone faces very old and worn looking down on the chancel, and an oak door that has been swinging on its hinges for 600 years, a doughty veteran.

The Great House Empty and Forlorn

GRENDON. It is so quiet that life seems to have ebbed away from it since they cut the dial by the priest's doorway for telling the time of mass. The great house in Grendon Park, empty and forlorn, was fast becoming a ruin when we called. Its stables were deserted, the gardens overgrown with weeds, the fine gates rusted. It was all made new 100 years ago, but the Chetwynds were here 600 years ago and the church has their memorials.

Weatherworn but lovely still is the 14th-century doorway bringing us to their church, impressive with its wealth of oak carving. There is a panelled chest and a big chair with rich tracery. The pulpit, once a three-decker, is Jacobean. The old reredos, lost for many years (like the old font), has finely carved flowers and a head of Christ. On the altar rails, with their rich border of cherubs and birds, stand four figures in relief, one blowing a bagpipe and one a flute. Very striking is a fine canopied pew 300 years old, with a curious panel at one end showing Mercury with winged feet, a staff in one hand and a falcon in the other, and cherubs in the clouds above him. How the children must delight to sit in this stately pew!

The Chetwynd chapel, one of the small number of chapels and pews we have seen in England complete with fireplace, has a fine 17th-century oak screen with 12 cheerful cherubs between its arches and two more with trumpets, supporting a massive coat-of-arms. Round the walls and in the windows glow the Chetwynd shields. There is a weeping figure in the chancel in memory of Mary Chetwynd, who died in 1750, and two beautiful women in alabaster. One, perhaps a 14th-century Chetwynd, is a figure of slender grace, serene in simple headdress and a cloak enriched with roses, a tiny dog peeping from its folds. Her companion since 1538 is an engraved figure in a flowing cloak, sleeping with her child.

Great Packington C.P. Meriden R.D.,
Great Alne C.P., Alcester R.D., pop. 250
pop. 73.

Here John Ruskin Sat for Hours

GUY'S CLIFFE. It is the show-place outside Warwick, a lovely peep of a little mill and a big house. The house, which has an ancient core, is mainly 19th century, with Dutch gables and many little balustrades, and is a delightful picture in its frame of lovely trees, with gardens aglow, the sleepy waters of the Avon running by, fine old firs and oaks, and one of the biggest cedars in Warwickshire.

The story is that Guy, tired of love and war and pilgrimage, made a cave here and lived and died a hermit. An earl of Saxon England, he has become a legend. He is said to have killed a giant, a wild boar, and a green dragon. There is a much-damaged statue of him eight feet high carved out of rock about 600 years ago. It is in the chapel standing by the big house built in the 18th century on the ruins of the old. Close by the house (of which the road gives us a lovely peep through the trees) is Guy's Cave, with some Saxon lettering on the wall.

From Saxon days this scene has been a place of pilgrimage and legend. Here Henry the Fifth came; it is said he would have set up a chantry here had he lived. Here came John Ruskin and David Cox. Both loved to watch the old mill. Cox painted the mill and Ruskin would sit on the boulders for hours, thinking it all good to see.

A little way off across the main road is a column among the trees marking the spot where a gay young man met his tragic fate one summer's day six centuries ago; it tells us that "in the hollow of this rock was beheaded on the first day of July 1312, by barons lawless as himself, Piers Gaveston, the minion of a hateful king, in life and death a memorable instance of misrule."

The Curious Story of Piers Gaveston

PIERS GAVESTON, the favourite of Edward the Second, was the same age as his master, and was brought up at Court with him, in token of the gratitude of Edward the First to Gaveston's father, a landless Gascon knight who had served him with valour and fidelity. The son early fell into disgrace and was banished, to be instantly recalled on the accession of Edward the Second.

Edward loaded his friend with honours, made him Earl of Cornwall, gave him money, immense estates, and his own niece in marriage, and when he crossed to France he left Gaveston as Regent of the realm. The barons hated the upstart, as they called him, though he

Compton Verney
Richard Verney, 1526

Middleton
Richard Bingham, 1476

Compton Verney
Anne Verney, 1526

Wixford : Thomas Crewe and his wife, 1411

Middleton
Margaret Bingham, 1476.

Baddesley Clinton : 10 c.

Coventry : Mary Hinton, 1594

Barcheston : 16 c.

OLD WARWICKSHIRE FOLK ENGRAVED ON BRASSES

was no more upstart than other men of the time. He was artistic, witty, and gave the barons opprobrious nicknames; he was haughty and insolent and rapacious beyond precedent, and his influence on the degenerate Edward was wholly mischievous. The king robbed his queen to give to Gaveston, trampled down all who opposed the favourite, and set up complaisant toadies who tolerated him. The outraged barons and bishops assembled in council, succeeded in expelling Gaveston to Ireland, where he ruled for a year, at a greater cost than ever to the country, so lavish were the gifts the infatuated king made to him. In the end the anger of the barons and bishops grew, and the country was brought to the verge of civil war because the king would not dismiss his worthless associate.

For the moment the firm front of the opposition was effective and Gaveston fled to the Continent; but only for a few months. Then he stole back once more, skulking in hiding until Edward again defied public opinion by reinstating him at his side. Again the barons took up arms, and, though Gaveston was excommunicated, his militant opponents demanded his surrender to them. The king still remained loyal to him, and as the barons marched he retreated north with Gaveston. In May 1312 they parted for the last time, Edward to take refuge at York, Gaveston to stand a siege in Deddington Castle. The fortress was strong, but it was insufficiently manned and provisioned, and at the end of three weeks Gaveston was compelled to surrender, and one night he was seized and carried off to Warwick Castle, where he was summarily tried, hurried away to Blacklow Hill, and beheaded. Friars bore the remains to Oxford, where they lay for two years, and in 1314 Edward had the body buried with lavish ceremony at King's Langley.

The Strange Winged Creature

HALFORD. It is a lovely place half lost among trees where the Roman road crosses the Stour, with an ancient bridge and delightful views of a mill and a weir. But its prettiest corner is below the church, where lawns and flowers grace the wayside, and a quaint old timbered manor smiles across at a vine-clad cottage.

The church treasures a Norman chancel arch and two Norman doorways, one with an angel spreading his wings in the tympanum. A fascinating capital of one of its Norman columns has a strange winged creature and a little bearded man holding a sceptre in one hand while the other grips the jaw of a wild beast; a little face upside down looks on at his struggles from another capital.

Six heads of bishops have kept a long vigil from the oak cover of the ancient font. The embattled tower has a huge gargoyle of a man with arms about his head, and among the bells is one that has been ringing for over 400 years. In a corner are two big hooks, relics of the oldtime village fire brigade, which used them for drawing burning thatch off cottage roofs.

As We Like It

HAMPTON-IN-ARDEN. It is the countryside as we like it, the scene of As You Like It. Here is Shakespeare's forest with woods more free from peril than the envious Court, those woods where a man may find tongues in trees, books in the running brooks, sermons in stones, and good in everything.

There is charm at every turn in the quiet ways of old Hampton, in the very heart of all that is left of the forest the poet immortalised in one of his loveliest plays. Here are steep streets with 17th-century houses looking quaint and charming with their overhanging storeys and decorated walls, and only a little way off is one of the few pack-horse bridges left in the Midlands. With fine arches about 500 years old, it is a delightful place from which to see an English landscape.

The bridge and the church have been companions for centuries, the church with round buttresses, a modern porch sheltering a splendid old door, and almost every style of architecture known in our churches.

Standing finely on a hill, it had a spire till it was struck by lightning in 1643. The chancel walls, two windows, a north door, and the pillars of the nave are all Norman, one of the pillars enriched with finely carved heads. The arches of the nave are 700 years old. The base of the tower is 14th century, some of the windows are 15th, and the aisles are 16th. There is a very old font like an hourglass, an ancient stone seat against the south wall, and a recess with a battered figure of an angel where the heart of the lord of the manor may have lain long ago.

A rare example of old craftsmanship is a clock wound up for the first time about 300 years ago; it tells the time no more. Behind the altar are lovely old blue-and-white tiles with Calvary scenes on them, and near the pulpit is a small brass portrait showing a man in a long robe trimmed with fur. He has a rosary and a girdle with a purse and is probably Richard Brookes, a bailiff who worshipped here in the 15th century. At the sides of the altar are paintings of the Madonna and St Bartholomew. On an 18th-century monument is a shield with three porcupines.

One of the windows in the chancel has precious fragments of old glass with panels of delicately drawn birds; but the most striking of all is the glorious east window to Elizabeth Peel, a niece of Shelley. It is Hampton's finest possession, for it has not only a wonderful company of saints, kings, and singing angels, but a group of poets rarely met in our churches. Here in the heart of the Forest of Arden that he loved is Shakespeare holding a red rose, with Milton in a rich blue robe, William Langland the forerunner of Chaucer, and the great Chaucer himself with Dryden and Cowper and Shelley. We have seen no better group of poets in our journeyings, and they could have no happier meeting-place.

A Multitude in Stone

HAMPTON LUCY. A charming bit of Shakespeare's countryside, it has a glorious thing that Shakespeare never saw, an impressive 19th-century church built by Thomas Rickman, who made his name 100 years ago as a pioneer in the revival of those Gothic ideals that have never been surpassed.

It is noble inside and out, and fills us with surprise by its multitude of bosses and corbels, angels and animals and men. They must be here in hundreds, and truly magnificent many of them are. One of the corbels has a laughing fellow like a jester in a fool's cap, facing a very prim Miss with a deep collar round her neck.

The lofty vaulted roofs have all fine bosses, the east window is rich with scenes of Peter's life in glowing colour, and the windows of the clerestory glow with red and blue. There are 21 great lancets in the chancel, which has an apse by Sir Gilbert Scott. From the finely carved oak pulpit, set on a base of Devon marble, old John Lucy, who largely bore the cost of the rebuilding of the church, preached for nearly 60 years after Waterloo. He must have seen growing the great elms of Charlecote Park from which these pews were made. There is splendid ironwork on the door, and worthy of all this grandeur is the carving on the alabaster font. It shows Adam and Eve, Noah coming out of the Ark, the Baptism, and the Sending Out of the Disciples.

The Marvellous Group of Friends

HANDSWORTH. Birmingham has gathered it in its great arms and is proud to share its monuments. It should be so, for here was the workshop of three famous inventors who helped to build up the industrial era on which the city depends. Here these three sleep.

The church in which they lie has a tower about 500 years old, and a chapel of Tudor days. It is a church of striking monuments. One has a stone figure of William Wyrley, in armour with a lion, and his wife is in an Elizabethan gown with a dog. Another stone figure, perhaps older still, is of William Stanford, who has his feet on a helmet and has had through all these years to keep him company a carved skeleton.

Near the porch lies Francis Eginton, who made beautiful things. He was one of the men who worked for Matthew Boulton at his Soho factory, and he made a stir in his day with what were known as sun pictures, paintings reproduced in a new way. He afterwards became a painter on glass, and his fame grew so fast that he had a school of pupils to help him with his windows. We have come upon his work in two of our cathedrals, at Lichfield and at Salisbury, and his remarkable Last Judgment is in Magdalen College, Oxford. Nelson took Lady Hamilton to see him at his work, and it is recorded that a company of the prettiest girls for miles round threw flowers on their path while the bells rang out a welcome. Eginton did much work for William Beckford of Fonthill, who paid him £12,000 for 32 figures of knights and kings, and he made a fine window for the banqueting hall at Arundel Castle: it covers 200 square feet and shows Solomon receiving the Queen of Sheba.

Working with Eginton were the three friends lying with him in this place, James Watt, Matthew Boulton, and William Murdock. It was at the Soho factory that Watt and Boulton made their first steam-engines. Pioneers of the Industrial Age, it seems remarkable that after their great work together they should still be undivided here, Matthew coming in 1809, James in another 10 years, and William 20 years after. Their names are Handsworth's greatest pride and their monuments its chief possession. The bust of Boulton is by Flaxman, and shows him wearing a plain cravat and with winged figures on each side. One holds an inverted torch and the other has a tablet-picture of his factory. The Murdock bust is by Chantrey and the

Watt monument is a statue, one of Chantrey's best. It shows the inventor, dignified and earnest in thought, with his compasses and a plan of his engine on his knee. It brings back to mind the wonder of the industrial rise of England; has any other church three monuments like these to three men who did so much to change the world?

The Three Wonder Men of Light and Power

IT is a rare combination of circumstances which called together these Three Musketeers of Invention, Matthew Boulton, James Watt, and William Murdock. Boulton was a Birmingham man who was born in 1728 and died in 1809; Watt, born at Greenock in 1736, died in 1819; Murdock, a son of Old Cumnock, Ayrshire, born in 1754, died in 1839.

Boulton unconsciously prepared the way for the coming of the others. After a grammar-school education he was admitted to the works of his father, a silversmith, and with inventive ability created a business which outgrew the original premises and demanded the great works at Soho. There he made inlaid steel buckles and buttons and watch-chains, and invented a process for the reproduction in metal of classic works of art, which made him rich and famous.

He had the services of the best workmen in Europe, who, under his guidance, produced not only his works of art but machinery for coins, astronomical clocks, and telescopes, and drew to his hospitable home visitors from all parts of the Continent. During his leisure Boulton invented a steam engine but never perfected it, for chance brought him in contact with a man with a better idea than his own.

James Watt received a first-class education, including a knowledge of classical and modern languages, but inclined to drawing, and became a maker of scientific instruments, in which capacity he was appointed to Glasgow University.

There a model of Newcomen's steam engine was brought to him for repair. Like all its predecessors, it was an atmospheric engine; steam raised the piston but gravitation was responsible for the fall, for the power-stroke of the piston. Watt had learned from Joseph Black the principle of the doctrine of latent heat, and he attempted to make an engine in which the two strokes of the piston were actuated by steam. He had as partner Dr Roebuck, who, just when Soho needed mechanical power for its works, owed Boulton £1200. Roebuck could not pay, so he assigned Boulton his share in the engine Watt was making. His other creditors thought so little of the matter that they released the other share to Boulton for nothing, and so began the association between Boulton and Watt, developing into a famous partnership. Boulton dropped his own steam engine and financed that of Watt, and was within sight of bankruptcy before the scheme was brought to success and made to pay.

The two men fitted ideally. The splendid courage and fine generous spirit of the Englishman were essential stays to the delicate, sensitive, suffering Scot. Neither could have attained final success without the other; together they brought about a revolution in industry and enriched invention with a score of things that, commonplace now, were marvels as they left the brain of Watt and the workshops of the illustrious firm.

Murdock had been ripening his faculties as a farmer and wheel-wright, and turned up one day on foot at Soho asking for work, and during a conversation Boulton found that the young man was wearing a wooden hat that he had turned on a lathe of his own making. That decided it; Murdock was engaged at 15 shillings a week and, proving a treasure, was packed off to Cornwall at a pound a week to supervise the stationary engines the firm had installed there.

The young Scot was soon improving the engines, keeping the steam pumps of the mines going, delighting his friends with his experiments and soundly cuffing into politeness the churls who resented his intrusion into the county. When he was 30 Murdock completed his model steam locomotive, and at night he would let his friends see it at work in his room, tugging a load of shovels and fire irons.

Here Murdock made his first retort for coal-gas. He knew from experience in Scotland that lighted coal gave off a combustible vapour, and now he charged his retort with it, attached a tube with a perforated thimble for burner, and lit his home at Redruth with gas. He used to light himself on his way during winter nights with a flame from a little retort carried in his hand. Boulton and Watt would not hear of his proceeding with his steam engine: they needed his skill for the stationary type, and, although the mine-owners of Cornwall offered him a thousand a year to remain with them, back he went at the firm's summons to Birmingham. There, at the celebration of the Peace of Amiens in 1802, he lit up the whole works at Soho with gas, and two years later he installed his system for a cotton factory in Manchester.

The three geniuses proceeded on their several ways for several fruitful and prosperous years, the most wonderful combination of brains, good nature, and joyous cooperation in industrial history. Fortune smiled on them, and they all died practically in harness, delighting in their happy labour to the end, and found a common burial-place here within sight of the scene of their triumphs.

The Blacksmith's Son and His Legacy of Colours

HARBORNE. Except for a timbered house its massive tower of the 15th century is all it keeps of antiquity, for Birmingham has swallowed it up. But Harborne has woven itself into Birmingham with the dignity of one of the earliest garden villages, with hundreds of homes that were a model long before the garden village was so fashionable.

The old house still left is Tennal Hall, in which the Pearmans lived without a break 300 years. It is one of the hundreds of places where we are told Queen Elizabeth came.

The church, in a tranquil corner a mile away, has lost everything old except the tower, but its black-and-white roofs and dormer clerestories give it a touch of quaintness. It has a fine alabaster pulpit with canopied figures, and saints on the ends of the choir stalls.

In a window recess is a book with the names of those who fell in the war. The little oak panels are bordered with roses, thistles, shamrocks, and daffodils, carved and painted, and red-robed figures of Peter and John the Baptist guard this charming memorial. Windows by a 19th-century Belgian artist have scenes from the life of Christ in dainty colours, and one in the chancel is in memory of a Harborne blacksmith's son who made himself famous and whose works are in the city's great Art Gallery. He was David Cox. Here he sleeps under one of these chestnut trees he loved to paint.

This painter of wind-blown skies and wide expanses of the English scene was, like more than one of our English water-colourists, an artist who found his true calling in spite of all the obstacles of his birth.

The son of a blacksmith at Deritend, he was a delicate boy and had the misfortune to break his leg, so that he could never help his father in the smithy. That was really why he became a painter, but he had a long way to go and many ups and downs on the journey. He began by decorating lockets for a jeweller, but the jeweller died after 18 months of this employment and David had to begin again. After seeking other employment far and wide he found it in painting scenery at a Birmingham theatre, and here he was lucky enough to attract the notice of the elder Macready, who engaged him as scene painter. With Macready's company he toured the country for four years, and then came to London in the year before Trafalgar.

The tide now turned. He continued to make a living as a scene painter, but he took lessons from John Varley in water-colour, and sent a drawing to the Academy. It was accepted, and he was launched on the career that suited him best. He made many journeys to revisit places he had seen with the theatrical company, but it was now to find subjects for his brush. He taught drawing first at Dulwich and then for 11 years at Hereford, but when he returned to London to live at Kennington he was a recognised master of his art, and his water-colours commanded a ready sale.

He settled at last at Harborne, near his native place, and interested himself in oil painting; but it was his water-colour, at first delicate but stiff, and later freer and filled with air, that gave him his place in fame.

A Monster and a Lady

HARBURY. Here lived a monster about a hundred million years ago, a huge ichthyosaurus buried 40 feet under ground and now with some of its ancient companions at South Kensington.

And here, too, lived a lovely lady in the days of Queen Elizabeth, Jane Wagstaffe. Her memorial in the nave of the church must have looked very fine in its day, but it has lost the brass portrait which showed her in her lovely Tudor dress, and it has lost the brasses of all her children but one, a poor mite no longer than a pencil. A little gem all alone (named Jane after her lost mother), she wears a flowing robe.

A pleasant spot to come to is Harbury, with a windmill above its cottages, the beams of its sails like four huge arms. Long the home of the Wagstaffes, the village still has a school they built in Shakespeare's day, a grey building between two giant chestnuts. An old inn, a tall yew, and a magnificent chestnut 14 feet round (a small hamlet's population could sit under it) keep company with the 13th-century church, which is not without a touch of grandeur. One of its vicars was Richard Jago the poet.

Forty Churches in Sight

HARTSHILL. From the ridge on which it stands the rows and rows of its miner's cottages and plain little houses sink out of sight in a spacious view which on a clear day takes in the faint peaks of Derbyshire.

Forty churches can be counted on the plain, and just over the border in Leicestershire is one more significant than any other. It is at Fenny Drayton, where was sown the seed which was to grow and spread throughout the world, for George Fox was born there, founder of the Society of Friends. One of the shoots of his planting stands above Hartshill, a Quaker meeting-house and a Quaker school. In the village itself Michael Drayton was born. He sang in his Polyolbion of the river Anker which sauntered past his birthplace to join the Tame, "trifling betwixt her banks so slow."

The story of Hartshill before his day was long but is clouded in the mists of time. The Romans may have built a station here; the site is one they would have chosen, and their kilns have been found, and pottery stamped with the maker's mark.

Then Hugh de Hardreshull found it a convenient height for the Norman castle he built in 1125. Traces of its chapel are left, and some of the walling of a 14th-century strengthening of the defences. This and Oldbury Camp, not very distant and older than the Romans, comprise the historic record of this small place.

By the rectory lawn stands the 19th-century church, with a remarkable west front. It has a deeply recessed doorway occupying nearly the whole width of the church, one of the biggest doorways we have seen, in stone and blue brick, with arches and pillars and carved capitals. Above is a great wheel window, four stone roundels with symbols of the Evangelists, and at the base of the bell turret are two quaint heads, one a gossip with two tongues.

It is one of our most captivating literary figures who saw the light here, one who went round England in poetry.

Michael Drayton Who Went Round England

FRIEND of Shakespeare and Ben Jonson, Michael Drayton was born here in 1563, and at an early age was admitted as page into the Goodere household at Polesworth. From his cradle, he tells us, he "inclined to noble poesy," wondered what kind of men poets were, and, clinging to the knee of his tutor, begged the learned man to make him a poet too.

His first works, a metrical rendering from the Scriptures, were burnt at the behest of the Church; he combined a love of Virgil and of Spenser in his Idea, the Shepherd's Garland; he stood forth as a sturdy lover of his motherland in the long historical poem which eventually became the Baron's War.

His magnificent Ballad of Agincourt was inspired, it is thought, by a rough ballad he had heard sung by a minstrel at Polesworth. It remains still an unmatched martial lyric. He loved history, and feared that unless he sang the glories of his country they would die forgotten. Therefore he gave half a lifetime to his greatest work, Polyolbion. It is a great pity it is not to be bought today. In this he makes a survey of the country, and with a great song for each county tells of its rivers, its hills and dells and smiling meadows, its birds and beasts and flowers, its history and legend. He must have travelled far afoot, and up and down the rivers, for roads were bad and few. This is his opening picture:

> *The sundry varying soils, the pleasures infinite,*
> *Where heat kills not the cold, nor cold expels the heat,*
> *The calms too mildly small, nor winds too roughly great,*
> *Nor night doth hinder day, nor night the day doth wrong,*
> *The summer not too short, the winter not too long.*

The poem was illustrated with footnotes, each county had its map, and running through all the maze of detail was a trilled melody sometimes rising to strains of exquisite beauty.

The poem runs to 30,000 lines, a thousand times too many for poor Michael's generation, which would not read it but left a later age to discover its abounding charms. Yet he was not discouraged, but after all this labour wrote his delightful Nymphidia and the Muse's Elysium, bright, blithesome, and musical as he had never been before.

He sang to Elizabeth, he half ruined himself by celebrating James with indecorous haste, he sang to Prince Henry, he sang on into the reign of Charles. It is possible that he was the "rival poet" of Shakespeare's Sonnets. Certainly he was Shakespeare's friend and Ben Jonson's. On the completion of Polyolbion Jonson wrote him a noble tribute beginning with the lines,

> *It hath been questioned, Michael, if I be*
> *A friend at all; or, if at all, to thee,*

and praising this poetic journey through England in a splendid eulogy.

Drayton was a year older than Shakespeare; when he died in 1631 Milton was 23, reading him and modelling himself to some extent on this lost master, who had given us almost the finest sonnet in the language, that beginning, "Since there's no help, come let us kiss and part." He lies in Westminster Abbey, with an epitaph Ben Jonson is believed to have written.

The Brasses Far From Home

HASELEY. It is trim as a well-kept garden, and has spacious views of pastures and many noble trees. It has a new manor house, charming in grey stone and with a Tudor look about it; and it has part of the old manor house where the Throckmortons lived when Shakespeare was a boy. On the porch of the old house are the initials with olive branches and lover's knots of Clement Throckmorton and his wife. We meet them in the simple church, where on their high tomb are their portraits in brass, he in armour with head resting on a tilting helmet, she in a beautiful gown. At their feet is a brass of their 13 children, boys and girls in two ranks facing each other.

The brasses are interesting to antiquarians because they belong to what are called palimpsests, old brasses astray, far from home, used a second time so that they are now engraved on both sides. There are more of these brasses in this country, bought or stolen from Flanders, than there are now original brasses there. On the back of this Throckmorton brass is the figure of a 15th-century civilian and some Flemish 14th-century canopy work. It is odd to remember that when the 14th-century craftsman was engraving this brass in Flanders our builders were raising this tower at Haseley, where the brass was to find its way.

The tower has a 15th-century window with fine old glass showing the Annunciation, St Catherine with the wheel, St Winifred with a cross, and a priest—little gems of colour, probably as old as the 15th-century font. There is another window with a few old fragments of glass in delicate colours, and a fine old black-and-white wagon roof, a kind rarely seen in this countryside, but familiar elsewhere.

A cottage by the church has the remains of a timbered tithe barn.

Old Parr

HATTON. It is spread among the quiet lanes in the heart of Warwickshire's beautiful woodlands. The fine lychgate to the church has four gables and winged lion gargoyles. A yew which may have been a sapling when the 15th-century tower was built still throws its shade across the graves. The rest of the church has been

Haselor C.P., Alcester R.D., pop. 145.

made new since Samuel Parr was vicar here. There are two painted panels of Moses and Aaron, and some fragments of Flemish glass in the west window. In another window are fine portraits of the Disciples with their emblems, and from golden glass two angels look out, one with a trumpet and the other with a scythe. There is an old font on a new base, and a peal of six bells old Samuel Parr put here.

There is an inscription to the memory of this remarkable man, who was in many ways Dr Johnson's double, and a portrait which makes us think they must indeed have been very much alike. He was a robust countryman who is said to have had the Herculean intellect of Johnson without his prejudices or his temper. He was here for 39 years in the 18th and 19th centuries, and during that time he built up a library and was much visited by literary friends, who delighted to make pilgrimages to the parsonage across the fields.

In his forty years in this village Dr Parr was a European celebrity. He was born at Harrow in 1747, son of a doctor, became head boy at the school, helped his father, went to Cambridge, and was driven home by poverty. After some years as usher at his old school he applied for the headmastership, supported by a petition signed by every boy in the school, but he was unsuccessful and went off, followed by 45 Harrow boys, with whom he set up school for himself.

All his savings were converted into books and he built up a library of 10,000 volumes. Classical studies were his delight, and although his writings under his own name were insignficant, his pen has been traced in many pages of works which added to the fame of other authors. He was an intellectual institution ; he knew everybody, had 1500 correspondents, and left 8000 letters.

Parr had a horror of the east wind, and his friend Thomas Sheridan, who loved him as a guest, once kept him his prisoner for a fortnight by fixing the weathercock showing the wind dead east. Cambridge made him a doctor of laws ; his admirers furnished him an annuity of £300 a year, and here he dwelt among his little flock, with his guests, his Greek, and his letters, loving, next to them, church bells and old glass. He died in 1825, and here he lies in the chancel, within sound of bells he often helped to ring.

A Mile of the Medieval World

HENLEY-IN-ARDEN. It is as lovely as its name, an open, friendly place, with a mile-long street of many glimpses into the medieval world: who could pass it by? Nowhere in Warwickshire shall we find a street more varied in timbered walls and crazy roofs, in ancient windows and hoary gables, in doors and doorways so gracefully grown old. Along these pavements we step into Tudor England; almost we expect to turn a corner and see the Morris dancers.

He who chooses his time will come when all is quiet here; entrancing it is then to spend an hour or two looking at Henley's old houses and inns, built when there was no lack of sturdy oak from Arden forest. Aptly indeed Henley has been called a museum of domestic architecture. It has one splendid old house with five yews in a row casting their shade over its timbered gables, and it has a wealth of ancient carving in fine staircases and doors. There is some of the best linenfold carving we have seen, and in the floors are immense beams of oak, all wondrously worn and smooth. It speaks of Tudor England from every nook and cranny, a wonderful home which we hope has been rescued from the uncertainty hanging over it when we called, for it was deserted and filled only with the strange sense of long ago.

Stand under the yews and look along the street to where the church tower rises above the gables and the crazy roofs, with the timbered walls of the old Guildhall beyond. It is a perfect picture, such a scene as would have greeted Shakespeare if he came this way. It is so very English, this street of contrasts, all its cottages striving to be different yet with that rare harmony which age and old associations bring.

Forgetting that cars are rushing past, we let our fancy fill the street with tumult of another kind. We picture Henley full of excitement at the news of the death of Simon de Montfort on Evesham Field, every doorway agog. Peter de Montfort had fallen too. He was lord of the manor of Henley and lived at the castle which stood on the hill behind the church of Beaudesert, 100 yards or so from Henley's church. In his time Henley was an exciting place, for he was one of the King's most famous captains, Warden of the Welsh Marches and Ambassador to the French. He allied his fortunes with his more famous namesake, whose great friend he became, and under him the men of Henley helped in the fight to establish the right of the burgher to sit in Parliament with the knight, the baron, and the bishop. We may feel that this village in Arden took its share in the

awakening of that democratic spirit which was to shake England to
its foundations.

Not least among the ancient treasures are the inns. We look
through the timbered porch of the Old Bell to a courtyard which
must have been busy when the horse ruled the world of speed. The
White Swan, with 1358 on its pleasant gabled front, is said to have
been the resort of poets and writers 100 years ago; Boswell thought
that here the poet William Shenstone wrote his most familiar lines
(perhaps his only familiar ones):

> *Whoe'er has travelled life's dull round,*
> *Where'er his journeys may have been,*
> *Must sigh to think he still has found*
> *His warmest welcome at an inn.*

A place of rare charm is the Guildhall, where the people of Henley
have met for 500 years. Ralph Boteler's arms are over the fireplace;
he built the hall in 1448. Particularly fine is the roof of old timbers,
and there is old oak everywhere, in the Elizabethan sideboard, the
refectory table, and the chairs. Here are the ancient maces and symbols of all the civic offices Henley once maintained, the truncheons
of the old constables, some good pieces of pewter, and an old candelabra. One gem of medieval painted glass shows Antony the Hermit. But perhaps the best of all the relics here is the charter granted
to Ralph Boteler by Henry the Sixth, with one of the best examples
in the country of the Great Seal of England of that time, in green
wax. Lovely is the little Dutch garden of the Guildhall, overlooked
by the tower of the church.

In the church porch we are greeted by a king and queen, two fine
corbel heads worn by the passing of nearly five centuries. They are
probably of Henry the Sixth and his Queen, and both have flowing
hair. Under them is a holy-water stoup.

The glory of the church is the beautiful tracery of the 15th-century
windows, the splendid roof-beams, and the great stone carvings on
which the roof timbers rest. The carvings show figures in costume
of the time when the church was built, and there are grotesque
animals. The 16th-century pulpit has linenfold panels, and there is
an old processional cross from the Continent, set with precious
stones. An old painting shows Christ bearing the Cross. The fine
oak panelling in the sanctuary is of our own time; so is the glass
which fills the east window with a harmony of soft colour.

Henley's old cross is five centuries older and five hundred times more beautiful than its ugly petrol pumps, but only the steps and the slender shaft remain.

The Wonder That Came to Watling Street

HILLMORTON. Of all that came along Watling Street to Hillmorton, Roman chariot and Roman legion, priestly procession and knightly cavalcade, none was so strange or made so great a stir as that which came to it last of all, the great wireless station with masts 800 feet high, the Voice and Ear of the British Empire in the Wireless Age. The Romans came and went and left not more than a name, some coins, and a few tiles and potsherds. The Normans came and left the church, and stone portraits of their great families, the church's founders and benefactors, within it. These were the Astleys, still a fine old name in England.

Thomas built the church in the 13th century and died fighting at the battle of Evesham. Other Astleys rebuilt it in the 14th century and enlarged it in the 18th, and all left their memorials, though mostly little but names and dates. But among them is a cross-legged knight who is probably Sir Thomas who died in 1336, and with him lies his Margaret in long sleeves and a close-fitting gown. In his priestly robes lies William Walton, who was serving his church before Chaucer rode to Canterbury.

In one of the very big pews is a curious thing, a trapdoor which can be lifted by a ring. Under it is a brass of an unknown lady, very dignified, with a mantle over her gown and a veil down to her shoulders. She may have been Lady Katharine Astley. The shaft and base of a 14th-century cross still stand on the main road.

For many miles round Rugby and Hillmorton can be seen the towering wireless aerials. These great aerials, veritable symbols of our Age, tower above historic Watling Street, which runs close by. The Rugby Radio Station of the Post Office is four miles south-east of Rugby and occupies 900 acres. From it telegrams can be sent to any part of the world and to ships on any of the Seven Seas. It is the world's telephone exchange, for it has the power to link the instruments of the majority of telephone subscribers in the five continents. Many big liners also may be spoken to from here while they are crossing the Atlantic.

The outward and visible signs of all this wizardry are the 12 great masts and, to a lesser degree, the clusters of shorter masts which appear to nestle comfortably at the feet of their taller brothers, away on the east. These shorter masts support the aerials used for the Beam system of directional wireless, in which short waves are used for long-distance telephony. The tall towers support the aerials used in long-wave transmission. Each of these 12 giants is 820 feet high; when we called there were no higher wireless masts in the world. They are a quarter of a mile apart, and each weighs about 200 tons. They are of steel, and triangular in shape, the three vertical posts in each being 10 feet apart and braced together.

It would be expected that great slim structures like these would run some distance into the ground into solid foundations, but as a matter of fact they are not fastened at the base at all. The new idea of foundations in architecture was adopted here in its very beginning. The base of each mast tapers and has a ball-shaped end. This rests in a socket in a big granite block which is firmly mounted about six feet above the ground. Each tower is held upright by 15 wire stay ropes, arranged in five groups of three. These stays are firmly anchored in the ground some distance from the mast. Mounted in this way the mast is capable of free movement at its base and unknown stresses are avoided. If it were fastened rigidly the swaying of such a tall and heavy structure in the wind would probably cause the steel to snap; as it is the masts are designed to withstand wind pressure of 140 miles an hour and a horizontal pull of 10 tons at the top. The bracing is so efficient that the sway is no more than five feet.

Each mast has an electric lift capable of carrying three men to the top in about 12 minutes, so that inspection and maintenance can be carried on with little waste of time. Painters are always at work somewhere on the masts, for it is important that they be fully protected against the ravages of weather.

A Picture in Two Chapters

HONINGTON. It is in two chapters, a lovely street that hides itself away like a true piece of England, modestly set among great trees growing from trim green verges, and a rare building of the 17th century, a classical church with all the fashionable ornaments of a conventional day.

The way to it has been cut through a park; we come through the stone piers of the vanished gateway, over a bridge with 22 stone balls adorning it, until we reach the parting of the ways, with the rural England of all time on the right and the classical 17th century on the left. But everywhere are the great English elms, a long line of them, sometimes five yards round their trunks, throwing their shade on the grass verges and on the lovely stone cottages with thatched roofs.

The church is tucked away in a corner of the park, cut off from the 17th-century house. It has formal vases standing on its parapet, a little apse, four weathervanes on the tower, and a noble elm rising above it all. The lower part of the tower has been here about 700 years; all else is 17th century or since. Looking up the aisle from a pompous monument at the west end are two 17th-century men in loose cloaks and buckled boots. We have seen such men many times in pictures of Charles the Second and his friends; they are two Parkers, father and son, almost comical in their great curly wigs.

Most of the monuments and windows are in memory of the Townsends from the great house. One is perhaps the most unpleasant cherub in all England, a nightmare of sculpture with a mass of crossbones worse than anything by Mr Epstein. Two of the fashionable sculptures of Richard Westmacott show a weeping woman at an urn in memory of Lady Elizabeth Townsend of 1821, and a pilgrim resting with his staff and knapsack, in memory of George Townsend who ended his pilgrimage a few years later. There are two old chairs in the chancel, charming twisted altar rails, and an elegant brass lamp hanging by four dainty figures.

Honington Hall, built in the 17th century with the church as its neighbour, has a remarkable front looking into its park, for peeping out from oval recesses in its brick walls are six busts of Roman emperors, a surprising sight in our English countryside. The quaint octagonal dovecot near the house has a sundial.

The Window in the Buttress

HUNNINGHAM. It is by the river and has an ancient bridge, a dreamy and beautiful place with thatched and timbered cottages and a little church among the fields. Very odd its tiny wooden tower looks rising from the sturdy masonry of the 13th-century walls. The bell which rings out from its small chamber was ringing in the days of Agincourt.

A fine old black-and-white roof protects the nave and chancel.

There is a built-in Norman doorway, and that most unusual thing, a window in a buttress. Among the stone faces looking down from the arches of the nave are two we imagine to have been crusaders.

IDLICOTE. The quaint church and the big house are like good friends sharing the beauty of a glorious park. The house was a grange belonging to Kenilworth before the Reformation, and there are still fragments of the moat and an ancient tower, standing alone.

Most of the church is 14th century, but it still preserves a simple Norman doorway and a Norman font. The aisle has an oak screen five feet high, and a very old stairway of solid oak climbs under the arcade to a tiny gallery. Low box pews line one side of the nave, the other having one huge pew enclosing the clerk's desk, a canopied two-decker pulpit, and three benches, a very odd arrangement.

The Old Fiddler

ILMINGTON. There was music in the air when we came one summer's evening to this romantic spot. With stone cottages where the lovely plains of Warwickshire rise up to the Cotswolds, it has winding ways, a 17th-century gabled manor house, and the church the Normans built with a battlemented tower among the trees.

We found in the churchyard old tombstones richly carved and shaded by a yew which has been here about 300 years. The fine old porch has a Norman doorway with a canopied niche, and everywhere its massive walls remind us of the Normans. In the nave are Norman arches. In the tower is an impressive arch and lancet windows cut through more than six feet of stone. The chancel arch has a stone face like a bit of Egyptian sculpture. On another arch is a queer face showing its teeth, with colour on its cheeks and its eyes.

There are three stone seats for priests, a tiny piscina, two fine old chairs, an ancient font, and an iron-bound chest like a family trunk. A tablet tells us that the Brents of Stoke have been buried here since 1487. Perhaps to those days belongs the lonely, nameless praying figure with a fine face and wearing a long simple garment. The modern sculpture of a youth weeping at an urn is in memory of Francis Canning of the manor house. By the porch is an unusual 18th-century tomb with a canopy and spire.

We found villagers and visitors at Ilmington being entertained, as they had been for years, at the cottage with a maypole in the garden, close to a small stone building called the Old Fox House, with quaint carvings over its doorways of a fox chasing a fowl and being chased itself by huntsman and hound. It is a cottage Cecil Sharp knew well, and here we found his fiddler friend. Everywhere in Warwickshire is the fame of the old fiddler, for he fiddled his way down many years and in many places. We found him playing his 300-year-old fiddle to a group of children, as if we were in Merrie England once again. He had played in Canada to old folk who love the tunes of Shakespeare's country, and, dressed in his century-old smock and Morris hat, he has been seen at every folk-dance festival for miles around.

Here Sir Thomas Overbury, an unfortunate poet of Shakespeare's day, was born at his grandfather's house.

Murder Most Foul

SIR THOMAS OVERBURY, son of a judge, distinguished himself at Cambridge University, and returned from abroad master of several languages and of a ready gifted pen. He was recognised as a foremost influence in introducing art and culture into Stuart Court life, but to secure his foothold there he had to stoop to subservience to one of the most ignoble of James's creatures, Robert Carr, afterwards Lord Rochester and Earl of Somerset. Carr, who preceded Buckingham as royal favourite, had good looks but no education, so the brilliant Overbury was an indispensable ally, as Carr, all-powerful as the fount of office and honour in that corrupt age, was in turn indispensable to Overbury.

Carr fell in love with Frances Howard, wife of the Earl of Essex, and Overbury wrote to her glowing letters and passionate poems which the illiterate Carr sent as his own. Overbury furthered the intrigue, but when he found that a divorce and the marriage of the countess to Carr were intended, he took fright, and incensed Carr by seeking to dissuade him, and denouncing the profligate beauty in unmeasured terms.

Carr fell a victim to the wiles of his imperious lady and her great-uncle, the Earl of Northampton, and the three carried out a plot of unparalleled complexity. First Overbury was cunningly offered a mission abroad, which, being poorly paid, would have involved him in pecuniary loss as well as removing him from Court. Carr himself counselled Overbury not to accept it, and two days later had him flung into the Tower for disobeying the King's command.

Isolated from his family and friends, Overbury was submitted to a course of slow poisoning. Outside the Tower they had an apothecary to compound the poisons, and a woman of infamous life to test their effects on animals. The end came on September 14, 1613, and a jury of ignorant men having certified that death had resulted from natural causes, the emaciated body was secretly buried. Rochester married his lady and was created an earl so that she might not suffer in rank by her divorce. For two years she ruled at Court, where her husband was more powerful than the king.

Then suddenly retribution came. A boy living in Flushing who had worked for the murderous apothecary let slip the fatal secret, which was at once communicated to England, and the guilty parties were arrested and charged. The lieutenant of the Tower, his henchman, the apothecary, and the woman were hanged. Carr and his countess were tried with as much ceremony as had attended their wedding. Bacon, who had formerly been a suppliant to Carr for favours, led for the prosecution. They were both found guilty and condemned to death, but James revoked the sentence and committed them to the Tower. He released them after five years, so striking a wounding blow at the monarchy, and inducing many to believe that he had been privy to the whole foul plot, which is probably not true.

The Great Sights Kenilworth Has Seen

KENILWORTH. If we come to it from Coventry we have come by what was still when we called one of the loveliest four-mile roads in England, and it brings us to a ruin as historic as anything in these islands. It is not beautiful as many ruins are; it has not the loveliness of Tintern or Fountains, or the grandeur of Corfe Castle, but who can come to it and not be stirred by these gaunt red walls with their doors and windows open to the sky, and such a march of great events starting in the mind as may bewilder us?

It is a place to dream in. Here has been heard the gay minstrelsy of centuries ago, the tumult and the shouting of the pageant. Here was something of the intensely human drama of the life of Queen Elizabeth. Here have been heard a thousand boasting and beseeching voices of history. Here imagination sees again the pomp and vanity of our great age of pageantry; here echoes something of the shame, the pity, and the pride that have mingled through the centuries.

A place of pilgrimage for all our English-speaking world, home of kings and queens, old centre of wars, it is enshrined imperishably in our island story. Eight hundred years have passed since men quarried the stones to build these walls. Geoffrey Clinton, watching his castle grow on the rock rising from Kenilworth's gentle slopes, must have reflected on the good fortune that had come his way. A man of lowly parentage, his talents alone had won for him a high place in the favour of the King. He was made Treasurer and Chief Justice of England. Here, he would say to himself, should rise a home worthy of the holder of so great an office. But he built too well. Henry the First had made it possible for him to build; Henry the Second looked on the castle with covetous eyes and took possession of it. Now began the long story of strife, of tottering thrones, of schemings and rejoicings, that Kenilworth has known.

Let us look at Caesar's tower and its great keep, the best remaining symbol of Geoffrey Clinton's days. The building is of immense and awe-inspiring size. Partly rebuilt in the reigns of the second and third Henrys, it has withstood the storms of the centuries and the passions of men. It stands about 80 feet high, its walls 14 feet thick, with a well 70 feet deep. The roof has gone, but there are windows and arches as the Normans left them. Other windows it has on which a curious change was wrought, for Robert Dudley, eager to flatter the vanity of his Queen, had them made new so that when Elizabeth came she might see nothing but the hand of Tudor times.

When Henry the Second's son rebelled against him a garrison was placed in the castle, and from this tower the soldiers of Henry would look out on the wide Warwickshire fields for a sight of their enemies. Thus it tells us of a father and son at war with each other. But it tells, too, of a father and son in arms together, for in the wars of the Barons it was Simon de Montfort's home. Within these walls the French champion of our English liberty would hold many a council of war. He was fighting for the road to Kenilworth when he fell at Evesham, and his son Simon was waiting at the castle to receive him. A little later Henry the Third was camped here with a great array of troops, and the siege went on for six months till hunger and disease forced surrender. Simon fled to France and the barons with him were given four days to leave. The generous treatment by the King was regarded as a sign of the royal moderation which was ultimately to reconcile the opposing forces in the Barons' War.

A stirring scene it would be when the King rode in, brave music

Knowle   **Grimshaw Hall**

Warwick   **The Castle**

Kenilworth   The Castle Ruins

Kenilworth   The Ruined Walls and Windows

from the walls and much fluttering of flags. He came in triumph, but Kenilworth was soon to see a sight as mournful as this was splendid, the entry of a king to whom events had brought the final bitterness of defeat. Edward of Carnarvon would gaze in dismay on these stout walls when they brought him here from Wales, where he had been hiding. Here he came to spend some of the unhappiest of his last unhappy days, so soon to be ended at Berkeley Castle by an act as brutal as any that stains our history.

We walk from the Norman tower across the inner court, past the crumbling walls of the Presence Chamber, into the Great Hall. It is open to all the winds that blow, yet there is grandeur in its fine lofty windows, and beauty is in this doorway enriched with sculptured foliage which Queen Elizabeth may have seen.

Here we cannot be far from the spot where Edward himself would stand to receive the deputation that had come from London at the bidding of the Queen. They brought him in dressed in a plain black gown, all his kingly bearing gone. While his son Edward of Windsor was receiving in London the acclamations of the people, the temporal peers and the prelates, this Edward would hear from bishops, earls, barons, knights, and burgesses the command to yield up his throne. A despot in his day of power, it was he who was now bullied and despised. It is said that at the sight of the prelate Orleton, his implacable enemy, Edward sank to the ground: but he soon recovered, so that the pitiful ceremony came to an end with the steward of the royal household breaking his staff in front of Edward, an act performed at the death of a king.

This, then, Kenilworth saw: a king deprived of his throne, bereft of his friends, denied the sight of his children, with the knowledge that his wife was chief among those against him. Bitterly Edward must have longed that his days might close. The country round Kenilworth would be calm and lovely then as now. He would find much to reflect on as he gazed from his window before his captors came to take him away to more indignities. The rooks wheel mournfully above where we stand; it is as though they are mindful of the doom of the mighty dead.

We turn to think of a happier chapter. Now comes on the scene the famous John of Gaunt, Duke of Lancaster, to whom the 14th century owed so much of its improvement in domestic architecture. He redeemed the character of Kenilworth from its severity as a fortress. His buildings extended all round the inner court, some of the walls of which we see. A corner tower he built is here today, and from it we look over the green valley where lay a great lake. Sir Walter Scott has called it Mervyn's Bower, and made it the refuge of Amy Robsart. The mullioned windows of the ruins known as Leicester's buildings are one of the glories of the castle. These rooms were built by Robert Dudley for the Queen. He spent £60,000 preparing for her.

Four or five times Elizabeth came, her most famous visit in 1575, when the magnificence of Dudley knew no bounds. The Queen's pleasures were to have all that the arts of pageantry could devise, and all that money could buy. There had been nothing like it in England before, and we may doubt if there has been anything to equal it since.

From the roof of the gatehouse Robert Dudley built we look on the tilt-yard and imagine the scene as the Queen arrived. Six trumpeters sounded a fanfare from the walls as she entered on a white horse. From a pool bright with many blazing torches came one representing the Lady of the Lake, attended by nymphs to greet the Queen. All along the bridge which she crossed were great posts; some bore cages filled with birds, some were laden with baskets of rare fruit, others had sheafs of corn. There were clusters of grapes and silver wine vessels, arrays of armour and weapons. They were the offerings of all the pagan gods of peace and war. Everywhere the Queen would see the armorial emblem of this proud man whose guest she was, his two ragged staves in silver. As she reached the castle a great peal of music and the thunder of guns burst forth, and fireworks brightened the sky; we are told that they included flying birds and fighting dogs and cats, with a dragon flying three times as high as St Paul's before it scattered its fire. For 17 days the Queen remained and the feasting and rejoicing went on. The Queen's capacity for amusement must have been as marvellous as Dudley's ingenuity in providing it. Every hour had its event. Minstrels played and sang in every corner of the castle; the park was full of mimic gods and goddesses.

Shakespeare would be a boy at this great festival, and it is thought he may have looked on with the boys of his school, gazing astonished at the fireworks, peeping entranced at the plays. Looking on these ruined walls, and thinking of what he would see, we may reflect how all this pageant faded and left not a wrack behind. Strange indeed it seems that in three centuries and a little more so great a change should have come to pass in a once royal home; but there was a change soon after Elizabeth's time which to the one woman it concerned must have seemed tragic and complete.

The castle would be still a noble building, unharmed by Time, when Alice Leigh walked here with her children. She would think how the first Robert Dudley had filled the place with music and gay company, and all the pleasures he could think of, for the entertainment of his Queen; and she would think, perhaps bitterly, how her husband, the second Robert Dudley, had left it for her a forlorn and empty place. Here with their four daughters she and her husband lived happily for a time, and then, when the suit he brought to prove his birthright ended and failed in the Star Chamber, he deserted his young wife, went off to Rome, and scandalised the court by marrying Elizabeth Southwell, maid-of-honour to James's Queen, who had gone with him dressed as a page.

Less than 100 years were to pass before the magnificent castle became a ruin. Cromwell gave it to Colonel Hawkesworth. The Parliament troops pulled down many of the walls, some of them 10 feet thick. They melted the lead off the roofs, broke the glass in the Gothic windows, cut down the woods, drained the lake, and wrought havoc in the park. For years the destruction went on. Yet even this could not deprive Kenilworth Castle of its grandeur, for the gatehouse is almost as perfect today as then, a charming example of Elizabethan architecture. It is habitable and we can go inside.

Robert Dudley's initials are cut in stone above the finely carved porch of this fascinating house. Just inside is a bronze tablet, a little touch of American pride, erected a year or two ago, telling of the Underhill family who lived at Kenilworth and from whom descended John Underhill who founded the family afresh in New England. Here also are two chests, one with 1669 upon it, the other a small one, both richly carved. Above is a great armorial shield of iron, richly carved. The entrance is a delightful introduction to a house so full of treasures and oddities that merely to name them would take many pages.

In the drawing-room is an immense alabaster fireplace, sculptured with Elizabeth's monogram and Dudley's arms, and an inscription in Latin telling us that his virtue lives beyond the grave. The guardroom has huge beams of 1570 and charming panelled walls, two old chairs carved with the heads of eagles, and lovely fragments of old glass. Here is a collection of pewter including immense chargers with the Tudor rose, said to have been used by Elizabeth.

In one of the bedrooms is one of the finest tester beds in the country. Charles Stuart slept in it. It is richly adorned with carvings. One panel at the head contains the Madonna, two others have female figures carrying cornucopias. Four small faces exquisitely carved are in the corners of the top, probably the Evangelists on whom we call:

> Matthew, Mark, Luke, and John
> Bless the bed that I lie on.

In this room is a bronze portrait of Charles Stuart. There is a dower chest of iron said to have been used by Henrietta Maria, with an amazingly complicated lock. Another fine mantelpiece is of cedar adorned with skilfully wrought wreaths, with an unopened Tudor rose at the centre.

The house has much medieval and modern glass, among the old being an excellent figure of St Nicholas, surrounded by modern panels with quotations from Goethe and Shakespeare. There are many pictures by famous artists, landscapes by Gainsborough and Constable and portraits by Reynolds, Lawrence, and Kneller.

We leave the gatehouse with its store of fine things, and a few steps away is Leicester's barn, another unspoiled survival of Tudor days. Probably it was the stables when Elizabeth came; it has been admirably restored. The lower part is of stone, the upper part of brick with timbering unlike any other we remember, for it is in the form of Robert Dudley's emblem, the ragged stave. Inside, the roof of sturdy timbers is a striking sight. Many of them are the original beams.

Much has been done in our own time to recapture the beauties of the gardens. Rubbish heaps have been cleared away, trees planted, and thousands of bulbs made a glorious show when we called. On some of the lawns exploration still goes on, and the spade has brought to light the foundations of the Norman fortress. In the inner courtyard the crypt of a Norman chapel has been discovered. Wander where we will among these ruined walls, with their deep mysterious cavities, arched doorways, narrow stairs, lofty oriels, each corner has its captivating interest. There is no stone uncared for now, and, remembering this, we are grateful to one whose pen did much to stay the progress of desolation and neglect. For it might all have been very different had there not come to Kenilworth, a little more than 100 years ago, a man of middle age, with lofty forehead and keen grey eyes, leaning on a stick. He came in through the gatehouse many times, and spent many silent hours among the lonely walls. Nobody took much notice of him, but Walter Scott would go quietly back to the King's Arms to write a few more glowing pages of his Kenilworth, a novel which still brings thousands to Kenilworth every year. We may still see the room at the inn where he stayed, with the furniture now as it was then.

We leave the castle with a parting look at the lofty windows of its Great Hall, fitting background for the stirring drama of people and events emerging out of the past, and filling this solitary place with a vivid and ever-restless pageantry.

A little walk through the friendly town brings us to the church, a small, snug place in a hollow. Geoffrey Clinton walks with us, for the work of his time is here too. At the end of an avenue of trees from the church are the ruins of the priory he built, under which it is said he is buried. It is sad to see what havoc Time has wrought in this once lovely place, for lovely it must have been if we are to judge by fragments. One gem of its architectural beauty remains in the arch of the gatehouse. It was built of red sandstone like the castle, and has one charming small window. A stile leads through the arch, and round the corner is the old guest house, containing some of the priory relics unearthed in our own time. The foundations of many of the walls can be traced.

The church has one sight that holds every traveller entranced— its thrilling doorway, the work of Norman masons and probably from the priory. The arch is framed in a square of richly carved stone with diamond, zigzag, and beak-like mouldings, and there are panels carved with flowerlike patterns. The smaller treasure of the church is its plate, a silver chalice given by Robert Dudley, and a flagon, plate, and chalice given by his deserted wife Alice Leigh, exquisitely engraved. In the chancel are three seats for priests and a canopied piscina very old, with fragments of carved stone from the vanished priory.

The chancel screen is fine and modern, enriched with grape-vine and arcades. The lectern and the pulpit are of the same admirable workmanship. There is much modern glass in the charming 14th-century windows, one with a good Resurrection scene. There is a graceful white monument of 1817 to Caroline Gresley, with a woman reclining on a couch watched by her husband and child; the figures are by the fashionable sculptor Westmacott. Beautiful, too, is the white figure in the memorial to Sophia Cave, who lived in Kenilworth for a time.

An odd relic for a church is a great ingot of lead, boat-shaped, with the seal of Henry the Eighth's Commissioner, weighing nearly half a ton and probably part of the lead melted down from the priory roof.

Kenilworth is full of interesting old houses. On the castle green are timbered cottages which were doubtless here when Elizabeth came. In the town are charming Georgian houses with delightful doorways. One dwelling opposite the church has the name of Latimer House above its doorway. It has been much altered in modern times, and there is now, perhaps, not much left of what was there when Latimer preached from the steps not long before he walked to the stake at Oxford. The news of his coming would spread through the Warwickshire villages; we may imagine this street thronged with a great crowd eager to catch his words. It is a scrap of Kenilworth's story and England's history that we ought not to forget.

The castle has its glories, and its pity and shame; we think of it as a place which has seen a vast multitude and is now a great solitude. It has much that we never can forget, but we may think of this small house close by, keeping alive its memory of a man who preached the Word and kept the Faith, and gave us for evermore those glorious words that cannot die:

Be of good comfort, Master Ridley, for we shall this day light such a candle in England as I trust by God's grace shall never be put out.

Charles Stuart's Banner Waves on Edgehill

KINETON. It is one of the pleasantest old towns of Warwickshire, a place much liked for its wide streets, its charming red and grey houses, its old inns and stable yards. Pure English is the scene by the church, with a row of dormered cottages in the shadow of the tower.

It was all very much like this, no doubt, on that October day when the banner of Charles Stuart was waving from the top of Edgehill and the great army was assembling in the fields below. On the heights above the fields of Kineton the King addressed his troops before the battle, declaring his love for his whole kingdom but asserting his authority from God. Standing not far from him would be Sir Jacob Astley, who lifted up his eyes and hands to heaven and cried : "O Lord, Thou knowest how busy I must be this day: if I forget Thee do not Thou forget me"; and then—"March on, boys!"

Kineton's streets were blocked with carriages and wagons after the battle. The fight had waged thickest between Battle Farm and Thistle Farm, and soon they were laying 500 dead in one great grave in Kineton fields. It was while the fight was at its height here that William Harvey sat down under a hedge with the young Prince of Wales and the Duke of York, his pupils. There the immortal discoverer of the circulation of the blood "took out of his pocket a book and read: but he had not read very long before a bullet of a great gun grazed on the ground near him, which made him remove his station." Thus old Aubrey tells the story. Both these boys lived to be kings, but their tragic lives can have seen few days more terrible than this so fraught with destiny for their dynasty.

Again the fields of Kineton come into history, for here, one July day in the following year, Henrietta Maria met Charles near the scene of his first battle, having slept the night before in Shakespeare's house, the guest of his daughter Susanna. We may imagine that the bells of Kineton Church rang for the king and queen then, as a year before they had tolled for Kineton's dead.

The church has a 14th-century tower which seemed to be perishing when we called; the rest of the church was refashioned in the 18th century. But it has one relic as old as the church itself, the fine stone figure of an unknown priest. Very dignified he looks, and beautifully carved are the graceful folds of his long gown. Near him is an old ironbound chest. There is a beautiful Jacobean altar table with two fine chairs in the chancel. The east window has a great Crucifixion and on each side of the altar are windows with three saints, St George in one and in the other Elizabeth with a bunch of roses and Cecilia with an organ. On the chancel wall is a tablet to Diana Bentley with a little story of her life from which we gather that she was the ornament of her own sex and the admiration of the other, cheerful without levity, virtuous yet easy, engaging and inimitable, but, sharing the fate of the eminently good, she was cropped as a blooming flower.

Those who died in Kineton's fields in the Civil War are a nameless host; but those who died in the Great War have their names on a column standing on a pleasant green at the head of this old town. An ancient avenue of elms on the Kineton high road has been saved from destruction by that great friend of our highways the Roads Beautifying Association.

The Man Who Did Not Come Back

KINGSBURY. It is on a hill above the River Tame, where it is said the kings of Mercia had a palace. A hint of vanished greatness is near the church, a crumbling wall round Kingsbury Hall, now a farmhouse, but still with a touch of its Elizabethan splendour.

It was the Normans who built the first church here, and there is much of their work to see. In a charming corner of the village, keeping company with a fine old house, it has a Norman doorway, a 14th-century tower with a 16th-century belfry, and a nave arcade of lofty arches with two capitals which have a thrilling interest, for they still have the roughly painted outline for the medieval mason who never came back to finish his work. Half a dozen times in our tour of England we have come upon unfinished work like this.

The arch into the chancel, built after the Normans, has two grotesques which have been watching over it for centuries, one with its tongue out, the other with a monkey peeping over his shoulder. Another old arch has deep grooves in which it is thought the bowmen sharpened their arrows. The old font is unusual for having 12 sides.

In an aisle is a wall sculpture in memory of Sinmo Luttrell, Earl of Carhampton, who died in 1788, his crest having a dog with a fish in its mouth. In the east window is a great array of figures, a heavenly company about Our Lord: Peter and Paul, scenes from the last days in Jerusalem, the Good Samaritan, the passing of Dorcas surrounded by weeping widows, and (the gem of them all) Christopher crossing a stream by torchlight. Another charming window, in memory of a woman kneeling in the corner of it, shows a woman standing with a shawl over her head and her children round her, a boy clasping the hand of Jesus and two girls leading a tiny tot with a golliwog (the only golliwog we remember finding at church).

The School That Made a Mistake

KING'S NORTON. Those who love it think of it as a village trying bravely to keep the spirit of its wonderful past in the midst of the restlessness of a modern city, for it is perhaps the best of Birmingham's suburbs.

Antiquity lingers serenely about its splendid church, set on a hill. For nearly 500 years men have looked up to this tall spire, a graceful sight from many a field. Perhaps as old as the spire are the yews on which it looks down and the fine oak beams in the black-and-white house close by, once an inn, perhaps once the manor house, and now a social centre for the church. Its ceilings have wonderful timbers.

A little walk beyond the yews brings us to another hoary relic, a schoolhouse with a curious touch of history. A tiny and half-timbered building, with a rare 14th-century window of oak tracery, it huddles rather forlornly under the trees, grey and worn by the centuries. It was one of the schools endowed by Edward the Sixth, but it has lost much of its importance because (so the tale runs) King's Norton took its endowment in money instead of in land, while the school at Birmingham took the land instead of the money; and so Birmingham school grew rich while King's Norton remained poor.

Well worth while it is to take a closer look at the beautiful spire, one of the finest in the Midlands, rising from a magnificent tower. Of the many crockets adorning this spire hardly any two are alike. The porch is charming. Great carvings face each other from the corners, symbols of the Evangelists, weirdly hewn and deeply furrowed by time. Two small windows still as the Normans left them are the oldest possessions of the church. The east wall is 700 years old. The beautiful enrichment of the chancel arch is the ballflower ornament beloved by 14th-century craftsmen. The low chancel screen has in it some 15th-century oak carving. The east window has splendid modern glass.

The tower opens into the nave with a lofty arch from which quaint heads look down, one wearing a coronet, the other in a horned helmet. On an altar tomb in the tower are the engraved portraits of Humphrey Lyttleton and his wife as they were in the 16th century, he proud in armour over a coat of mail, with flowing hair, she in a gown and ruff. Between them is the face of a little child. There is another engraved portrait of a 15th-century priest with a chalice and a book—he is Humfrey Toye; and there is an entrancing monument to Sir Richard Greves and his family, a perfect 17th-century group. Sir Richard's helmet has an eagle, his wife's head is on a richly embroidered cushion, and the dresses are all charming; it is an exquisite piece of work, of which any church might well be proud.

In a panel of the tomb are shields from which come hands that clasp each other, and two vine tendrils spring from the figure of the lady, pass through the clasped hands, and put forth leaves and fruit, one branch entwining itself round small figures of four kneeling sons, another round five kneeling daughters. It is as if the sculptor has been thinking of the Psalmist:

> Thy wife shall be as a fruitful vine
> by the side of thine house.

Of Sir Richard Greves himself we are told that:

> His heart was fixed on Heaven, and he stood
> Not for his own but for his country's good.

Some bitter tragedy befell one of Sir Richard's kinsmen, for a stone tablet says:

> Ascension Day on ninth of May
> Third year of King James reign,
> To end my time and steal my coin
> I, William Greves, was slain.

There is a monument without a name under an arched recess, with a husband and wife kneeling, dressed as in a Vandyck picture.

Here lies a poet, scholar, and preacher of Shakespeare's day who long served this church and school, Thomas Hall.

The Scholar in an Age of Strife

THOMAS HALL, minister and poet, classical scholar and lover of books, was born at Worcester when Shakespeare was living at Stratford. He led an astonishingly active life. His church and his school were not enough; he wrote many books, collected a great library, lectured in Birmingham, and threw himself heart and soul into the Puritan cause. Five times he went to prison for his principles. He was plundered and hustled by Royalist soldiers. He saw Henrietta Maria arrive at the head of the troops on the march from Yorkshire to camp outside his church, and we imagine his indignation when they tore the lead off the roof of the church to make bullets. Two years later he would see King Charles himself march through King's Norton.

Amid these scenes of war he remained devoted to his church and school, spending his spare time writing or collecting the rare books now treasured in Birmingham Library. He was buried near the church and the school he served so well. When things had gone well with him his doors were always open to the poor. He had been seen to take his coat off and give it to a beggar. Brown bread and the Gospel, he used to say, make good fare.

The House of the Doves

C.P., Alcester R.D., foh 3.1.

KINWARTON. A rare place tucked away in the fields by the River Alne, its church, its parsonage, and its old farm buildings are a delightful picture. Well may Kinwarton be proud of its big dovecot and its little church.

The church has a small wooden tower, a fine black-and-white roof, an ancient studded door, old candelabra still used to lighten its darkness, and a font which still has its staples and bar from the days when it was locked to prevent witches from stealing the water. Very charming are two 14th-century windows, one with fragments of old glass showing the Madonna and Child, a winged dragon, and two saints. One window has oak tracery and another lovely window has St George and St Richard of Chichester with his cathedral. But the greatest treasure here is an alabaster panel which shows the dedication of the Madonna, Joachim and Anne bringing Mary to the Temple, with five veiled women standing by, their hands clasped in prayer, and a priest with an angel at his feet. This gem of 15th-century sculpture, probably once part of a reredos, was found over 100 years ago by a rector of this church among the rubbish in a carpenter's shop at Binton, four miles away.

On a grave by the gate is a stone perhaps 1000 years old, part of a Saxon cross, with carved knotwork.

We have to climb over a stile to come to one of the finest round dovecots in Warwickshire. So old that it is thought to have been here 600 years, it is alone in a field and has a charming roof and a lantern with two dormers for 500 birds to come and go. It is so big that a cottage could be built inside it, and its walls are strong enough for a fortress. Whoever would enter must bow his head, for the door is not four feet high. It is all older than the church, for it is a precious fragment of a moated grange which once belonged to Evesham Abbey; it saw the life of the old monks in the spacious days when the Church was lord of England, and it has seen the fall of the Church from secular power, and the coming of our new world.

Proud Monuments of Old England

KNOWLE. Proud of its two ancient monuments, its guild house and its church, the centuries have given it a rich store of treasures that all may see. It has a fine old inn with the sign of a white swan hanging over the street in one of the best bits of wrought iron for miles around.

The guild house has fine old timbers and is a link with the guild Walter Cook and his friends formed about the time of Agincourt. He had begun to build the church a little while before and he founded a college for 10 priests who looked after his guild, which became amazingly popular. It had thousands of members, among them dukes, abbots, and knights, and the illuminated register of their names is one of the treasures of Birmingham's great library.

Walter Cook builded well, but much of his fine church has vanished. Even his brasses have gone from the round stone marking his last resting-place. But the church has noble work in wood and stone. Its greatest possession is one of the most spacious screens in Warwickshire, a precious example of wood carving 400 years ago. It rises in perfect proportions, slenderly carved pillars growing into beautiful ribbed arches on which rests a canopy projecting four feet. It is all richly decorated with vines, and is a marvel of preservation.

Much carving worthy of its screen has this clerestoried church. Two of the choir stall misereres have quaint animals; we looked at a fox reading a book and an ape with a bag, which it is showing to another ape, while a bear looks on. On some of the stalls are tiny silver plates with the names of choristers who went to the war and did not come back.

There is a beautiful Soldiers Chapel with a magnificent traceried stone screen, a rich cornice, and the Crucifixion above it. A fine window shows three of Knowle's heroes kneeling by the trenches before the demon of war wreathed in flames; a battered church is in the background, and Christ and a host of angels above. Other windows have the Ascension in glowing colours, and St George fighting the dragon outside city walls; but the loveliest of all shows Jesus with the children, one asleep in His arms, one with a ball, and another with his pet dog and a pigeon.

Two richly carved kneeling-desks have friendly pairs of animals at their base, panther and goat, lion and ox, bear and cow, wolf and lamb; strange companions as symbols of peace. In a corner is the most pathetic symbol of war in our countryside today, a wooden cross from Flanders. The altar table is Elizabethan, and two chests fastened with iron clasps are from the ancient days when such things were hewn from solid oak. The roof keeps some of its fine old timbers, and the splendid pulpit with its hourglass in a wooden frame is worthy of the ancient screen. There is a triple sedilia and a moulded niche.

In the tower the lion and the unicorn adorn iron brackets two centuries old, and we are glad to see here also a bronze portrait of Walter Cook, the priest who loved this place and gave it most of what it has to see. His guild house has a few lovely old places to keep it company, one of them Grimshaw Hall, with many timber-framed gables and carved bargeboards. It has a projecting porch of two storeys, windows on carved brackets, and the elegant chimneys that add so much to the comeliness of 16th and 17th-century homes. It lies a mile out of the village, but would be a rich reward for a longer and duller walk.

A Lesson for All Mankind

LADBROKE. Old and unspoiled by changing time, its timber cottages grouped about its church, this small place opens its heart to all the world, for in remembering the men who gave up their lives for us it tells us of the price paid on the battlefield in money and in men by all mankind.

It remembers the nine who died for us, the 32 "who rendered dutiful service in various fields and divers ways," and all those others who "kept open the door of hope and bright the lamp of charity which endureth all things." It has, engraved on a great brass set in a Norman arch recess, the terrible figures of the cost of the great world war, a lesson for all nations that we should like to see in every church. These noble lines we read on this memorial:

> All witness bear as men go by
> That greater things than life and death
> Are Truth and Right which cannot die.

This church set among black-and-white houses, with a noble old yew at the door, belongs to all our chief building centuries; the chancel is 13th century, most of the walls 14th, and the clerestory 15th. The grey-and-white tower rises 120 feet.

The porch has a sundial which has been marking the hours for 300 years, and a group of queer sculptures which must make the porch a great delight to Ladbroke children. There is a weird man with curly hair, one wearing a crown and showing his teeth, one with odd devices round his mouth, and other comical figures, all from the vanished church of Radburn, where the tie-beams of the roof rested on them.

Indoors is an ancient sculpture of deep interest worn away by the hand of Time through 20 generations. Six hundred years ago it was a fine figure of the first rector of Ladbroke, John de Pavely; now it lies, poor worn-out thing, forlorn beneath an arch. It has had its adventures, for they dug it up last century under the floor.

The nave rises to a remarkable height and the chancel is dominated by a great east window, in which Christ sits in majesty with 100 figures about Him, a finely drawn group with faces full of expression. There is another modern window with Our Lord and two disciples; and in another is St Nicholas with his three little men and his three bags of money. We noticed near one of his feet a curious small drawing of a spider's web. In a tiny aumbry is a charming silver chalice of 1638, and near it is a crucifix covered with old mother-of-pearl delicately engraved with figures. The big brass almsdish has on it two men who appear to be wearing Puritan hats and are carrying an enormous bunch of grapes on their shoulders.

Little Red Riding Hood and Little Boy Blue

LAPWORTH. Coming down the lane we passed Little Red Riding Hood and thought her charming. She was coming from school in her hooded cloak, and behind her was Little Boy Blue in his cloak without a hood.

It is all the idea of a friend of the village who is now gone, and who paid for new cloaks for the boys every other year and for the girls in the years between. At Christmas time the school choir in their gay cloaks tour the village with lanterns, singing carols, and it is a pretty sight. Today the cloaks are paid for by a lady whose name is a secret, and we thought it fine that Lapworth should have its Little Red Riding Hood and its Little Boy Blue with a fairy godmother to find them cloaks.

It is a delightful church that these little ones come to on Sundays, a beautiful casket of stone inside and out. Its grey walls with their pinnacles glisten in the sun and are clearly much beloved. It stands on a hill with a lovely yew hedge round it and views of some of the gentlest wooded slopes in Warwickshire, and has a quaint chapel which tempts us but does not lead us in, for it would seem that the builders never finished it. It is the small and charming chapel at the west end, and has unfinished vaulting in its roof and no doorway into the church. Two doors under its archway lead us to the room above.

The church goes back 800 years, its Norman nave having received new arcades in our three great building centuries. Above them is a gallery of angels and grotesques. The oldest thing we see is a small Norman window. The most striking thing we see is a modern window in the chapel of the chancel; it draws us to it by its colour and its scenes. It is a memorial to Captain Adie Wale, one of the men Lapworth gave to England. It shows a young student in his study at college, having laid down his pencil, tearing off his gown as he listens to the call in 1914. We see him next as a soldier marching in France, with St George at the head of the troop. Then comes a young man at the beginning of his career with his foot on the first rung of the ladder of success, and after this is a little picture of this church set in green fields, while in a darkened scene a battery is at work and we see the stricken soldier with the Master bending over him in white robes.

There is a memorial of a mother and child on a stone relief in memory of Florence Bradshaw of Packwood Haugh, one of Lapworth's great houses, and an alabaster carving of the Last Supper on the reredos, an animated scene showing Judas drawing his cloak and hiding his face behind one of the disciples. A lovely modern screen has fine rose-tipped tracery and a magnificent cornice of grapes, an Elizabethan altar table, choir stalls made from the old rood screen, heads on the font carved 600 years ago, and a massive chest dug out from a block of oak.

Making History for New Zealand

LEA MARSTON. Far over the earth, on the other side of the world in New Zealand, are those who would love to walk among these black-and-white cottages and old barns, on this green in the shade of two cedars, and into this almost-forgotten church, tucked away at the end of a grassy track and dim with the diffused light of painted windows.

For here it was that a chapter of New Zealand history was made; here its first Constitution was framed. The old house has gone, the old Hams Hall where Lord Norton worked out this Constitution, and what we see in its place are the great cooling towers, among the biggest in the country, of the Hams Hall Power Station of Birmingham.

Here before the great transformation lived Lord Norton, a colonial reformer in the days when our great Dominions were just colonies and little thought of. Here Lord Norton, for nearly 40 years a member of the House of Commons as Charles Adderley, gathered about him a group of people, among them that strange genius Edward Gibbon Wakefield, and planned the development of New Zealand. It is traced back to one evening in 1850 when Adderley and Wakefield paced up and down the terrace at Hams Hall, "concocting the New Zealand Constitution."

Lord Norton's zeal knew no bounds. His wife used to say he thought more of the colonies than of his children. He sent labourers out from Lea Marston to a settlement at Canterbury, and he lived to realise the triumph of his dreams, for, born on the eve of Waterloo year, he lived to see New Zealand and Australia and Canada and South Africa united in the 20th century.

He lies in the chancel of the church, where his children have put a window in memory of his noble life; it shows the Presentation in the Temple. There is also a marble tablet on the wall with his wife's portrait. In a modern window is the portrait of one of the sons of the house, a kneeling knight before the cross, in memory of his falling in the war. The village peace memorial is a painted panel with a small figure of John the Baptist. A small portrait in brass is a tribute to the founder of the S.P.C.K. and the S.P.G., Dr Thomas Bray, who was vicar here for some time.

The avenue of trees which led to Hams Hall from near the church has been saved, and has an imposing cross near it, 20 feet high, which we understand was set up in memory of Mr Gladstone's visit. About Hams Hall grew great oaks planted by a Charles Adderley who knew Charles Stuart and was his equerry. Charles Adderley, who became Lord Norton, lies with his ancestors.

The Fairest Modern Town in Warwickshire

LEAMINGTON. It is the fairest modern town in Warwickshire and one of the finest in England for the calm dignity of its streets, the beauty of its gardens, the unspoiled loveliness of the little river from which it takes its name.

The Entrance to Jephson Gardens

The Parade

The Lovely Town of Leamington

Welford-on-Avon   **Old Thatched Cottages**

Luddington   **A Street Shakespeare Knew**

No more than a village three lifetimes ago, now it is known the world over as a town with healing in its waters and beauty in nearly all its ways. Its tree-shaded pavements are charming; its gardens are wonderful; it is a town with the brightness and fragrance of flowers in its heart.

Americans delight in it. It was known and loved by Thackeray, Dickens, and Ruskin, by Nathaniel Hawthorne and Washington Irving. Friendly and intimate, it charms every writer and every artist, and by roads mantled with wide avenues of trees it joins company with Warwick and Stratford and Kenilworth to make this part of Shakespeare's country irresistible.

Happy indeed would Benjamin Satchwell be if he could walk in Leamington now. If William Abbots could walk with him they would both rejoice to see how their devoted efforts to bring fame to their village had been crowned at last. Both were strong in their conviction that the waters of Leamington must prove of value to the world, and tireless in their enthusiasm for declaring it and building for the future. With a mind above the shoes he made and mended in his cobbler's shop, Satchwell was for ever writing or telling the praises of this place, while William Abbots built the first spa bath in 1786. They lie together in the churchyard of Leamington's church. They died within a few years of each other, and their graves are near, both marked by simple stones.

The great modern church of All Saints has a lofty western tower, 145 feet high. The nave is of cathedral-like spaciousness, with the tower resting on four colossal piers each with 20 round shafts, and the six bays on each side supported by piers of clustered columns to match. In the chancel are five east windows 35 feet high, almost the highest in any parish church in England, all with conventional glass except one, which is superb in its glowing colours of subdued red, blue, and gold. It is by far the best window in Leamington, a miracle of loveliness from the 15th century, and it has in it 12 panels of Bible scenes difficult to recognise owing to the dazzling richness of the glittering fragments, though we found in it the Feast of Cana, the Baptism, with Our Lord by a lake in Galilee and on the Road to Calvary. In other windows are many saints, angels, and patriarchs; one shows Paulinus baptising our people in the days of St Augustine, and another shows Augustine himself. One of the chapels has a wall-painting of the Nativity, and another has a brilliant triptych painted by an artist with crippled hands, a truly remarkable achievement, for it is big and fine, with our four patron saints, Our Lord in majesty, and angels playing harps and blowing trumpets.

There is one glory of glass and another glory of stone, and a veritable marvel of stone tracery is the rose window over the south door. It was copied with slight modifications from one of the finest rose windows in Europe, that of the famous church of St Ouen in Rouen. The magnificent wheel window in the north transept is also after one in Rouen. Both these windows still wait for the glowing colour such windows need.

These are things of which any church would be proud, yet there are greater treasures still, the silver chalice and plate by goldsmiths of the time of Henry the Eighth. On the chalice is the English hallmark of 1532, a date suggesting that they may have been given to Calais by Henry in the year of his marriage with Anne Boleyn, when he visited the French king. The chalice is exquisitely wrought, with much detail in which we see Jesus washing the feet of the disciples; figures of Faith, Hope, Charity, and Justice; the temptation of Eve; Moses striking the rock, and the Israelites gathering manna in the wilderness. This alluring treasure was probably the work of a Flemish goldsmith. There is another chalice of unknown origin, but very old and beautiful, and if Leamington had nothing else the pilgrim here is repaid if he has the fortune to see these gems.

The oldest possession of the church is probably the small red sandstone figure of a mitred bishop, with almost all its details worn away. It stands in a porch by a holy-water stoup. There is a good carved Jacobean chest and a picture of Emmaus by Guercino of Bologna, painted in the 17th century. The mosaic reredos in the lady chapel also represents the supper at Emmaus. The sanctuary roof is fan-vaulted in red and gold, seven brass lamps hang above the rails, and the reredos at the high altar is a fine stone carving of the Last Supper, in which Judas is turning away frowning, carrying the bag. Very striking are the lofty iron screens with heraldic shields, and the marble crucifix under which are the names of the Leamington men who did not come back. A window given by a Leamington mother is in thankfulness for her son's return.

No lover of dreams and flowers can resist the gardens of this gracious place. An hour spent in them is an hour of beauty whatever the time of the year may be. The Jephson Gardens are the floral crown of the town; we wonder if anywhere in the world a penny can buy more. Nathaniel Hawthorne spent many hours here, thinking, no doubt, of fresh tales. The French Riviera has little that is better to show than these shady walks by the River Leam, with their broad lawns, their spacious flower beds, their terraced rockeries, their roseries, and the fountains copied from Hampton Court. In these gardens stands the bronze statue of Dr Jephson, who brought much fame to Leamington by the use of its spa waters.

The most delightful of Leamington's social centres, the Pump Room, is in its own acres of gardens, with rhododendron walks and lime tree promenades, a rare place to come to when the crimson chestnuts and red mays are out, and music fills the air. The fine town hall, in front of which Queen Victoria stands, has windows with portraits of Shakespeare, Milton, and Byron; the museum and art gallery has a collection of Roman and medieval pottery; and the library has 30,000 volumes. The peace memorial stands among flower beds, with a bronze statue of a British soldier by Alfred Toft.

A chapter of history closed here with the death of Admiral Sir George Cockburn, the man who took Napoleon into exile.

He Took Napoleon on His Last Journey

SON of a London baronet and uncle of the famous Chief Justice Cockburn, he entered the Navy in 1780, as a mite of eight, and served it for 73 years. He sailed all the seas, he fought in all the wars of his era, a typical figure of the Nelson tradition. He served on the Victory before Nelson hoisted his flag on her.

He captured many a ship in single-handed fights, and in the American War he planned and helped to effect the capture of Washington. Peace summoned him home in 1815, and he arrived to find that Napoleon had escaped from Elba, and that he had been chosen to go to Plymouth in the Northumberland and convey the fallen giant to St Helena. At first Napoleon refused to leave the Bellerophon, the ship to which he had surrendered, but Cockburn was a model of tact and courtesy, and when he had to remove the arms of Napoleon's suite he left Napoleon with his sword, and made the official examination of the baggage a mere gracious pretence, with good results.

Napoleon expected to be treated as Emperor, but Cockburn was under orders to treat him only as a General. Yet by his obvious goodwill he won over the unhappy exile. The voyage lasted from August 8 to October 15, and many times during its course Napoleon opened his heart to his generous captor. He told the admiral that he had really meant to invade England from 1803 to 1805 and to dictate peace in London. He contrasted our political system with that of the Continent, and said that while a Parliament was ideal for England, it was impossible for the irresponsible peoples of Europe.

St Helena reached, the two men explored together, and it was Cockburn who planned Longwood, and his carpenters who made it habitable. He remained as governor of the island until the arrival of Sir Hudson Lowe in the following summer.

Madonna

LEAMINGTON HASTINGS. A delightful spot by the river Leam, it has a lovely manor house for the rich, 17th-century almshouses for the poor, and a beautiful church for all.

Its tower, looking down on yews and a fine chestnut tree, has an ancient sundial and two stone arches reminding us of Egyptian carvings. The centuries have given a touch of beauty to the fine arch of the north doorway, which has sculptured foliage and faces, a perfect setting for the oak door so weather-worn. Six angels have kept watch at the font for centuries, and a roof of fine old beams has looked down all this time on the imposing arches of this spacious nave. The pulpit and the chancel screen were made by Jacobean craftsmen, and keeping company with them are three fine old chairs, one with a beautiful rose carved among its foliage.

One of the windows has the Good Shepherd, a gem of a window in the tower has some old heraldic panels of glass, and the east window has scenes of Calvary. Its light falls on the tomb of one of Charles Stuart's Barons of the Exchequer, Thomas Trevor, who is here in his robes of office; another monument shows his son with his wife. A wall inscription tells of a mother who saw her little one for a moment before she died; she was Sarah Stockley, hardly more than a girl when she died 250 years ago, and we are told that she was:

> *A mother sadly thus described:*
> *Her babe she saw, kissed, blessed, and died.*

A Romantic Corner

LEEK WOOTTON. In that lovely piece of countryside which runs from Kenilworth to Warwick, it has some good old houses and a modern church approached by an avenue of limes and protected by a fine hammerbeam roof spanning its grey walls.

Two fragments of the past are at one church door, a portion of a stone coffin and a plain round font, much worn. The vestry has an 18th-century window remarkable for the wealth of its colour; it shows Our Lord, Paul, and Peter. It once graced the east window, now filled with modern glass showing Isaiah and Isaac, the two Johns, and scenes from the Nativity and the Crucifixion. The chancel screen is a splendid piece of work, with elaborately carved grape-vine, and matched by the handsome choir stalls and lectern. They were all the gifts of the Wallers of Woodcote, a house of fame in Elizabethan days; we found the name of Sir Francis Waller, to whose memory the screen was set up, on the peace memorial.

The quiet road from here to Blackdown Mill leads to a strangely romantic spot. The mill, long unemployed, has a fine wheel and two wooden balconies enriched with carving and supported by stout pillars. We look round and see the strange stone creatures which seem to have taken possession of this charming corner, for there is sculpture everywhere. Along the top of a pretty bridge a lioness watches a lion lick his paw, and a seal and a mermaid keep them company. A dragon clambers round the chimney opposite, and two monkeys climb a roof. It is all odd and queer and unlike England, rather like a page from some old fairy tale.

At Bannerhill, a farm two miles away, is an oak hollow enough for eight people to sit in. It is said that Cromwell once hid in it.

Sebastian Bound

LIGHTHORNE. It is charmingly set in its green hollow, with the village smithy hammering away under a thatched roof. The little church was made new last century, and only the tower is old. One rare possession it still has which has been shining here for centuries, a window of old glass showing Sebastian bound to a stake and pierced with arrows, the victim of that Diocletian who tried to stamp out Christianity. His companion is a modern figure of St Lawrence, to whom the church is dedicated, with flames about the grid on which he stands.

St George in the Middle of England

LILLINGTON. They call it the middle of England and so it may be, the middle of this dear, dear land set in the centre of the greatest land-mass of the earth. Other places claim to be the middle of England: Lillington by Leamington, which has an oak-tree said to mark the spot; Meriden, which has set up a memorial stone; Copston Magna, where the oldest inhabitant will tell you that the centre is just there; Minworth, where the boys of King Edward's Grammar School at Birmingham have proved it by demonstration. Perhaps we shall never know, but Lillington has marked it by an oak which she does not treat exceedingly well, for we found it stuck with notices to motorists and made to look like anything but a noble tree.

Yet we were glad to find an English oak growing on this spot and St George's flag flying from the 14th-century tower close by, and two old flags in the church which may have braved the battle and the breeze of some great day.

It was thrilling to find four wooden crosses here, brought from some corner of a foreign field that is for ever England; they are by a peace memorial with 29 names that live for evermore, and the name of Ronald Irwin, a vicar who died in peace from wounds he received in war. And more than good it was to find here, in the very heart of our land, a witness to that spirit of goodwill which truly men bear to men the whole world over. It is a moving little thing, a simple piece of wood with the words cut out with a penknife and inked over, saying in German: "Here rests an English flying captain." He fell from the sky into the German lines at Joncourt, St Quentin, and the men who brought him down put this inscription on his wooden cross. He was Captain Archibald William Field, who lived at Blackdown Hills round Lillington, and here this touching inscription hangs with its story below.

The church has a Norman doorway into the vestry, some neat carving on the front of its choir stalls, and two stone seats for priests with a window at the back of one; but it is mostly new and has no history except for the history of our time, which makes it at once the pride and the tragedy of our human race.

An Old Man's Memory

LITTLE COMPTON. Is there in Warwickshire, we wonder, a more charming example of our English Group than this church, this manor house, this rectory, and these small grey cottages? And where is a more fascinating saddleback tower than this, presiding since the 14th century over a church all white and wonderful? It keeps its 13th-century font in excellent preservation. It has a white stone pulpit and low white arches in the thick walls of the chancel. The small windows are delightful.

But it is a name in the floor that thrills us here, carrying our minds back to one of the stirring pages in history. It is the name of Juxon, and it comes to mind as we look at the splendid manor house in which the Juxons lived, its gables and mullioned windows overlooking the church. It has a gracious dignity, a gateway with magnificent stone pillars, and an aspect most impressive with wide and lovely lawns.

Here there used to walk about an old man with the most pathetic and dramatic memory of any man in England. He was Bishop Juxon, who came to this quiet place after he had stood with Charles Stuart on the scaffold. Walking about these gardens he would think of it all again; kneeling in this little church he would think of his king and remember. It was Juxon who, when the summons came for Charles to walk to Whitehall, burst into uncontrollable lamentations so that Charles exclaimed, "Leave all this, my lord; we have no time for it." Juxon was there when the King bade farewell to his children; he was at his right hand when they led him down Whitehall; he was on the scaffold when the King said, "I go from a corruptible to an incorruptible, where no disturbance can be," and it was to him that Charles spoke his last word, *Remember*.

Little Stonehenge

LONG COMPTON. Roses and old grey cottages, and a story running back to the dim twilight of history—that is Long Compton. It is the village with Warwickshire's Stonehenge.

Warwickshire folk come here to see the Rollright Stones just across the border in Oxfordshire. They are far above the village, on the top of a hill which is a bit of the Cotswolds, where the view is inspiring on a clear day. All Shakespeare's country lies at our feet, and much more of England is fading into blue. For miles the road runs on the top of this ridge across the heart of the Midlands.

On this windswept height, a little awe-inspring whatever the weather may be when we see them, are the Rollright Stones, a great circle of about 60 monoliths rough-worn by the winds and rains of centuries. They are of much greater age, the experts say, than Stonehenge, but they can tell us little of the purpose for which they were erected, ages before the Romans came. They were a mystery then and remain a mystery now.

The highest stone of the circle is a little over seven feet, the smallest four feet, and there may be more stones in the turf below. Four hundred yards away is a group of five stones called the Whispering Knights. A little away from the big group is a solitary stone nearly nine feet high, the only stone actually in Warwickshire. Called the King Stone, it is so placed, they say, that when seen from the centre of the circle on June 21 the rising of the sun is immediately in line with it. It may therefore have had, like the smaller group, some astronomical significance; but another suggestion is that it may have been the sepulchral monument of the chief of an ancient tribe.

We leave this windy height and its ageless mysteries of stone, and go down to the friendly village again. Very quaint is the old gatehouse over an arch which leads into the churchyard. It has two storeys and is made mostly of stone with bits of wattle and daub; it has a thatched roof and crazy little windows; and it was filled when we called with old pictures and furniture. But its history is nearly all forgotten. It may have been a priest's house, but in our own time it has been the home and shop of the village cobbler, and we envy him the fine view he had of the long village street as he sat at his last.

In the battlements of the church are loopholes which may have been used by marksmen in the Civil War. There is a sanctus bell turret, a Norman arch to the porch, and a door made in 1620. The nave is 15th century and the chancel 100 years older.

The most remarkable thing in the church is the stone figure of a lady who lies by the porch. For 500 years her face has had this curious stare, and her figure is oddly distorted where the stone has worn away. She has no name and no inscription; she lies here all forlorn, the unknown lady as mysterious as the Rollright Stones.

Queen Elizabeth Calls for Dinner

LONG ITCHINGTON. The River Itchen flows by and Wulfstan the Saxon bishop must have played by its shining waters, for he was born here 54 years before the Conqueror came. Others have found it a pleasant abiding place, or one in which to tarry by the side of the wide green and its tree-bordered pond.

There is a gabled house with timbered sides which Queen Elizabeth would see, for she was once at Long Itchington and was feasted in a tent "which for number and shift of large and goodlye rooms might be comparable with a beautiful pallais." Among those present on that famous day may have been some of the Odingsels, whose home, one of several beautiful English homes here, has stood at Itchington 700 years.

The church is chiefly 14th century, though it keeps some of its 13th-century lancets. On the massive 14th-century tower the broken fragment of the old spire shows above the parapet; it was struck by lightning in 1762 during a service. The chancel has much that is fine: an oak screen 600 years old, canopied sedilia, and a richly moulded Easter sepulchre. Under a stone canopy is a brass with a kneeling figure of John Bosworth, a 17th-century yeoman, and his wives Ellenor and Isabella. There is a Jacobean altar table, and an ancient chest with five locks. Quaint men look down from the modern hammerbeam roof, and little grotesques gaze from some of the arches and the walls. The chancel arch, which has a peephole at the side, has on its capitals a jester and a monkey with a young one nestling in its arms.

Here were the Romans, and their relics have been found; among the fine things we may see in Warwick museum is an ancient British urn discovered here.

The village boy Wulfstan, who rose to fame from here, was one of our first great statesmen, and helped the Conqueror with his Domesday Book.

Wulfstan the Great Saxon

BORN early in the 11th century, Wulfstan was to write a chapter of the close of Saxon days. He received what was considered in those decadent times a good education; and who could doubt his acquirements when, becoming a monk at Worcester, he was appointed schoolmaster there? His fine qualities made him Prior, and, a friend of Lady Godiva as well as of Harold, he was consecrated Bishop of Worcester in 1062.

When the Normans came, however, although Wulfstan swore fealty to the invaders, the great Lanfranc objected to him as too ignorant for the high office of bishop. Truly he was not learned, and he had to fight hard for the see he had unwillingly accepted, but he had the courage to maintain a right he had not sought, and the nobility of his character won him fast friends. He stood loyal to the

Little Packington C.P., Meriden R.D., Feb. 56

Conqueror, and to Rufus, and won back manors that had been filched from his bishopric. If he could be spared from history he should be in Ivanhoe, for he is the last of the Saxon princes of the church. If a monk came late to service Wulfstan beat him; if the young gallants about his palace wore their hair at what he thought an effeminate length he cut off the locks with his knife.

But he went about preaching, teaching, baptising, building churches and schools; and when the Normans stood aghast at the slave trade in Bristol Wulfstan went there and stayed until the unholy traffic was stamped out.

He was a man of abstemious habit, for whom water and plain fare were a banquet, but his palace was like a Saxon hall. There he was attended by a train of knights; there the sons of nobles came as pages to be initiated into the rules of chivalry; and the first thing he taught them was to serve with humility and deference the poor who fed daily at his table. From noon to sunset he feasted his guests in the old Saxon way, and kept the wassail bowl circulating, without himself tasting its contents. He was the most jovial saint in the calendar, a man of spotless life, maintaining the extravagant hospitality of his ancestors. He lies in his cathedral at Worcester, and was canonised St Wulstan. For a generation he helped to bring Saxons and Normans together, and one of his services to the Conqueror was to contribute to the making of Domesday Book.

The Clumsy Cook

LONG MARSTON. Who does not know the story that has made it famous? It is one of the best stories told of Charles the Second's flight after the Battle of Worcester. Here he came, the story runs, in disguise as Will Jackson, servant to Mistress Jane Lane. With Jane and several others he reached the house in this village which is still called King's Lodge, and was sent to the kitchen to work. There the cook bade him wind a meat-jack. Enraged at his clumsiness, the cook, little dreaming that before her stood the fugitive King, struck him as Roundhead troopers came in, saw a cook buffeting a yokel, laughed, and turned away.

Near the house of this story is a fine little deeply-thatched and timbered cottage with low doorways and stone floors. It must be much older than the house, and would be much as we see it now when Charles passed through. The village itself, in leafy lanes, has a group of charming old houses and cottages which are pictures of contentment in their lovely gardens. Perhaps Shakespeare, strolling along the few miles from Stratford, may have seen them.

The church has a quaint sight, a bell turret built up from the floor of the nave on great oak beams seamed with the passage of centuries. It must be nearly as old as the chancel arch, which has stood for 700 years. The fine cradle roof of the nave looks just as old, and so do the sturdy porch timbers. The round bowl of the font is Norman; in the east window are fragments of 15th-century glass with something of a Madonna; and the oak pulpit is Jacobean.

LOXLEY. Years ago the glory of this leafy hollow was a mighty elm, one of the biggest in Warwickshire, and its trunk is still here, though its glorious branches are no more. Near the hoary trunk stand Loxley's cottages looking across a deep wooded valley.

The small church was made new 700 years ago, and is still a humble place with candles and lamps to light its dimness. The village stocks have been brought inside and monuments have been taken out. There is a sundial on the tower saying "I die today and live tomorrow," and a very odd pulpit set high against the wall, with a small door into the vestry which the children must watch to see the parson come out, something like a jack-in-the-box.

Here Judith Shakespeare Loved to Walk

LUDDINGTON. On the Avon three miles from Shakespeare's home, a little off the beaten ways, it has little or nothing for us that is old—nothing but a stone from a font or a cross. Yet it might have been so very different. If the old church had still been here, and if we knew for certain what Luddington folk like to believe, this would be one of the most visited villages in the world, for it is believed here that in the vanished church Shakespeare married Anne Hathaway. If that is true the old stone is a very precious thing.

The church we see is less than a century old, and it has lost not only its ancient walls but its ancient registers, which would have proved the truth or established the falsity of the story of the marriage. Only the tradition remains, but one thing we know which makes a walk here memorable. It is known that Judith Shakespeare loved to walk in these fields by the river, and there can be no doubt that not once nor twice but many times she must have been here with the poet and her mother.

Caesar's Legions and Alfred's Men

MANCETTER. In this gracious countryside two people live for ever through dying for their faith, but older far is Mancetter in fame. It has known Romans, Vikings, Saxons, and Normans. Near by ran Watling Street, the famous highway down which Caesar's legions marched long before Alfred made it his boundary between the English and the Danes.

A wealth of trees, a charming black-and-white manor house with an imposing gateway, a group of cottages and almshouses, all cluster by a church among old yews, the impressive tower keeping watch. The tower still has an old sundial to mark the bright hours, and bells still ringing which have been pealing about 600 years. Many times they called to service those brave villagers Robert Glover and Joyce Lewis, who went out from here to die by fire. It was from this charming manor house close by that Robert Glover went; its rows of yews may be the offspring of yews he looked on, and his old home is almost as he left it, with its steep roofs and small gables and a belfry crowning its timbered walls; one of the rooms is still called the Martyr's Chamber.

Much of this beautiful church is 13th century, and it has all the marks of the days when our English building was at the height of its glory, for, standing by a great chancel arch to see the fine east window, we see the splendid black-and-white roof, 15th-century tracery, and the wide chancel walls, a splendid picture of the work of 14th and 15th-century men. The east window, with a canopied niche on each side, is a marvellous pageant of rich colour in glass six centuries old. It is crowded with beauty, with thousands of fragments pieced together, the remains of a Jesse tree, with David and his harp and other kings wearing their crowns, quatrefoils with saints, canopies with angels, and many familiar figures. Here are St John and St James, Paul and Bartholomew, and St Margaret in a red robe and yellow mantle.

The chancel has other windows with 14th-century glass, one showing St James in black and gold. By this window is a 17th-century marble of Edward Hinton with his wig and cravat. There is a tablet to a vicar for 56 years of last century, and a group of monuments to the Bracebridge family, a family with a very remarkable record, for its members have made their home in Warwickshire since the 12th century. On the monument of one of this proud family is a boast that they were descended from Egbert, Alfred, John of Gaunt, and Robert Bruce, and we read that he who lies below worthily closed this noble lineage, a proud boast indeed, even for an epitaph.

Under two crowns in the west wall are inscriptions to the two heroic neighbours of Mancetter, Joyce Lewis and that great scholar of Cambridge and lord of the manor here, Robert Glover. There is a chained book in one of the aisles with a picture of Glover in the fire.

Bravely They Lived and Gladly Died

A TRAGIC story of this Village Beautiful is the heroic surrender of these two lives. There is a sigh from every heart for Robert Glover and Joyce Lewis, who were led from here to the stake during the bitter days of Mary Tudor. Glover was one of three brothers who left Cambridge ripe scholars and converts to Protestantism; Joyce was moved by his example to follow in his steps.

In 1555 Robert was a husband and father of a family when Ralph Bayne, Bishop of Lichfield, ordered the arrest of the three brothers. The Mayor of Coventry sent friendly warning and two of them escaped, but Robert was ill in bed, and was seized and condemned. To his comfort there came Augustine Bernher, the uncanonised saint, Hugh Latimer's servant, murmuring consolation and succouring the victim's wife and hapless children.

Glover was depressed and wondered whether divine favour was denied to him, but on the way to execution he clapped his hands and cried, "He is come, He is come," and stepped with joy and alacrity to the stake, dying in company with a poor capmaker of Coventry. His example, following on the teaching of the three brothers, converted the strict Roman Catholic household of Thomas and Joyce Lewis, who owned part of the manor here, and Glover's persecutor forwarded to Joyce a summons which her husband compelled the officer to eat.

The arm of the Church was unwearying and terrible, and Joyce was taken to Lichfield gaol and imprisoned for a year. To her as to Glover and other martyrs appeared the unfailing Bernher, with words of sympathy and inspiration that bore her with unflagging courage to the stake. He was at her side to breathe a final prayer and benediction.

Undaunted by the sufferings of other martyrs, unmoved by menace or threat, Joyce was resolute to the end; and one who saw her chained to the stake said that she manifested a cheerful serenity and countenance so unchanged as to astonish all who beheld her. She died triumphantly, her hands lifted up to heaven.

John Middleton's Bridge

MARTON. A bright little village on the busy road to Coventry, we come to see its bridge across the Leam, both old and new. It was first built by John Middleton, a wealthy London mercer of the days of Agincourt, to free his native village from tolls. It has been widened for our Motor Age, but the old stones have been used again on the outer walls, and from the meadows by the river we see this bridge as it looked when packhorse and stage-coach passed over it, even perhaps as the Cavaliers saw it as they sped along the road one August afternoon in 1642 after being defeated in a skirmish at Bascote Heath.

But Marton's church has been here much longer than its bridge, for its south arcade and its red and grey tower are over 600 years old and the porch shelters a doorway by the first English builders. In a corner of the church are photographs of the men who never came back to this corner of England, and near by is a simple Flanders cross.

The Last Night of the Plantagenets

MAXSTOKE. In this little world of its own is a fortified castle with many treasures, one of the biggest tithe barns in the county, the ruins of a 14th-century priory, and a 14th-century church.

The castle is six centuries old, built by Sir William de Clinton in 1346, and from his day to ours it has been a private house. Set in the midst of lovely meadows, its magnificent oaks, sturdy chestnuts, and towering elms remind us of the vanished grandeur of the Forest of Arden.

A long straight avenue of trees leads to the gatehouse set up by the old knight about the time of the battle of Crecy. The solid oak gates, 5 feet wide and 12 feet high, hang on six of the strongest iron hinges we have seen. Across the middle of the gates runs a heraldic band. The groove for the portcullis is still here and the moat still has water in it; in places it is 18 feet deep and is crossed by an old stone bridge. The gateway, the battlemented walls, the turreted towers are perfect, seeming defiant of time. The courtyard, closed in by turreted and battlemented walls from which grotesque faces look down, seems the very heart of peace, lovely with its lawns, its flowers, and its doves.

It is hard to believe that the beams in the great hall of the castle have been here 600 years, so little worn are they. The drawing-room has Tudor panelling and a magnificent oak mantelpiece. There is a Whispering Doorway with a door superbly carved. It came from Kenilworth, and Richard the Third is said to have admired it on the night he stayed here on the way to Bosworth Field. It would be one of the last beautiful things he saw in his ugly life. There are three octagonal rooms, one with an unusual carved wheel ceiling.

The treasures include the gold watch Charles II gave Jane Lane for helping him to escape after Worcester, and a box said to be made from a limb of the oak in which he hid at Boscobel. There is a pair of Queen Elizabeth's silk stockings, salmon pink, with very tiny feet. There is a superb dining-table carved of solid oak, and a sideboard made, it is said, from a tree at which Cromwell used to practise shooting.

Round another fine table here, made of carved oak and once belonging to Sir Everard Digby of Coleshill, the Gunpowder plotters are believed to have sat weaving their plots. There is a shovel board table nine yards long with the quoits still on it. There is an elaborately carved four-poster bed six feet square in which Amy Robsart slept. There is much old furniture and many suits of armour, one with the story of Samson engraved on it by a 15th-century craftsman, many paintings by old masters, and many lovely miniatures. One of them has the quaint face of Tom Grainger, the last jester at Maxstoke; he died in 1681, and his descendants still live at Fillongley a few miles away.

It is a wonderful collection, truly, for any house in the land, and it would be more wonderful still if we could believe that what is called the chair of Henry the Seventh was actually the chair in which he was crowned on Bosworth Field. It seems too good to be true, but it is true that Maxstoke Castle has the room where Richard slept on the eve of Bosworth, and to which Henry came the evening after. Surely no other room in any English house has seen a swifter change in history than this—a Plantagenet king one night, a Tudor king the next. The room is in the Lady Tower. The massive wall and the rafters are still as the two kings would see them in these dramatic hours. Little has been changed since the fearful Richard slept here, hardly thinking that after one more waking he would be crying on the battlefield:

> *A horse, a horse, my kingdom for a horse.*

Here Richmond was to come when the fight was over, to sleep the sound sleep of a king-to-be:

> *God and your arms be praised, victorious friends,*
> *The day is ours, the dog is dead.*

In the park of the castle stands the great tithe barn as it has stood since Elizabeth's day, with its open-timbered roof and eight bays. A mile away is Maxstoke Priory, built about the same time as the castle, perhaps by the same men, but now a ruin. The noble gatehouse is still here with huge doors and two carved heads, one of a knight with the vizor of his helmet down, the other of a monk with a cowl. There is a farmhouse, formerly a gatehouse of the priory, with a painted ceiling copied from one taken down in 1868 which had 64 panels with coats-of-arms.

A quaint place is the church, close by the crumbling priory walls. Its best possession is the slender tracery of the 14th-century east window. There are fragments of ancient glass in one of the windows, and in the paving of the chancel are some tiles from the priory. An old chest bound with iron is six feet long. The pulpit and the gallery are both about 200 years old. Behind the altar is a modern oil painting of the archangel Michael. A small crucifix is a memorial to the men of Maxstoke who did not come back, and to seven flying men of the R.A.F., who perished in a terrible accident at Maxstoke during the war. In the churchyard is the nine-feet shaft of a cross 600 years old.

The Splendour and the Dream

MEREVALE. Glorious are its hillsides on a summer's day, its richly wooded landscape spreading out for many miles, and by the quiet road off Watling Street nature and man together have made a beauty unforgettable. We are bound to think of Wordsworth, the splendour and the dream.

Easy it would be to miss the small turret of the church, half lost in the trees, but not so easy to lose the noble gatehouse which leads us

Curdworth   Coleshill   Two Views of the Norman Font

Charlecote   Rowington

Lapworth   Wolston   Wootton Wawen

Stoneleigh   Sutton Coldfield   Oxhill

Old Fonts of Shakespeare's County

Hampton Lucy
Modern Font

Brailes
14th Century Font

Charlecote
Modern Font

there. Did ever gates open more charmingly than these? Before us lies a lake ringed with rushes and lilies and young trees that sway in every breeze. We are in the presence of a lovely house bathed in sunshine, and a church with turf running along its ancient walls.

Above the lake rises a thickly wooded bank, crowned with the turrets of Merevale Hall. It is the home of a descendant of Sir William Dugdale, whose library has in it the quaint diary kept by the old historian, a great friend of Pepys. The Hall itself is less than a century old, with fine views over five counties.

Standing before this beautifully wooded hill, we are looking at a fragment of the Forest of Arden as Shakespeare must have seen it. It has some of nature's most magnificent old gentlemen, giant oaks raising their heads here when Shakespeare was a boy, from whose ancestors came the sturdiest oak in England, for ships and cottages, manor houses, churches, and inns.

Worthy of its gracious corner of the world is the ancient church with its possessions. It offers a great contrast, for it is in two parts, one dim, the other bright with treasures kept like jewels. There is an odd charm in its unusual design. The west end, an empty space but for the gallery and the tombs, is part of a chancel built perhaps 700 years ago, and has two blocked arches on each side. The extraordinary gallery stands on eight tall and richly moulded pillars, and has a projecting centre bay. A finely panelled and massive piece of ancient carpentry, it is sometimes thought to have been a roodloft.

Here lie three unknown people in stone, two sleepers on a high tomb, and a headless figure facing them. The woman on the tomb has a tender expression that is breaking into a smile. She is wearing a fine necklace, rings on her fingers, and a rich headdress. Her head is supported by two angels, and at her feet are two dogs, one holding up the hem of her garment. Her husband is an imposing figure, wearing 15th century armour, his head on a fine helmet with a plume of feathers. Time has worn the hands that wielded his brave sword, but he has his gauntlets and at his feet is a lion. Round the sides of the tomb are six angels. It is thought these two medieval figures may be Edmund Lord Ferrers of Chartley and his wife, but nobody knows, though we may all feel grateful to the sculptor, for these monuments are beautiful work, a fine example of a period since which English sculpture has rarely been excelled.

Time has dealt harshly with the nameless solitary figure on the other side, for head and both its feet are missing. Yet it has the interest of being perhaps the earliest armoured figure in Warwickshire. It is believed to be William Ferrers, Earl of Derby, whose family were buried here in ox-hides before coffins were common. We see through him the type of man who fought for Magna Carta, for he wears armour as it was worn by knights who fought in the Wars of the Barons, with chain mail under a long sleeveless coat falling in graceful folds.

We leave him at the hoary wall that shelters him, and come through the great arch to the nave which has echoed with five centuries of praise. A flood of light streams through its east window, a beautiful mass of 14th century glass. It is one of the rare Jesse windows. In the lowest panels are the five good kings of Judah, above is another row of kings with David carrying a harp, above these are five more figures with Our Lord in the centre, and at the top are later fragments of saints and angels, roses, and horseshoes of gold. Through all the lower panels run the winding branches of the tree which stands for the rise of Our Lord from the House of David. The glass of this superb window is said to have been bought from the old Abbey of Merevale, of whose walls we may still see something near the church. There is a story that two ladies of Merevale worked these fragments of glass into their wonderful setting.

Not alone is it in its splendour, for there are two windows in the north aisle filled with glass 500 or 600 years old. At the top of each is a small round panel of the 18th century with colours like glistening jewels, one showing the hosts of the Children of Israel at the Red Sea and Pharaoh in a chariot with a dome of gold; the other showing the Ascension and a girl whose hair falls about her face. These roundels are set in medleys of fragments of glowing glass. There is more rich 14th-century glass in the south aisle (with lovely leaf tracery old and new). Here is a small and bright figure of a mitred bishop in armour, carrying his Bible and pastoral staff.

The church is proud indeed, for its nave has eight tall and slender columns, so exquisitely moulded that they would grace a cathedral. Their arches make a perfect example of church architecture 400 years ago. The nave would be as we see it when Latimer came here to preach. It took him three days to ride from London, but he must have thought it well worth while to be in a setting so noble. There is a filled-up arch with stone carvings of a man's head with a turban, and on the arch of one of the windows near it is a splendid stone owl. A great monument adorned with pinnacles is to members of the Dugdale family.

We look up in this fine nave to see a roof of cedar-wood enriched with bosses and framed by ancient beams; we look down to find two of the most beautiful brasses in all Warwickshire. They have no name, but are believed to be of a lord and lady of the Ferrers family in the 15th century, and are marvellously preserved. He is in armour, with a fine tilting helmet and a plume of peacock's feathers, and has a long sword which almost touches the dog crouching at his feet; she wears a lovely headdress, and the folds of her long garment fall round a small lap dog, looking up at her. On one of the choir stalls, all made from the stoutest Arden oak, is a tribute to Thomas Clarke, a chorister for 67 years.

So much has Merevale in glass and stone and brass that we might well overlook one of its interesting possessions, the small organ on which Handel is said to have played. One of Handel's great friends was Charles Jennens, a writer of verse and a wealthy descendant of Birmingham manufacturers. He entertained his friends in London on so lavish a scale that he was called Soliman the Magnificent.

He had a country seat in Leicestershire, Gopsall Hall, ten miles from Merevale, and among the treasures long kept there were several of the composer's original scores, and a full-length portrait of him. While staying at Gopsall Handel was frequently a guest at Merevale, and played on the organ in this church, as he did also on the organ at Great Packington. It was played for us when we called, and we were much impressed by its beautiful tone.

We go out by the lovely lake, and wonder if there is in all this glorious Warwickshire a village with a richer store of interest and beauty from the past.

The Village Green on Empire Day

MERIDEN. If we would view Meriden aright there is a day above others when it seems a corner that is for ever England. It is Empire Day, when thousands of cyclists come from all over the country, many travelling all night, to be present on the village green at the service beside the memorial to British cyclists who fell in the war. The memorial is very near to the centre of England, for Meriden disputes that pride of place with Minworth and Lillington and all the rest of these central villages of Warwickshire.

There is a piece of ancient turf here, at Forest Hall, where the Woodmen of Arden, the oldest Archery Society in England, hold meetings. The turf is said to have been undisturbed since the trees of the Forest of Arden cast their ancient shade over the archery butts. Here these ancient archers have been thrilled to shoot their arrows, for at Forest Hall is kept a horn which legend says belonged to Robin Hood.

The village itself lies low and its pretty name means only miry valley, but it has always been well beloved and many old farmhouses and inns attest its comfortable hospitality. It had renown, too, as a healthy spot, for when the Great Plague came to England in 1665 few there suffered from the visitation.

It is a stiff climb to the church half a mile away, but the square tower and the churchyard itself command a noble view over deeply wooded country. From beside the ancient sundial, or from the yew with mighty trunk, the eye roves for miles. Birmingham smokes and glitters in the sun below; far away are the hills of Worcestershire, Staffordshire, and Shropshire. But the church rewards us for our climb. It has some well-preserved 17th-century monuments and two older still. One is a boldly sculptured figure, in chain mail with richly ornamented sword, of John Wyard, who founded a chantry here in the 15th century. The other is of Sir John Walsh, lord of the manor in 1440. He has a dagger suspended by a chain from his girdle. Still earlier is the 13th-century chancel arch, and legend puts the first foundation back to Saxon days. But authentic beyond legend is the carved alms-chest, with the inscription on its lid that Henry West gave it in 1627, and the admonition, "This chest is God's exchequer; paye in, then, your almes, accepted both of God and men." In the chest is a chained book of Bishop Sewell, as old as Queen Elizabeth; and there is a 17th-century brass of Elizabeth Rotton.

Four clappers from the ancient bells lay in the tower when we called, silent but saying:

> *Our duty done in belfry high,*
> *Now voiceless tongues at rest we lie.*

A Pilgrim Through the Kingdom of Nature

MIDDLETON. A little place at the end of a lonely road, it was the home of a great naturalist who was born here, loved it all his life, and passed out of the world near where he came into it.

We come to a churchyard wall with the gentle hand of Time on its massive stones. It is shaded by four yews centuries old, friends of a sturdy tower which has stood 600 years and has several quaint faces wearing away. The small porch shelters a Norman arch with zigzag in its beautiful yellow stone. The oak chancel screen, carved about 300 years ago, has three quaint faces and small painted and carved medallions, a Tudor rose, a man with his tongue out, and a face wreathed in oak leaves. The pulpit has old panels showing winged heads, and an odd candle-holder. The peephole, about 12 feet long, was discovered only last century.

In the chancel are two noble 15th-century brasses of Sir Richard Bingham and his wife, she in a gown with ample folds, the knight in his judge's robes and skull cap with his feet on leaves and clover. Stone busts of Samuel and Benjamin White, companions for nearly 300 years, look out from a canopied monument reminding us of the front of a Punch and Judy show.

There is a 17th-century armoured figure of Edward Ridgeway with long sword, helmet, and gauntlets. On a wall is a monument, bedecked with skulls and ugly cherubs, to Francis Willoughby who in the stormy days of the Civil War, caring little for the tumult and much for knowledge, went on quietly with his studies of insects and birds. His brief life was long enough for him to lay the foundations of Natural History as we know it.

From childhood he was passionately interested in the life of the country, and on going up to Cambridge came in contact with the great John Ray, to whom, for the rest of his life, he was friend, collaborator, host, and patron. His course at Cambridge completed, he went on to Oxford for the study of rare books on his special subject.

At 27 he accompanied Ray on memorable tramps surveying the broad field of Nature and its free, wild creatures, which live recorded by Ray's admirable pen. Willoughby's bent drew him to animal life, Ray's to botanical, and together they determined to re-write the imperfect book of Nature, to clear it of all obscurities, to banish

Milcote C.P, Stratford R.D, pph. 41.

"hieroglyphics, emblems, morals, fables, presages, or aught else pertaining to divinity, ethics, grammar," and in fact to resolve Nature into genera and species, with descriptions of each rendering them capable of identification by all. They travelled far on the Continent, and the fruit of their labours, given to the world after Willoughby's death by the loving hand of Ray, was a system of ornithology which forms the foundation on which Linnaeus was to build.

Willoughby also did inestimable work in the description and classification of fishes and insects. He worked too hard, he travelled too much in broken health, and he died a martyr to knowledge.

The Middle of the World

MINWORTH. Strange it is that our master Englishman should come to us from the very heart of England, from very near the middle of our Motherland. What the centre of England is has never been determined with exactness: perhaps it cannot be. Many places in Warwickshire have claimed this alluring distinction; Lillington by Leamington, which has an oak tree said to mark the spot; Meriden which has set up a memorial stone; and Copston Magna where the oldest inhabitant will tell you that the centre is just here.

It may or may not be; as for ourselves, we raise our hat to the schoolboys of King Edward's Grammar School at Birmingham who have tried ingeniously to solve this problem, and have done so to their perfect satisfaction. They drew 40 maps of England on cardboard and accurately cut them out. Then they determined the centre of gravity on each map by careful balancing, and it was found that Minworth, this little place six miles north-east of Birmingham, was the centre of gravity on all the 40 maps.

The schoolboys, of course, could make no allowance for rivers and mountains, lakes and hills, or any other factor that breaks the surface of the land, but as far as it seems likely to be possible to solve it the experiment does seem to solve the problem of what is the exact centre of the face of England if it were all level. All this being so, have we not something like the very centre of the world if all the Earth were level? If you take up a globe of the world and hold it so that you see the greatest possible space of land, you will see a red spot in the middle. It is England, and it seems that the exact centre of this little red spot must be the exact centre of the great land area of the Earth.

The Wonderful Gates

MONKS KIRBY. Ancient camp, monastery, and monastic church have all had their foundations laid in Monks Kirby, a mile from the Roman Fosse Way straddling the Leicestershire border. Now the church alone remains.

Of all its possessions the village has nothing more beautiful than a piece of craftsmanship which lies outside it, at the seat of the Feildings, Newnham Paddox—the iron gates famous for their strength and ornament. They have been called the biggest and most beautiful in the kingdom, with none to compare with them but the gates at Eaton Hall, but they were once famous in Spain as well, for they were brought in 1793 from a Spanish monastery.

Yet they were made by Englishmen. The brothers Roberts fashioned them in the 18th century, and these craftsmen probably learned their art from the master Tijou. They were fond of mingling eagles, masks, and acanthus leaves with scrolls of wrought iron, as may be seen in the Eaton Hall gates; these at Newnham Paddox, which stood at Berwick House near Shrewsbury before coming to Warwickshire, have decorations of cockatoos with beaks and feathers, dragons complete from head to tail, and bearded faces with wreaths or open mouths. The wicket gates at the side were made by a later Derbyshire craftsman, Robert Bakewell. These stately iron portals are 13 feet high. The piers are garlanded with flowers and foliage. What processions of priest and politician, soldier and noble, have passed through them!

Some who passed through to wedding bells or funeral bells lie in the 14th-century church, which is full of monuments of the Feildings, Earls of Denbigh. One broken bust of a 14th-century knight is older than theirs; it may be that of Geoffrey de Wirce, who rebuilt the church and whose munificence established the monastery, of which now no traces remain unless the blocked doors by the chancel led to it.

The church is impressive, with lofty arcades, and its tower imposing with magnificent arches and a vaulted roof, sheltering the baptistry. Inside the porch is a beautiful doorway. There is an Elizabethan cup of 1584, and an ancient chest with studded iron bands. The costly plate was given by Duchess Alice Dudley, benefactor of many Midland churches.

But the significant treasures here are monuments which are in part the annals of the lords and ladies who sat here in something approaching high state. On the wall hangs a plan of the seating as allotted by the Commissioners of Queen Anne, the nobility and gentry in the front pews, the domestics at the sides, labourers and servants at the back.

There is a small tablet to a Countess of Denbigh which brings to mind the picture of a great lady going about among the village folk, for it was put here by the peasant boys of Monks Kirby and its neighbouring village, to whom she had shown much kindness. There is a group of sculptures more beautiful, but none more moving. One is to the young Lady Augusta Feilding, who has been here nearly a century and sleeps with a thick plait of hair over her shoulder. A 19th-century monument shows William Feilding, the 7th earl, lying in a loose cloak and lace cravat with his wife, and two others are to 16th-century ancestors, William in armour with his wife in a stiff gown, Basil in knightly armour with his wife, who has two dogs in the folds of her gown. Their family is grouped about them—daughters in elaborate Tudor dress, sons in armour, and five infants. A strong, adventurous family this was; one went to India 300 years ago for the love of it; two fought for Charles Stuart and one against him, and another fought in the Crimea.

There is an inscription to a 19th-century vicar who ministered here for 52 years, and in the records is an extraordinary item of news from 1720, when there was buried here Elizabeth Mott, who was married 44 years and was the mother of 42 children. On her stone they set these lines, which we may well believe true:

> *A loving wife, a tender mother,*
> *Scarce left behind her such another.*

The Poet, the Patron, and the Jester

HERE was born Sir Henry Goodyer, himself a minor poet and boyhood friend of Michael Drayton. The Goodyers preserved the ancient custom of maintaining a minstrel or jester, John Hewes, who was the constant companion of the two boys Michael Drayton and Henry Goodyer, and was remembered in later days by Drayton when, in dedicating his Odes to Goodyer, he reminded him of

> *John Hewes his lyre*
> *Which oft at Powlsworth by the fire*
> *Hath made us gravely merry.*

It was this John Hewes, chanting his rough dactyles to the boys, who inspired Drayton to his battle ballad on Agincourt.

Goodyer was something of a poet, but lives as the patron of poets rather than through his own writings. He kept open house at Poles-worth for men of genius. Donne was his closest friend and he figures repeatedly in the writings of that poet, but Ben Jonson often made the rafters ring, and Inigo Jones was another welcome guest. His attendance at the courts of James and Charles the First, where he was once Gentleman of the Privy Chamber, seems to have reduced Goodyer to poverty, and he appealed to Cecil for help. He was granted a little estate of £50 a year, but still pleaded (in vain) for a post at court which would secure him "meat, drink, and lodging with some dignity in that place where he had spent most of his time and estate."

Silver Chalice and Brass Squirrels

MORETON MORRELL. As charming as its name it lies by the Fosse Way, all its treasures old. It has fine houses, and Moreton Hall amid beautiful clipped yews, where Amy Robsart is thought to have walked. By the little gate from the Hall to the church is a big stone with Norman carvings of a cross and a circle, perhaps the oldest thing in the village.

The church has a tower with red brick above its grey stone and an oak porch sheltering a 13th-century doorway. There is a chest with a curious heavy lock, and in it is a pitch-pipe used by the choir in the years before the harmonium came; it is beautifully made, and has a sliding stopper engraved with the notes of the scale. There is some fine old pewter, and another treasure is an exquisite silver chalice perhaps older than the Armada. Richard Murden and his wife have been kneeling here since 1635, the portly Richard in armour, the lady in mantle and gown.

Francis Bagshaw's brass (hidden under the harmonium when we called) is Moreton Morrell's great possession. It shows him as friends knew him in the 17th century, and with him on the brass are dainty squirrels engraved by the hand of a masterly craftsman. He must have seen such squirrels often, for they are on his heraldic shield, a charming touch of heraldry.

The Home of Joseph Chamberlain

MOSELEY. Two interesting places has this fine suburb of Birm-ingham, a church with a battlemented tower looking out on

Morton Bagot C.P., Alcester R.D.,
nob. 42.

the modern world as it looked on the old, and Highbury, the home of Joseph Chamberlain. Almost unknown to this generation is Mr Chamberlain's sensational career, yet we may be sure that history will say of him that he made the British Empire real to millions. His home, a modern house, now belongs to Birmingham, and is used partly as a Chamberlain museum and partly as a home for aged women.

The church has much interest for architects, for its 16th-century tower has traces of ancient roofs and its foundations are among the oldest brickwork in Warwickshire. Of the many windows, one which attracts us most is a peace memorial with scenes of the battlefield, soldiers in hospital blue, and Christ with his feet on the dragon of War. Below are the names of five houses in Moseley which were turned into war hospitals. Here is a brass crucifix which was used in the small chapel at Highbury where soldiers who died here were taken to lie in peace. The chapel this window adorns is a place of beautiful white stone, with fine screens carved with lilies and roses. The alabaster reredos shows Christ attended by a heavenly host, delicately carved in deep relief.

A brave tale of the war is simply told in a beautiful brass to Lieutenant Douglas Greenway, killed in the Dardanelles while gallantly bringing in a wounded soldier.

Looking Out on Seven Counties

NAPTON-ON-THE-HILL. It stands so high above the flat country round that seven counties can be seen from the summit of the windswept hill on which they set the church 700 years ago. As the centuries have passed the houses and farms below the church have been gently touched by the hand of Time, and their strong stone walls are mellowed to brown and gold. Charming they look with their thatched roofs. Below the crest of the hill are red barns, and away on the ridge is an old windmill, its unmoving arms outstretched against the skyline.

The old church standing so proudly on its hilltop has a tower added in the 18th century. A trim avenue of limes leads to its porch with stone seats each side and a Norman doorway within. Over the priest's door is a sundial, and in the ancient vestry door is an iron grille with a wooden shutter. There are lofty arcades and many fine 13th-century lancets. Under two arched recesses in the north transept are ancient stone coffins. A portrait in slate of John

Hillmorton
Unknown 15 c. lady

Coventry: John Whitehead with his two wives
and nine children, 1600

Compton Verney
George Verney, 1574

Solihull: William Hill with his two wives
and eighteen children, 1549

Haseley
Throckmorton, 1573

Whichford
Asheton, 1582

Shuckburgh: Thomas and
Elizabeth Shuckburgh, 1549

Merevale
Lord Ferrers, 1413

OLD WARWICKSHIRE FOLK ENGRAVED ON BRASSES

Shuckburgh is a solid presentment of a solid figure of the happy days of Charles Stuart, before the great storm broke. An oak chest was given 300 years ago by a man and his wife "in token of their love of this place."

Handel's Friend

NETHER WHITACRE. It has a fine old house and a new church, and the memory of two men of small fame. The great house (a mile away) is Whitacre Hall, which still has the mast of its timbered Tudor days, with fine stone towers, an ancient wall, and a quaint little gatehouse. The house was much rebuilt in the 17th century, and while one side has a Dutch gable the other has a straight gable with ornamental woodwork carved with fleur-de-lys.

Here lived the Jennens family, early iron-masters of Birmingham, and here was born Charles Jennens who built Gopsall Hall, where Handel used to stay with him. He would take Handel round to the churches near by, and in one or two of them the composer would play the organ. Jennens, who sleeps in the chancel, succeeded in early middle life to rich possessions, and built a stately house at Gopsall. He never married, but lived in such luxury that he was called Soliman the Magnificent, a satirical term not unjustified by his method of life in the country, by the extravagant splendour of his London house, and by his habit of summoning his coach and four with four gorgeous footmen to drive to a shop a few minutes away.

Nevertheless he exercised unstinted benevolence to all of his own creed, whose voluble gratitude redounded to his fame and exalted his reputation as a master of music and letters. The one fine friendship which ennobled his life was that for Handel, to whom he was a constant support throughout the composer's blackest hours of difficulty and defeat, when Italian opera and its champions in London overwhelmed the genius of the master.

Here, long before Charles Jennens, was born Francis Holyoake, rector of Southam, who suffered so cruelly in the Civil War. He was 21 when the Spanish Armada came and he lived through the great days of Drake into the great days of Cromwell. In the Civil War troops killed his servant, ill-treated his wife, and threw him from his house; and Parliament took away his estates. They laid him in peace at last in St Mary's at Warwick, where he sleeps with his only son Thomas and his grandson Henry. Henry was headmaster of

Rugby, and Thomas remembered his father by finishing a Latin dictionary he had begun.

The treasures of the church, with only its tower old, are a few queer things in stone and a few small gems in glass. The glass is ancient— a few fragments in two windows, one with a white angel with green wings ; the stone grotesques are on the tower, big ones and small ones, with four odd little faces on one side all in a row.

A Sculpture Gallery by the Avon

NEWBOLD-ON-AVON. Here are people of Shakespeare's day by the Avon Shakespeare loved. On a hill coming down to the river are Newbold's cottages and farms, many of them centuries old, and in a garden of roses is a church that has followed the good counsel of the poet :

> Let me grow lovely growing old,
> So many old things do.

Most of it is 15th century, and its porches are exquisite. One has six canopied niches, the faces in them almost worn away but still visible guardians of a massive door. Four old heads look down from the south porch, which has a splendid vaulted roof and an old sundial on the gable. The nave has lofty pillars and fine arches, and there are three windows with good glass, a delightful doorway to old rood stairs, a pulpit with linenfold panelling of our own day, two 17th-century chairs, and a fine old ironbound chest.

A quaint sculpture gallery shows the Boughtons of the 16th and 17th centuries, Here are Edward and his wife, a daughter, a son in armour, William and his wife with five small children, and another Edward with his wife and daughter and four small shrouded figures. Below them is a knight with his wife in Elizabethan dress, and at their side a little black-gowned man. A pompous 17th-century monument with cherubs and skulls has a marble figure of Sir William Boughton, a member of Queen Anne's Parliament, wearing high-heeled shoes and a wig falling over his cravat, his wife in flowing gown and veil. Some of the Allesleys who came to Newbold five centuries ago are here in alabaster. Galfrid Allesley is in civil dress, and his wife in a horned headdress has a smile. Thomas Boughton rests, armed with two swords, a fine helmet under his head and a dog at his feet. Two dogs pull at the hem of his wife's gown, and six angels guard the tomb.

Her Thirteenth Day

NEWBOLD PACEY. It cherishes precious things in the church, set in a pretty green corner of the village. It has two Norman doorways and a splendid modern reredos 10 feet high with a wealth of fine carving and three canopied and painted panels. They show Christ seated above a rainbow in a starry sky, and the warrior saints with dragons on either side, one in black armour with wings of red and gold and a golden sword, the other in silver with flag and sword.

In the chancel lies Thomas Castle Southey, a nephew of the poet and vicar here when the church was rebuilt last century. The most impressive memorial is to Edward Carew, showing him elaborately clothed, and above him a painted helmet with the strange crest of a heraldic lion in a palisaded enclosure. Beneath him, also in marble, lies the little shrouded figure of Felicia Carew, who "died in the 13th day of her age." He loved her greatly, we may well believe, though her days were so few, and they look down into the nave together, father and daughter, as they have looked since 1668.

Charles Stuart Kneels

NEWTON REGIS. This village with mellow brick houses was called Regis because it belonged to Henry the Second, but seems to have been Newton-in-the-Thistle when Charles Stuart called to kneel by the altar before fighting at Seckington; then they changed the Thistle back to Regis.

The 14th-century church, with slender spire and beautiful windows, stands at the head of the village. It has a fine old porch with ribbed roof, a peephole in an extraordinary position (through a buttress of the tower), a splendid piscina, and fragments of old glass. There is a mutilated portrait of a priest in alabaster, with a boy at the foot. The altar stone was long buried in the chancel, and with it was found a stone coffin lid elaborately carved. The head of a priest appears in the centre; above him are two angels, a little Baptism scene, and rich ornament, and below are two kneeling figures and a lamb.

In the very place where Charles Stuart knelt we came upon a link with another king, a rich gold and blue altar frontal which missed a coronation. It was once at the heart of our national shrine, laid on the altar of Westminster Abbey for the crowning of Edward the Seventh which did not take place, the ceremony being postponed owing to the king's sudden illness.

The Children's Flowers

NORTHFIELD. It fascinates us by its contrasts, this suburb of Birmingham with an old world living on serenely amid the new. The main road running through it is one of the busiest in the Midlands, and a mile or so away is a factory where cars are made under the shadow of the Lickey Hills.

A turn from the road brings us to charming peeps of old Northfield, an ancient inn in company with a village pound, and the splendid old tower of the church rising above elms and yews in a churchyard where the busy world seems far away. The church has a fine timbered porch which has been here while many generations have grown old, and above the doorway are stone heads of a king and queen. The north wall of the nave, which has stood 700 years, has the remains of a Norman doorway, and the 13th-century chancel has kept its dignity unspoiled through all the centuries. There are ancient timbers in the roof.

A modern oil painting much treasured here shows children bringing offerings of flowers to the Master; it is the work of a local artist, William Spittell, who took village children as his models, and the picture is a memorial to Elizabeth Bentley, a lady much beloved.

NORTON LINDSEY. A poor old windmill watches over its cottages and the thatched inn that has kept them company so long, but the village has been shorn of the inspiration which gave it a place in the poems of Theodore Shurt, a vicar in whose memory they built the vestry.

The church has the unpardonable sin of a country church, for it is dark. The pulpit has a panel from the old 17th-century altar rails, and the font has a bowl smaller than the shaft. It is the oldest possession of Norton, for it was made by the Normans. The most beautiful possession of the village is its Elizabethan chalice.

The Abbey Falls on Evil Days

NUNEATON. The lovely corner of the countryside in which George Eliot was born is still as she knew it, but the chimney-stacks and the dingy streets of Nuneaton town have spread themselves until the beauties of Arbury are almost in their shadow. Yet Arbury remains apart. Nuneaton has three fine buildings, an old church and a new one, and modern civic offices with a handsome colonnaded entrance.

St Nicholas Church, embattled and pinnacled, with clipped yew trees all about it and the charming old rectory close by, has a 15th-century doorway with trailing ballflowers and an ancient roof of glorious beams from which, among the panelling and carvings, one face has been grinning at the people in the pews for 300 or 400 years. On an immense corbel is a strange head crowned. The lofty chancel arch has fine corbels of leaves and heads. There are beautiful canopied saints and angels on the reredos, and more saints in niches on the altar, including St Nicholas, who appears again on the carved pulpit, which has a fine canopy.

In the arched recess of the chancel Sir Marmaduke Constable lies on an altar tomb in all the splendour of his armour as he wore it in 1560. He has a beard, rests his head on a helmet crested with a ship at furled sail, and has a lion at his feet. The centuries have barely touched him, and his figure is rich with detail, a picture of perfection. The old abbey he owned has fallen into ruin, but Sir Marmaduke remains.

In the chapel is an ancient canopied niche in which the sacred vessels were placed, and a stately modern screen exquisitely carved. Here, too, is lovely glass, New Testament scenes and a richly coloured window of Christ with saints and martyrs.

The ruins of the abbey at the other end of the town were rising to greatness again as we called, a new church being built about them on the lines of the old. The new nave has kept the four great piers supporting the old tower; the rough-hewn granite in them is here as the Normans left it. Round the base of each pier are fragments of carving, here a head and there a grotesque or a bit of graceful foliage. The abbey had fallen on such evil days that people carried away its stones as from a disused quarry; but much remains, and something of its ancient glory will come back. Among the relics is a massive stone coffin lid with an engraved cross, and one of its new treasures is the peace memorial east window, showing Christ with the archangels and a Madonna in blue and white.

The Serpent at the Window

OFFCHURCH. It is said that the Saxon Offa was buried in a stone coffin here. The conquering Romans passed this way, the Saxons left their jewels behind, but Offa, buried here or not, left the place his name and is of it for all time. He made his kingdom of Mercia, to which Warwickshire then belonged, the most powerful of all the Saxon kingdoms in the land.

Oldberrow C.P., Alcester R.D., pop. 35.

Wootton Wawen   Tysoe   Tysoe   Wootton Wawen

Nuneaton   Southam   Ilmington

Temple Balsall   Group of Medieval Carvings

Ilmington   Hampton in Arden   Hampton Lucy

Temple Balsall   Salford Priors    Southam

Medieval Carvings in Warwickshire

Coventry
Roof Boss

Salford Priors
Nativity Panel

Coventry
Guild Chair

Snitterfield
Stall-end

Brailes
Tudor Chest

Wormleighton
Stall-end

Stratford
Miserere

Knowle
Hourglass

Stratford
Miserere

Stratford
Miserere

Astley
A Seat 400 years old

Stratford
Miserere

Wootton Wawen
The Ancient Chest

Nuneaton
Boss

Wootton Wawen
Chained Books

Old Stratford + Drayton C.P., Stratford R.D., pop. 297

The church was started by the Normans. Their blocked-up doorway is still in the north wall, richly carved outside with several patterns, their windows are still in the chancel, and the chancel arch set up in the 13th century was set on Norman pillars, both with a round shaft worked into them, and both now leaning outwards as if they would fall. But the oddest legacy of the Normans is something almost comical, a little nature picture a child might have drawn at school; it is a serpent crawling over a narrow round window in the chancel, chased in the stone of the arch outside.

All our great building centuries have left their mark on the church since Norman days, for most of it is 13th century, the south porch is 14th (with two mullioned windows), the tower is 15th, and the fine beams of the nave roof (which is nearly flat) are 16th. One of the brackets of the chancel roof has a very strange stone angel. The pulpit is one of the rare two-deckers, neatly inlaid, with a seat below the parson for the clerk.

The tower stirs in us a memory of one of the greatest events in our history, for its stones are pitted with the bullets of Cromwell's soldiers. Two of the bells were ringing the people to prayer before Columbus found America.

A Soldier of the Civil War

OXHILL. It will reward any traveller in search of old and beautiful things, for it has much loveliness—stone cottages, and a Norman church so defiant of time that nearly everything the Normans left seems but a few years old. Somebody has said that Time must have taken another turning and missed Oxhill.

The Norman font is unique, richly sculptured with Adam and Eve at the Tree of Life, a splendid spectacle after its eight centuries of existence; but the church's finest possession is its south doorway, which stands as the Normans left it, with two shafts on each side on which are two queer faces peeping out of foliage, arches with fine zigzag mouldings with rosettes, and under a tiny arcade a row of six solemn faces and one grotesque.

There is another Norman doorway sheltered by the 14th-century porch with a man's face looking strangely down from above it, his long, thin hand in his mouth, as though he had been suffering agonies of toothache since the sculptor put him here. Very beautiful are the shafts of this doorway. The charm of the interior is the rich stone-

Over Whitacre C.P., Meriden R.D. pop. 265

work of the arches and windows outlined against the neat cream walls. The chancel arch is by the earliest English builders, some of the windows are Norman, and one of the 14th century has in it a deep stone seat and a hollow which may have been a piscina. The slender tower arch has a screen in which is worked some 16th-century oak.

The altar table is Jacobean, and some of the pews are carved by 16th-century men. Most of them were here when a soldier of the Civil War sat in one of them for the last time, a tablet in the nave giving us this brief story of him:

> When I was young I ventured life and blood
> Both for my king and for my country's good.
> In elder years my care was chief to be
> Soldier for Him that shed His blood for me.

The inscription is almost worn away by generations of feet walking over it in the nave.

Here Came the Two Charles Stuarts

PACKINGTON. Packington is Great and Little, and all its interest gathers about a magnificent stretch of 700 acres of woodland with Packington Hall in the midst. The park has three lakes and many small streams, and the lanes about it are delightful to those who love secluded ways.

Both the hall and the church have the mark of the Italian builder on them. The hall replaces an older house to which came the two Charles Stuarts, the first before the battle of Edgehill and the second after the Battle of Worcester. The house they came to was pulled down, and the house we see was built soon after, but there are noble trees in the park under which they must have walked.

Here lived and here lies Jane Lane, who became the wife of Sir Clement Fisher. It was she who saved King Charles the Second by riding with him as pillion on her horse after Worcester. There is no monument to her memory, but the entry of her burial is in the register.

The red-brick church, with a turret at each corner, was built in 1791 by the Earl of Aylesford. It has a bell which cracked in pealing out its thanksgiving for Trafalgar, and an organ on which Handel is said to have played. The organ came here from Gopsall Hall, the home of Handel's friend Charles Jennens. The great composer stayed with Jennens more than once and must often have played on this keyboard before the organ came to this church. It is in a handsome case of rosewood with decoration in the Adam style, and its natural keys are black while the sharps and flats are striped in black and white. We were told also that its range is peculiar, so that possibly it may have puzzled Handel when he sat down to it.

Little Packington's church stands by a fine old farm at the edge of the park. It has traces of the Normans, and its tower is unusual for its half-timbering. Some panelling of old oak adorns the chancel and pulpit, and a stone coffin lid is built into the wall of the nave with a much-worn cross engraved on it.

One of Warwickshire's many Shakespeares lived here and gave a shadowy fame to it by leaving behind him in the small stone church a memento of himself, George Shakespeare, with an inscription to the memory also of his father, mother, brother, grandfather, and great-grandfather. He was perhaps the last of his family, which lived here 200 years ago.

Michael Johnson Marries Sara Ford

PACKWOOD. It has a rare little road with a great surprise. We pass through a charming old gateway, and in one splendid moment the glory of Packwood House is upon us. It is a famous spot, one of the most wonderful in Warwickshire, and no traveller can forget its great company of ancient yews.

The house has all the dignity of ripe old age: the gardens with their statuary of lead and stone, the clipped box hedges, and the winding walks and terraces, are a sheer delight; but it is the yews that crown this noble place. We must count them as the great and proud achievement of an English garden. They are a mighty host, rank on rank, large and small, all perfectly trimmed and seeming to hold in their green depths the solemnity of the ages. They are Nature's monuments to the patience of man. They have been lovingly tended through the ages.

It was a lovely thought that came to the mind of the man who planted them, for they symbolise that day and that scene when the wisest words ever heard were spoken: they represent the Sermon on the Mount. The four tallest of them stand nearly 30 feet high and represent the Evangelists. Grouped around these are six tall ones for the Apostles, and at the top, in the centre of a wonderful arbour on rising ground, is the finest of all these noble trees. It symbolises Our Lord, and below is a host of smaller ones standing for the multitude. There can be few finer examples of topiary work in the kingdom; we have seen nothing to surpass them. Wonderful it is to think how many summers these yews have seen, how many times the birds among them have heralded the spring, how often autumn's tints have deepened round them while they have kept their perpetual green.

The house has not survived the centuries as these yews have done; it has been much altered from time to time since it was begun in the 15th century; yet it is still charming to behold with its timbered walls of Stuart brickwork and its fine grouping of chimneys. We counted seven sundials, some framed in moulded bricks and one dated 1667. Very beautiful is much of the lead work on the house, and there are splendid 17th-century iron gates. Over a door to the garden is a group of sculptured shields. In the piers of a terrace wall are 30 niches for beehives.

The house is magnificent with oak panelling, great fireplaces, and old furniture. It seems to have had a very peaceful life, and we can sympathise with that John Fetherstone who complained, in the Civil War, of being asked to provide the soldiers with weapons and armour, and sent his armour to a neighbour's house because he did not know which side to take. He loved his garden better than a battlefield.

Another delightful timbered house is Packwood Hall, with excellent chimneys and a moat surrounded by trees. Little seems to have happened to it since the days when moats were needed.

We walk through the fields to the church, which has a charming tower of the 15th century, an old timbered porch, and a mass dial on one of the buttresses. It would look like this 200 years ago when Michael Johnson brought Sara Ford to be married. Did Michael dream, we wonder, that the world would remember his wedding? He was a Lichfield bookseller, a zealous churchman, so full of knowledge that the country clergymen hereabouts thought him an oracle of learning. She, the daughter of a " little Warwickshire gentleman," was to be the mother of that poverty-stricken boy who, in tattered gown and wretched shoes, treated sneers at Oxford with savage scorn, and was to become immortal as the biggest talker in the world. Samuel Johnson was born three years after Sara Ford's marriage; the record of the wedding is in the register here.

It is a church of many contrasts. Everyone sensitive to the simple dignity of the 13th-century windows in the chancel will deplore the changes which have robbed it of much of its character and beauty; but it has two treasures left. One is the fresco on the wall of the Norman chancel arch, probably the work of Norman painters. Though only traces remain we can still make out a king. The other treasure is a small panel of glass, a Crucifixion in deep browns and blues. It is almost certainly 600 years old and may be older. It came from the graceful 13th-century east window which now has a striking Crucifixion in modern glass, with an angel below sitting by a stream and flowers growing in a crannied nook; on one side is a medieval scene showing the charity of a rich man, on the other a modern sickbed scene. There are fragments of old glass in other windows.

The chancel has a simple oak screen, and there are two massive old oak benches in the nave. Some of the immense beams in the roof have been here 500 years. There is a medieval font, and a dug-out chest so old that nobody knows its age.

The tower has an odd bit of history. Nicholas Brome paid for the building of it to obtain the pardon of the pope for having killed a priest near Barford. The arch of its doorway outside has two sculptured panels, very weatherworn, one apparently of a Tudor rose, the other of a head wearing a crown, as if Nicholas had to obtain the pardon of the king as well as of the pope and had this sculptured portrait made as part of his atonement. The rain of centuries has washed the king's face away.

Embroidery From the Manor House

PILLERTON HERSEY. Not far from the Roman Fosse Way are the two Pillertons, Pillerton Priors with splendid views of Warwickshire woodlands, a sort of compensation for having lost its church 300 years ago, and Pillerton Hersey with a small church of great charm.

The church is flooded with light from the green tinted glass of its ancient windows and without the aid of imposing monuments it has a simple graciousness unspoiled. Most charming is the chancel, with an arch like a horseshoe, five slender lancets, and a rare and elegant east window with shafts and sculptured capitals, framing the graceful sycamores we see through it. Above the three lancets is a deeply set quatrefoil and below is a pretty touch of colour in the narrow altar frontal, made by a lady of the manor house, on which are scenes of heather-clad mountains and green meadows with two angels in white kneeling before a golden chalice. It is a fine piece of modern embroidery.

The 500-year-old nave roof has lovely bosses of leaves and flowers in its panels and the chancel has a fine old hammerbeam roof, as also has one of the aisles. The oak rails and reredos of the south chapel are richly carved, probably by the modern craftsman who made the reading desk and the lectern. The extraordinary font cover, built up six feet high with a gate pattern, is also by a modern craftsman. There are a few odd fragments of old glass in a vestry window, a finely arcaded recess with a flower-shaped drain for a pillar piscina, a charming priest's doorway with five delicate columns on each side, and, quaintest of all the possessions of this small place, three curious iron candle-holders on the walls.

Michael Drayton Sits by the Fire

POLESWORTH. A thousand years before Polesworth became a miner's town Egbert, first Saxon King of all England, built a nunnery here of which his daughter Editha was abbess. The nuns are the first people we hear of in this countryside.

Later we hear of a boy who sat dreaming by the fire in a charming timbered house which has stones in its walls and beams in its roofs from the ancient abbey of the nuns. He was Michael Drayton, the poet we may believe to have been a companion of Shakespeare, and the house, now the vicarage, was the home of the Goodyers, to whose household little Michael was attached. Ben Jonson was later to sit by the same Tudor fireplace, and we may well wonder if Shakespeare also came here, for there is a strong tradition that the three were friends. The fireplace they may have sat at is still in the vicarage, set in a charming corner on the banks of the River Anker.

Fine black-and-white cottages nestle under the walls of the abbey gatehouse, opening to the peace memorial, and a splendid avenue of limes leads on to the old abbey church. The church still keeps its impressive Norman arcade with a Norman window over each of its eight arches, but it was rebuilt in the 14th century, and a doorway of that time has the original door on four great hinges.

But that is not the treasure of this church, for it has a 13th-century stone figure of an abbess, the oldest in England. She lies in a wimple and a long straight gown with hanging sleeves, on the tomb of Sir

Richard Harthill who died in the 14th century, when the church tower was built in his memory. Her staff is in one hand, her book in another, her feet rest on a stag. We may suppose she was Sara de Mancester who ruled the abbey 700 years ago, though she lies on a tomb that is not hers.

An alabaster figure of another lady in a charming headdress with three birds in its rich adornment is that of Isabel Cockayne who died in 1447, and whose family lived at Pooley Hall at the end of the 14th century. The present hall was built in 1509. A long rhymed inscription in the church recalls a grandchild of the house who died when only 14 weeks old:

> *As fine a child*
> *As ever parent's hopes by death beguiled.*

We are told that the little mortal was almost a yard long when he died, and that he dropped away like early blossom nipped by frost's decay. The little lad's grandfather sleeps by him; he is Sir Aston Cockayne, the poet. His works had hardly merit enough to keep them alive, yet they have a claim to remembrance that he could not have foreseen, for he named so many people in them as to make his verse a miniature Who's Who of Stuart writers.

An interesting west window with Egbert and his daughter, some 14th-century tiles, and an old chest hewn solidly out of a tree which grew in the days of the Conqueror, are the treasures of the church of Polesworth, celebrating its 1107th birthday when we called, and still flourishing among its colliery dwellings, its timbered houses, its tithe barn, and the old bridge which spans the river.

The church has an inscribed stone to Sir Francis Nethersole who, born of Kentish stock, died in 1659 and sleeps here.

First Moves in the Thirty Years War

FOR 14 years Sir Francis Nethersole bent his energies to the service of James's daughter, the Princess Elizabeth, who had married Frederic, Elector of Bohemia, and had just become the mother of a boy who shines in history as Prince Rupert. Knighted for his early services to the hapless king and his British bride, Nethersole sought to help them in a situation of great difficulty.

Not only was he an ardent Protestant; he was chivalrously devoted to the fortunes of his young princess, and strove by every means to bring England on her side when Bohemia was invaded by Roman

Catholics. But it was impossible; nobody knew or cared about Bohemia and its doomed king and queen. Nethersole knew and loved them both. What he did not know was that the events with which he sought to grapple, and in which he wished to induce England to take a commanding part, were the mere opening manoeuvres of Roman Catholics against Protestants in the frightful Thirty Years War, the horrible event which was not merely to ruin Frederic and Elizabeth, but to leave Germany a desert.

Under James and Charles the faithful Englishman did his utmost for the cause. To relieve the poverty of the refugee Electress, he sold his plate; he moved Charles to promise help, and sought to raise money in the City. But help did not come. The despairing Elizabeth, deserted by her brothers, still cried to Nethersole for help, whereupon he forwarded her appeal to the king's secretary and stated that her distresses were due to the inaction of Charles and James. For this he was imprisoned in the Tower and not released until Elizabeth had promised not to employ him again.

He settled down here on his wife's property, a scholar and a friend to learning, a friend of the king and still more of peace during the Civil War. He took no part in the fighting but imperilled himself in a series of scholarly pamphlets, urging peace and denying the right of anyone to take violent action against the sovereign.

PRESTON BAGOT. It has spacious views of green hills and armies of trees, and a mellow timbered manor house in the valley below. "Rest and be thankful" says a seat by its church, built on the hilltop by the Normans. It has a row of Norman windows, two Norman doorways, a pretty shingled bell-turret, and all the charm of simplicity within. By the lofty chancel arch is a headless brass of Elizabeth Randall who worshipped here in Charles Stuart's day; and close to the modern oak porch through which he walked so often lies a rector who ministered here for 55 years, preaching his last sermon in our own time when he was 90.

A Remarkable Collection of Glass

PRESTON-ON-STOUR. A turn off the road from Stratford to Shipston brings us to this enchanting place, where the Stour flows through the beautiful deer park of Alscot House. Nothing more graceful could we wish to see than the picture of this timbered house, its delightful gables and its clipped yews facing the green. It is mostly 17th century, though some parts are older, and the south front, in Gothic style, was built by James West when he bought the estate in 1747. He was a lawyer whose hobbies were science and antiques, and here and in his town house at the Piazza, Covent Garden, he collected old books and manuscripts which at his death took 24 days to sell. The manuscripts are now in the British Museum, and some of the books went to the Bodleian.

West was largely responsible for refashioning the church here 200 years ago. It keeps its lofty pinnacled tower of the 15th century, but the fine timbered roof, with nine gilded bosses, is 18th century. In the chancel arch is a lovely little green tablet to Gwendoline West, and James himself lies in the chancel. It was he who brought from the Continent the remarkable collection of 16th-century glass in these windows, which is like that in the east window of St George's, Hanover Square. There are 35 medallions in the east window alone. most of them with detail and colour perfectly preserved. We see Death with an hourglass, and again riding a chariot, one wheel of which has the face of a clock. There is a panel showing Jonah and the whale, another with a scene of the Last Supper, others with patriarchs and saints in glowing colour. The west window has heraldic glass, perhaps 17th century. There are figures of white marble by Westmacott in a memorial to another member of the West family.

Very quaint is the monument to a man of Shakespeare's time, Sir Nicholas Kemp. The sculptor has shown him cut short at the knees with his two wives kneeling on either side, and above them is a fine coat-of-arms and cherubs.

This Was A Proud Knight

PRIORS HARDWICK. Beautiful limes and old yews shelter the church, with a tower peeping just above the lofty nave and chancel, seven centuries old though much of it has been made new. The chancel has lovely traceried windows with small heads at the sides, and a lofty arch with lilies, ears of wheat, a vine, and a bird with a leaf giving grace to its capitals. Four angels guard the topmost corners of the nave, and between them are Paul with his sword, Peter with his keys, Judas with his moneybag, an Evangelist with his pen, and another disciple with his hand raised in blessing. There is a simple Norman font, a handsome 13th-century piscina and sedilia, 17th-century altar rails, and a modern pulpit with the Madonna, Gabriel, and St George. Engraved on a stone in the chancel floor is a pair of slender legs and spurred feet resting on a dog, all that is left of a once-proud Tudor knight.

Sixty-four years in the Navy.

PRIORS MARSTON. Its pleasant old houses shelter under a hill on the border of Northamptonshire. Fine cedars stand on each side of the church, and two shapely yews make an arch over the path. In this place stood a church belonging to the monks of Coventry in the Confessor's day. The lower part of the tower is Norman, and the chancel is 13th century, but most of the building has been made new.

The porch has a little gallery of pictures in glass roundels. We see a red-robed Jacob kneeling before Isaac, with Esau returning from the hunt in time to see his blessing stolen. In other scenes are six white-robed priests bearing the Ark, and Christ with the children and on the shore of Lake Tiberias.

We enter through an old doorway decorated with flowers to find more good glass inside. St Remigius, the Bishop of Rheims who baptised King Clovis, is dressed in green, and with him is his pupil St Leonard, the deliverer of captives, holding handcuffs. The church is dedicated to him, and we see him again releasing prisoners in the east window, which is in memory of Sir Henry Prescott. He was in the Navy 64 years, entering it at 13 in time to see the fights against Napoleon, and remaining in it as an admiral at 77, when he retired to live on till he was 91.

The Widow in Her Cell

QUINTON. We may be sure Shakespeare knew it well, for it is only a few miles from Stratford, still very much as he would see it, with thatched and timbered cottages, a village green, and a beautiful little church not greatly altered since his day.

It has seven styles of architecture. The rough walling between the arches of the nave is probably Saxon, the arcades are Norman, the north side of the chancel is English of the 13th century, the aisles and the lower part of the tower are 14th century, the spire and the clerestory 15th, and the porch is modern. The 15th-century spire rises 127 feet from a 14th-century tower and has a band of sculptured flowers near the top. There is a mass dial near the south door, and over the east gable is a graceful 13th-century cross with a ram's head to remind us that Quinton was once in the heart of a wool-producing country. Over the chancel arch is a fine 16th-century coat-of-arms, with a unicorn raging at a winged dragon with ferocious jaws and hideous claws, all in red and yellow and black, and underneath in bold black lettering is "God love our Noble Queen Elizabeth, Amen." It is painted over a fading picture of Doom in which the mouth of hell is still visible.

Very weird is the stone figure of Sir William Clopton, who has lain on his tomb here for over 500 years. He owned rich estates in four counties and in the Marches of Wales. We see him as he fought at Agincourt, in the armour he would wear for the battle; his feet are resting on a dog, his head on two pillows, and his hands are at prayer. His wife lies in the little chapel called St Anne's, under a magnificent brass which shows her in a graceful cloak and headdress, with a fine canopy, four coats-of-arms, a long inscription all round, and at the corners four curiously engraved emblems. When her husband died she took a vow of widowhood before a bishop and lived as an anchorite in a cell near the church, perhaps by the old timbered cottage near the churchyard. It is said that she paid for the building of the clerestory and the spire.

The font, 800 years old, has a wavy border round the bowl and traces of red colouring. The nave has a 15th-century roof, and three quaint stone faces looking down from the arches. There are seven carved Jacobean benches, and fragments of oak carving which may have come from the screens and the old pulpit. On the north wall arcade are traces of 13th-century painting.

In the east window of the Lady Chapel is 14th-century glass showing a beautiful Madonna in a cloak of gold; near it is a window with fragments 500 years old. St Michael in another window is a memorial to 24 Quinton men who did not come back.

Buried in the church but with no known memorial is Sir Thomas Overbury, whose famous uncle was murdered in the Tower. The Overbury family lived at Admington, close by, and their names are in the registers here. A small bronze plate tells of the pride of an American in this beautiful church. It is to the memory of the Underhills who formerly lived here, and from whom descended Captain John Underhill, who founded the family overseas in 1630. This long-honoured Warwickshire name is still found in New Hampshire.

The Rider on the White Horse

RADWAY. It must stir an Englishman strangely when he comes to this village of brown stone cottages in the shelter of Edgehill, for here was heard the tumult of the first bitter fight of the Civil War which was to rage through England:

> *In the heart of a sleepy Midland shire*
> *With the harvest scarcely in.*

Did ever bells ring more tragically than those in Radway tower as the king's troops rode by on that October morning? From matins to evensong the fight went on, and the war for our liberties reaped its first bitter harvest in these fields round Radway Church.

We may wonder what Jeremiah Hill had to say when he preached that evening to his flock, for the king was arrayed with his troops against his people. Some would be there to see the royal standard raised and Charles among his soldiers, his cloak of black velvet over his armour; they may have heard this proud man declaring his authority from God, whose substitute he claimed to be: "supreme governor under Christ I am."

The war was not over at evensong, and in his melancholy camp the king spent the long hours of the night "by such a fire as could be made of the little wood and rushes which grew hereabouts." Round him were his nobles, but brave old Lindsay, and Sir Edmund Verney his standard-bearer, were not there, for they were dead upon the field. One who lay dead with them is in Radway Church, Captain Henry Kingsmill. Here he lies, a grimly mutilated figure, resting his head on an elbow and his helmet gone, one hand and both legs missing, but still here in a loose leather coat with a scarf over his shoulder. He rode a white horse in the battle and was an easy target for Cromwell's men. It is thrilling to look at this brave man who died for his king in the fields about us, and to read on his stone those words of Paul after a nobler fight:

> *I have fought a good fight; I have finished my course;*
> *Henceforth is laid up for me a crown of righteousness.*

In the sanctuary is some fine old glass with scenes which appear to show the Good Samaritan and the Prodigal Son; and under this window is a stone priest whose hands have been at prayer for centuries; his head is lost, but the folds of his gown still fall gracefully about him.

Not far from the church is the gabled house called Radway Grange, its entrance charming with a group of thatched cottages round a green. It has a famous history, for here the great Lord Chatham planted many trees and here Fielding is said to have written part of Tom Jones, these distinguished people being among the many visitors to a house which was the centre of many social gatherings. It was as part of this estate that the Radway Tower was built on the height above.

We leave the dreamy village in its sleepy hollow (Sleepy Hollow with so great a past) and climb the road that runs up to the tower along Edgehill Ridge. We are on the ground where the king addressed his cavaliers. Stirring it would be for that alone, but it is stirring still for the marvellous piece of England seen from here, Shakespeare's country at our feet. The tower, built in the 18th century, marks the spot where it is thought the king's flag was raised. It was designed by Sanderson Miller, who lived at the Grange and built many churches hereabouts, and his poet friend Richard Jago wrote that Miller had "crowned with graceful pomp the shaggy hill."

The tower is poor enough inside, with a mean approach and littered with the scrawls of countless louts, but from it we look out across far horizons, to the Wrekin and the Clee Hills 60 miles away in one direction, to the Malvern Hills and Worcester's towers, to the chimneys of Birmingham 34 miles off, to Warwick Castle, and to the spires of Coventry. Few places are there where we can stand moved by so great an event in history and look across so great a scene, all the more thrilling because it is at the very heart of England, Shakespeare's own country.

RATLEY. It lies on the Oxfordshire side of Edgehill, a village of steep places and stone cottages with fine views of the hills about it, and mounds of a Bronze Age camp covering 18 acres.

The church belongs to the first centuries of our English builders, and has still ancient columns rising in the nave without capitals. They have been here 600 years. Some of the mouldings of the windows have quaint faces. The font is plain and very old, and the canopied piscina is a perfect gem of ancient carving. Hoary with age is a cross in the churchyard, broken, but still with its shaft on its old steps. About two miles away fine old yews shade a delightful walk in the grounds of the 18th-century Upton House.

Radway C.P. Southam R.D., pop. 143.
Ratley + Upton C.P., do ,, pop. 227

The Four William Shakespeares

ROWINGTON. One of Warwickshire's rare little places, it has a story of Saxon days and a link with Shakespeare. Hard to find among the winding lanes and tall trees is its Shakespeare Hall, a half-timbered house with good gables. Here, between 1560 and 1614, four William Shakespeares were living. They are said to have been kinsmen of the poet, and we may easily believe that Shakespeare visited them. As for the story that he wrote As You Like It in this house, we may believe it or not as we like, for there is no evidence anywhere.

One of the Shakespeares who lived here was Thomas, whose son John was apprenticed to William Jaggard the publisher, at whose press a collection of "Mr William Shakespeare's Comedies, Histories, and Tragedies" was printed in 1623. This was the famous First Folio. We know, therefore, that a boy of Rowington might have handled Shakespeare's pages as they came from the printer's hands.

A good half-mile from the village is Rowington's glorious church, with a tower that has seen six centuries come and go, and a portion of the wall raised by Saxons. The church has a beautiful setting, with groups of yew trees large and small, all perfectly clipped into the shape of cones. The oldest must be nearly 20 feet high. The tower has a fine doorway with four sculptured panels in the arch, and a splendid window.

We are impressed at once by the enormous dimensions of the pillars supporting the tower. Two stone faces look down into the small transept here; they are probably as old as the tower, and one is bearded, while the other is of a woman. There is a sturdy Norman font and an excellent stone pulpit of the 15th century. The north aisle has a flat roof of painted 15th-century timbers, and of the same age is a carved screen leading to the chancel. A lovely little chancel it is, with the bright figures of eight saints in the east window, three more in a side window, and Tudor roses among the shields in the tracery. A third window is filled with fragments of ancient glass. The roof is timbered and adorned with gilt suns and stars, and there are three 17th-century chairs.

A fascinating item of antiquity is the high pedestal of the almsbox, carved from one piece of timber 300 years ago. There is an Elizabethan altar table, and as many as five big and little oak chests.

The School Town of Tom Brown

RUGBY. Its fields were the scenes of war between ancient British tribes. Dobuni and Coritani fought each other across the Avon here. Romans and Normans marched where stand the masts of that great voice of Empire, the Imperial Wireless Station, 12 masts 820 feet high, a sight for miles around. Rugby throws a girdle round the Earth in less than 40 minutes, being much cleverer than Shakespeare's Puck; it carries the human voice round the world as it puts a girdle of affection round it with Tom Brown's Schooldays.

Filled with the memory of an illustrious company is this dignified town in the heart of our Midland shires. Who can walk in the shadow of its famous school without thinking of them all—of Thomas and Matthew Arnold, of old Thomas Hughes and young Rupert Brooke, born in this town? They left their mark on the English character, their charm in English literature.

But above all we think of Lawrence Sheriff, for 400 years ago his generous impulse towards the town of his childhood was the beginning of its eminence as a seat of learning which has made the name of Rugby known throughout the world. Rugby impresses us all by its great school; should it not impress us even more to remember it was started by a grocer?

We think of Sheriff in his London shop. He was only 16 when he left Rugby, with little learning himself, but he had the will to succeed. With patience and industry he built up a notable business, and soon he was selling spices to the Queen. As the years went on his fortune grew, and then his thoughts turned back to Rugby. In his will he left £100, a large sum then, for building a school and almshouses, and left eight acres of land in Middlesex to endow them. His almshouses are here still, but of his school, which stood near the church for 200 years, and to which boys came from all parts of England and abroad, not a trace is left.

He would stand in amazement if he could see the school today, with its many noble buildings and spacious playing-fields. The lofty, dingy room over the main gateway is where Dr Arnold taught his Sixth Form. Here we are at once in the atmosphere of his day, and it is easy to imagine the scene: we fancy we can see Tom Hughes there, in that "undignified kitchen chair," at that "undignified kitchen table." The actual table and the actual chair are in the museum close by.

From the windows of this room we look down on the old quadrangle where so much happened to Tom Brown. We cross it to reach the iron-studded oak doors through which Tom was carried shoulder high on his last night as a Rugby boy. It leads us to the dining room, with the fireplace before which the "roasting incident" in the book occurred. Here the portraits of Rugby's headmasters for 150 years look down from the wall, Dr Arnold among them. A few more steps and we are in the study where Tom spent his last days at school. It is now the study of the head boy of School House, a rare place for any boy to look upon as his own for a few precious years.

We peep into the dormitory where Arthur was slippered when he knelt down to say his prayers on his first night at school and Tom stood forth to protect him. We see one of the long oak table-tops from the dining-hall on which Tom Hughes carved his name when such things were still done by respectable people. We look up at the old clock in the quadrangle tower to which he climbed to scratch his name on the minute hand. The hand itself is in the library.

We stand in the Old Big School where Tom Brown and East hid in the master's desk and betrayed themselves by letting a marble roll out, the room where young Macready, who was to be the great actor and friend of Dickens, fascinated his schoolfellows with his art; where Dr Wooll, a small-built master believing in the birch, assembled the whole school with the idea of flogging everyone, but decided, when he saw them all, that he was not big enough for the task and had better flog every tenth boy only.

More perhaps than any other building the 19th-century chapel tells us of the fame of Rugby. Here is the pulpit from which Dr Arnold preached his stirring sermons. Here are windows with a wealth of colour from abroad. The east window has a 16th-century Adoration of the Magi from Louvain, and there is 16th-century glass from Rouen in a transept window. In the clerestory is old glass showing Christ before Pilate, and before Mary after the Resurrection. There is a beautiful window by William Morris showing a reunion in Paradise, and modern windows to boys of the school who fell in the Crimean War, the Indian Mutiny, and South Africa.

But we have yet to pause before the most hallowed spot in this great chapel, where we are moved by the simple way in which a great man is remembered. Under the chancel steps sleeps Thomas

Arnold. Here they laid him long before his work was done, but nobly he had enriched this place. He had changed the face of education through the public schools of England. He could have wished for no other resting-place than this, or that the stone should bear anything but his name and a cross. There is a sculptured figure of him a little way off.

Near him, in what is known as Poets Corner, is a white marble portrait medallion of Matthew Arnold, father and son looking out together on the place they knew so well, and under Matthew's calm and scholarly face we read his touching and inspiring lines:

> *Why faintest thou? I wandered till I died.*
> *Roam on; the light we sought is shining still.*
> *Dost thou ask proof? Our Tree yet crowns the hill,*
> *Our Scholar travels yet the loved hillside.*

And near Matthew Arnold is the white portrait medallion of his friend Arthur Hugh Clough, the inspiration of his lovely elegy Thyrsis; it is engraved with two short lines:

> *Young children gather as their own*
> *The harvest that the dead have sown.*

Here, too, is Rupert Brooke. We look on his fine sensitive face, exquisitely modelled in profile, and under it we read those immortal lines that have woven themselves into English poetry for ever and are known to all, beginning:

> *If I should die, think only this of me:*
> *That there's some corner of a foreign field*
> *That is for ever England.*

Very impressive is the beautiful figure of Dean Stanley lying under a canopied recess in white marble; it is by Sir Edgar Boehm. There are also medallion portraits of the two Archbishops, Dr Temple and Dr Benson, and of Thomas Jex-Blake.

From this chapel we pass to the sacred place enshrining the memory of 682 Old Rugbeians who gave their lives for their school and their country, four of them winning the V.C. Their names are on the walls, their records are in a register kept in a lectern richly adorned with inlaid wood. The windows of the memorial chapel glow with pictures, and the white stone reredos carved with corn and grape vine is guarded by two listening angels above the sanctus door. The windows have scenes of war on land and sea, with scenes of

Peace and Hope in which is a city set on a hill, a harbour of refuge, a lighthouse, and the setting sun. In other windows are scenes of the last days of Christ, and there are fine views of the school and impressive portraits of St Oswald and St Edmund with King Alfred and King Arthur.

We may go into the Close, where the host of boys and men who are remembered in the chapel knew their happiest hours. It is a splendid stretch of green and pleasant land, shaded by fine elms, a place memorable for those who recall Tom Brown's football and cricket matches. It has in it a mound which is a relic of the ancient British occupation of Rugby. On a granite tablet on the Doctor's Wall overlooking the Close is recorded the exploit of William Webb Ellis, who in 1823, "with a fine disregard for the rules of football as played in his time, first took the ball in his arms and ran with it, thus originating the distinctive feature of the Rugby game." Near the doorway at the base of the turret by this wall is an oak-tree planted by Edward the Seventh when he came to open the Temple Speech Room, the memorial to Dr Temple.

Many portraits of famous old Rugbeians adorn the Speech Room walls, among them one of Judge Hughes and one of Dr Arnold. Here also is a bust of Arnold holding a book, looking very calm and dignified. It stands on a pedestal carved from one of the great trees of the Close, under which he and Tom Hughes would have walked on summer evenings, and originally it was intended for Westminster Abbey. There is a bronze portrait of Dr Temple, and in the rich glass of one of the windows is Lawrence Sheriff in ruff and gown, holding a scroll and surrounded by armorial emblems. Another window has another portrait of Dr Arnold, with heraldic shields.

On the wide lawn of the Museum stands Judge Hughes, a commanding stone figure by Sir Thomas Brock. He has papers in his hand, and his grave and kindly face is turned towards the Close. As we enter the Museum we see in a glass case the hand of the clock on which Tom Brown and East scratched their names. There is a manuscript by Rupert Brooke, a letter written by Nelson on the Victory, and Dr Arnold's table and chair. There are relics of the battles of Edgehill and Naseby, a fine collection of fossils, alabaster pots of the time of Abraham, Greek helmets, a Roman nuptial ring, and many rare books.

The oldest church in Rugby town is St Andrew's, with a medieval tower said to be unlike that of any other church in England. Rising 70 feet high, it has all the appearance of a tower of refuge and defence. It has narrow lights, and a fireplace with a flue running to the top. It is thought to have been built by the Rokebys, the Norman family which settled here after the Conquest, as a place of defence as well as an ornament to the church, which was already a century old. Now the old tower is overshadowed by a new tower and a spire which rises nearly 200 feet.

Four ancient arches have been saved in the beautiful modern nave. The marble reredos has paintings copied from Fra Angelico. They were painted by the Cotswold artist Alec Miller, given as a memorial to her husband by Emily Bennett, a Rugby lady whose generosity has greatly enriched the church. She gave the magnificent iron screens and gates in the chancel and the chapel, among the finest examples of ironwork of our time, elaborately fashioned with the leaves and fruit of the vine and adorned with enamelled shields. There is a mosaic panel with a figure of the Baptist, and a lovely chalice of 1653.

A house in Hillmorton Road (Number 5) has become historic, and has a plaque saying, "In this house was born Rupert Brooke, 1887."

The four Rugby V.C.'s of the war were Geoffrey St George Cather, Christopher Bushell, Robert Gorle, and Frank de Pass.

Four Heroes of Rugby

THE immortal story of Philip Sidney is recalled and eclipsed by that of Captain Cather, who sacrificed his life while bringing water to wounded soldiers lying helpless in No Man's Land. After heavy fighting near Hamel in July 1916 he spent many hours crawling about the bullet-swept waste between the lines searching for wounded, and in full view of the enemy he carried four men to safety and repeatedly took water to others until he was shot down.

It was at Morlancourt in the opening attack of the last great offensive that Captain Bushell won his V.C. Although severely wounded in the head he refused to have his wound dressed and, walking about in view of the enemy, he reorganised the Allied troops, risking his life continually until he had placed the whole line in a sound position. When the men began to fall back he urged them to hold their ground, visiting every point of the line until he was taken to the dressing station, mortally wounded.

Through the remarkable dash and courage of Lieutenant Gorle a battle was won by the British about six weeks before the Armistice. Four times he brought his gun into an exposed position close to the German line and destroyed enemy machine-guns, stopping the German barrage so that our troops could advance. Later, when they began to fall back, he galloped his gun in front of the infantry and destroyed two more German guns. The men took courage and the wavering line rallied. What had seemed hopeless suddenly became possible, and the British retook the northern end of the village.

Many lives were saved by Lieutenant de Pass. Crawling down a German sap, which had been driven close to the British trench, he managed to blow up a barricade and put an end for 24 hours to intense bombing. With Private Smith he went out and rescued a wounded Sepoy lying 200 feet away near the German lines.

The Silver on the Stone

RYTON-ON-DUNSMORE. Beyond the church and the mill, both known in the Conqueror's day, stretches Dunsmore Heath, and on the heath stands Knightlow Hill. The hill is crowned by the barrow of some forgotten British chieftain, and on it medieval folk placed a wayside cross, of which a hollowed stone remains.

At sunrise on St Martin's Day people from 28 parishes within the Knightlow Hundred assemble for the payment of Wroth Silver. Each one casts into the hollow stone a coin or coins, amounting to a small sum in all, but a token for immemorial years of their indebtedness to the lord of the manor. The custom is said to have come down from Saxon times and the money is payment for rights-of-cattle way from one village to another. The Duke of Buccleuch receives this Saxon tribute which has never ceased.

On the hill once stood four fir trees about the cross. The older ones were torn down in a gale, and the long avenue of firs and elms stretching six miles to Dunchurch from Rugby suffered sadly from felling in the war. New groups of elms have been planted since in memory of men who gave their lives as the trees gave theirs.

Ryton's red-and-grey church has Norman doorways and a fine 14th-century tower with tiny pinnacles. It preserves an ancient font, Jacobean altar rails and pulpit, and old box pews, and a strange brass of an 18th-century vicar, Moses Macham, shows a skeleton clinging to a tree and a lantern on a coffin at the side.

Granny Clarke

SALFORD PRIORS. A charming little place it is, with black-and white cottages and a three-gabled house looking lovely behind a barn. It is the last village out of Warwickshire into Worcestershire, a perfect beauty, as if to make the traveller regret leaving Shakespeare's county.

The handsome Tudor hall, something like a castle at one end and a cottage at the other, has three fine gables, beautiful windows, and a lovely porch. Among its owners have been the Eystons, descendants of Sir Thomas More, and for 30 years after the French Revolution a little company of nuns found shelter here.

The oldest possession of the church is its richly carved Norman doorway with a Norman window in the west wall. The tower has fine 15th-century windows, and in the west wall are two small window-like recesses. Projecting from the south aisle is a splendid little embattled tower with the remains of what must have been three beautiful canopied niches. It has some of the quaintest gargoyles, a man holding his beard, a nightmare head, and a hooded figure holding his toes as he rides on the shoulders of a dragon. Other carved figures run along the aisle, a woman with her tongue out, two grotesque birds, and a woman clasping a winged creature.

The south aisle is also curious inside for being divided from the long narrow nave by an arcade of separate arches with walling between them, three of the 12th century and one of the 13th. The oak pulpit was made by a 17th-century carpenter, and a later craftsman gave it a panel of the Nativity, with scenes of the Crucifixion and the Ascension. In the Bethlehem scene the Child is in the manger with Mary kneeling and Joseph in an attitude of awe, shielding his eyes with one hand as he gazes on the scene. The chancel has 700-year-old lancets, the very fine triple east window having arches and slender columns with figures of St John in blue and white and Christ with the children.

Most of the monuments are to the Clarkes of Shakespeare's day, one to Simon Clarke's wife and sons having 18 shields; one of the boys lies in a tiny recess in a bodice and full skirt. Here also is Granny Clarke of 1669, a daughter of that Thomas Hobson, the Cambridge carrier, who gave us the familiar phrase we use so often, Hobson's Choice. A gracious old lady she must have been, for it was she who put here an inscription in memory of an old servant and a memorial to her grandchild. The old lady lies on a fine tomb, and opposite is the prim figure of little Margaret in red, only three when she died 300 years ago. The inscription Granny chose for her is very touching, for we read that Nature put the little one to bed:

> *As careful nurses to their bed do lay*
> *Their children who too long would play.*

The Midnight Murder

SECKINGTON. A village set on a rock which cannot be hid, its tower and spire are a landmark where Warwickshire meets Staffordshire. It has a fine earthwork of a Norman castle and a splendid monument from the spacious days of Queen Elizabeth.

The Tudor monument is in the 14th-century chapel of the church, a simple place with much charm, mottled stone walls, and a great chancel arch. Perhaps the most striking effect of the church is the rich glow of colour in the glass of the east window, with figures of saints, scenes of Bethlehem and Calvary, and the Ascension. There is also a little old glass with birds and a lion's head, but oldest of all is the coffin stone in a recess of the chancel wall with a very fine cross in memory of a priest of medieval days. On one side of the cross is a chalice and on the other side a book.

The great monument is that of Robert Burdett, who is kneeling on it in his captivating costume as Counsellor to Queen Elizabeth. He is in gold-and-white armour with his wife, looking charming in painted alabaster. The father has two sons behind him and the mother two daughters, and about them are arches and shields and pillars richly adorned.

It was here that Saxon nobles murdered King Ethelbald. Born to the throne of Mercia, he was driven from his court at the death of his father by the usurper Ceolred, and roamed a hunted fugitive in the wild fens. Ceolred died in 716, whereupon Ethelbald gained his throne without bloodshed and reigned for 41 years.

Except that he professed Christianity and counted the Pope among his friends, he stands out rather like a creation from one of the old pagan sagas, a man of herculean strength and impetuous valour, who, having made himself paramount king south of the Humber, took advantage of an invasion by Picts to seek the conquest of the northern half of England. Failing that, he marched against

Wales, which he ruled for many years with an iron hand. In 752 Cuthred headed a West Saxon revolt and the rivals met in a terrible battle at Burford, where Ethelbald, after feats resembling those of the legendary heroes of Scandinavian romance, was defeated. Here in melancholy humiliation he made his headquarters, soured, evil-humoured, and provocative. One midnight in 757 his exasperated thanes crept stealthily to his chamber and slew him as he lay.

The Chalice of the Last Supper?

SELLY OAK. It is one of the wonderful intellectual centres of England, for it has in its midst a marvellous group of Quaker colleges. As the University has grown out of the dreams of a maker of pens, Josiah Mason, whose Orphanage we see at Erdington, the colleges owe themselves to makers of chocolate, the Cadburys, whose spirit is everywhere in Birmingham. To Woodbrooke, a college for men and women, students come from all over the earth. Kingsmead is a missionary college. Westhill trains leaders for religious education. Fircroft is for working men. Carey Hall is for women missionaries. For years this remarkable group of colleges has been at work spreading throughout the world the spirit of goodwill. In Woodbrooke College at Selly Oak is a treasure almost beyond compare in our country.

It is one of six cups round which have been woven a legend which we may accept or reject as we please, but of which we must say that, however unlikely it is, its truth is not impossible. Each of these six cups is so beautiful and so old, and the known history of each one is such, that it is possible for it to have been used at the Last Supper. The six chalices are this at Woodbrooke, two in Berlin, one at Leyden, one in Italy, and one in the British Museum. The Woodbrooke chalice is of golden glass about three inches high, believed to have been made in Sideon either early in the first century or a little before it. It has round the rim a Greek inscription of which the first four words are the four words with which Jesus greeted Judas: *Wherefore art thou come? Rejoice.*

This beautiful cup was found in the Crimea and came into the possession of Dr Rendel Harris, who gave it to Woodbrooke, where he has been so long at work on ancient manuscripts. It was broken in pieces but has been repaired, and is one of the most precious things we may see in Birmingham.

At Woodbrooke is one of the rarest collections of manuscripts in the world, collected in the East by Dr Mingana. In it are writings lost to western readers for more than 1000 years, the work of famous scholars of the early Church.

Father of the S.P.C.K.

SHELDON. Neither clever nor great, one of its rectors accomplished a noble thing. He was Thomas Bray, the Father of the S.P.C.K. He would know many of Sheldon's old cottages, and the gabled Hall with Tudor chimneys, and the fragments of a moat.

The beautiful little church, in a churchyard like a garden, is in the fields. Although it has been made new since this 17th-century rector was here, its fine timbered porch has the original carved roof-beams and shelters the old doorway. The nave roof is a mass of ancient timbering, and in the north aisle is 14th-century canopy work. In the chancel are four old chairs.

The modern stone reredos, with canopied figures of Our Lord and the disciples at the Last Supper, is in memory of a rector for 61 years, John Jones-Bateman. There is a tablet to the famous Thomas Bray, who came here in 1690, and an old oak cupboard in the north aisle holds the books he left. He worked out a scheme to provide parish libraries throughout England and America, and out of his zeal grew the Society for Promoting Christian Knowledge. In 1699 he went to Maryland to start a mission, returning the next year to found the Society for the Propagation of the Gospel.

Like a Feast of Jewels

SHERBOURNE. It is an oldfashioned piece of countryside with a new beauty set in the midst of it. The village is almost lost in the woodlands, a charming picture seen from Barford Bridge by those who hurry by, but with a great splendour to unfold to those who turn down a lane to find the church, a new structure with a tower and spire of exquisite loveliness, rising from the green banks of the Avon. It stands with an old yew and a fragment of an ancient cross amid green lawns, a gorgeous place with a splendour of craftsmanship in wood and stone.

The tower has a spire and four tall pinnacles so richly decorated that they are like stone bursting into flower. It has beautiful windows with richly carved gables and eight saints in niches round the walls. The outside is charming; the interior is full of fine work. Outside

Selly Oak   The Library

Wootton Wawen
Saxon Arch

Oxhill
Norman Doorway

Curdworth   Norman Chancel Arch

Stoneleigh   Norman Chancel Arch

Snitterfield   A Shakespeare Village

Henley-in-Arden   The Street

Two Peeps of the Cottage at Shottery

The Fireside as Shakespeare knew it

Anne Hathaway's Cottage at Shottery, Stratford-on-Avon

the north wall is a king playing a harp, an angel on each side, all in a row under a fine canopy. The porch doorways are remarkable for their mass of beautiful carving. On the border of the arch outside is the branch of a tree with 11 birds among the leaves, all wrought with great cunning and astonishing detail. Some of the birds are pecking caterpillars and flies off the leaves, one is putting a worm into a fledgeling's mouth, one is feeding its young on the nest, one is singing, and others are preening themselves. At each side of this wonderful arch are a bishop and a queen. Peeping behind a fine border of leaves on the other side of the arch we find little birds and flowers tucked away, and across the porch on the inner doorway there are beautiful mouldings enclosing a door with fine hinges and ironwork.

The interior is a wealth of rich carving. There are lovely arches with clusters of eight shafts round the columns, and on the capitals and corbels are flowers and fruit with here a bird eating cherries, and there a bird hanging on in quest of food. The alabaster panelling of the sanctuary has more beautiful work of the same kind, and the alabaster reredos has the richest of canopies, crowned with a mass of pinnacles and with five niches under which stand Our Lord and the Four Evangelists. At each side, under still richer canopies, are sculptures of Gethsemane and the Burial.

The font has eight angels round it and a mass of inlaid coloured marbles, perhaps a little too clever and with too much colour. The oak pulpit is richly carved and has an angel for a book-rest. The best windows have Simeon in the Temple with Mary and Jesus, a woman in blue making gifts to children, and Christ with the doctors in the Temple.

The oldest thing we found in this new place was this inscription to John Smith who lived 300 years ago:

> Twice thirty years I lived till death me struck
> With fatal dart, and from me life he took.

We may wonder if there is anywhere a village church more magnificently adorned. It is not simple and has not the quiet charm of so many of our village shrines; we must think of it as rather like a rich man's table set for a feast.

The Traffic of Six Hundred Years

SHILTON. It is on a very busy highway, and the church has seen the traffic of 600 years go past its door. We were told that it had been made new so well that we must look closely to see what is old and what is new. Certainly it is well done.

The old piscina is quaintly worked into the splay of a window and the tracery of the windows has been largely renewed. The little church has two north aisles, the new one with sculptured heads of a woman in a wimple, a king, a bishop, and a few ordinary men. The walls of the nave seem to be leaning; the chancel walls have modern paintings of St Andrew and two angels. In the windows St Margaret is treading a dragon under her feet, but facing this window is a finer picture of "the widow of fourscore years who departed not from the temple but served night and day." She is sitting reading her book. There are fragments of old glass with shields in two windows.

We found that, although electricity is hiding in the corners, the church is still decked with its candle lights as in the days when they buried here Henry St Germain and his wife Anne. It was their son Christopher who went to London in the 15th century, became a great lawyer, and wrote a textbook which remained a standard legal work until Blackstone superseded it 200 years ago.

None to Write a Line for Him

SHIPSTON-ON-STOUR. The flavour of other days is in all its streets, where the houses and inns are of the Georgian period when the woollen industry made Shipston a more prosperous place than now. In many of the houses, older still, a stone over the door has the date and the initials of the builder; we noticed one with these two rather curious lines:

Here we pray for peace in our land,
And we success with this in hand.

There are charming weathered roofs of Cotswold tiles, quaint little dormers, and handsome doorways with old brass knockers. It is a fitting place to remember one who was keenly interested in Old England; here was born in 1860 Francis Haverfield, who visited the sites of Roman remains all over England, conferred with antiquaries, directed excavations, and, in short, laid thoroughly the foundations of our knowledge of Roman Britain.

Only by the 19th-century church, where the main road runs, does the modern world seem to intrude, but here a fine monument of the past looks down on the busy traffic. The tower, all that is left of the old church, has been here 500 years and the wind and the rain have left their mark on its massive walls, its pinnacles and battered carvings. Inside the church is an oak table made from the sounding-board of the old pulpit, set on an eight-sided pedestal and a massively carved base. The white stone pulpit has panels adorned with chestnut leaves. There is a white marble bust of John Hart, of whom we are told that he was 200 years ago a considerable improver and promoter of manufacture here.

With no memorial to keep his memory green, there sleeps beneath this chancel a man who was rector of Shipston in the 18th century. He was William Parry, famous for the skill and beauty of his handwriting. It is said that his work could be mistaken for print, and as some of his manuscripts are preserved in the Bodleian Library we may judge for ourselves. It seemed odd to us that one who could write so perfectly found none to engrave a memorial line on his tomb.

Proud on its Hilltop

SHOTTESWELL. Almost hemmed in by Oxfordshire, it stands proudly on its hilltop with its church rising above the roofs of the houses lining its maze of narrow lanes. The church, with a tower and spire and low lead-covered roofs, is a charming little place, with an air of ripe age clinging to its walls. It has a Norman doorway and Norman arches on one side of its nave facing English arches on the other. There is a crowned head and one draped at the ends of the Norman arcade, and under one of the arches still stands the font at which the Normans christened their children. The pulpit and the pews have 15th-century traceried panels in them, and two oak screens in the chapel have a little timber which has survived 600 years. There is an old altar table with a small figure of Justice, and an ancient chest.

The great possession of the church is its striking oak reredos, a fine piece of Flemish craftsmanship, its eleven panels having carved figures between them. In the middle is Christ enthroned, and at the sides are figures of Justice and Fortitude, the scene in the stable at Bethlehem, the serpent giving Eve the apple, and the Roman soldiers waking up startled at the tomb. We noticed on the outside a quaint little face looking doubtfully at a bishop across the window.

Who Plays While the King is Fighting?

SHUCKBURGH. It is Upper and Lower, both in or about the great park. In Lower Shuckburgh a shapely oak throws its shade over the village stocks, but the church was new last century and has nothing old save the 13th-century font. But Upper Shuck-burgh, in the park by the Hall, has a church that draws us to it, nobly set among these trees, with herds of deer about and within hail of spacious gardens adorned with statues. A great cedar throws its shadows on the walls from which stone faces have looked down for centuries.

Two stones in the south wall with skulls and crossbones are be-lieved to have come from Cardinal Wolsey's palace at Esher, of which only the gatehouse still stands, stones which verily may have witnessed one of the last chapters of that dramatic Tudor story.

Here sleep many generations of the Shuckburghs from the great house. Some of their 16th-century brasses remain, one of a knight in rich armour with his wife, another of a group of five sons and three daughters. Elizabeth is in brass by the side of her husband Thomas, a curious figure with his head in brass and the rest graven in slate. Of the brass of Margaret Shuckburgh only part of her dress remains, the rest of her, like Thomas, being cut in slate. The memory of other Shuckburghs endures in stone; John in armour and Mary in ruff and a flowing gown lie under a rich canopy on a painted tomb with glowing shields about them. Catherine has cherubs about her head, Julia has a sculpture by Flaxman, a death-bed scene with an angel hovering near. Stewkley has the figure of a weeping woman, and George a marble portrait.

But it is Richard Shuckburgh's monument with his canopied bust that interests us most, for he is a romantic figure in Warwickshire's story. They say that as Charles Stuart was riding to Edgehill he passed Richard out hunting and inquired who passed his time so pleasantly while the king was fighting for his crown. Richard was brought before him and so graciously received that he rode home, armed his tenants, and the next day was knighted after fighting for the king at Edgehill. Afterwards he fortified Shuckburgh Hall and made a brave stand against the Roundheads, fighting desper-ately until he was severely wounded and carried prisoner to Kenil-worth. He lived to see the bitter end of his royal master and Cromwell in his place, and when he died in 1656 they laid him here, not far from the place where he met the king on that day which changed his life.

At the Hall there are splendid portraits in stained glass of Richard and his son John on horseback, as well as fine paintings of the two Stuart monarchs they so faithfully served.

The Summons to Surrender

SHUSTOKE. One day late in the 19th century a flash of lightning struck the church built here 500 years before, and the church was almost entirely destroyed, except for two doorways and most of the tower. But one historic monument was saved, that of the most famous of the Dugdales who lived here, the great Sir William, historian and antiquary.

It was he who, beginning his researches with the antiquities of Warwickshire, left to us also an incomparable collection of material about English cathedrals and ecclesiastical establishments. His official position led him into important and even dangerous duties in the Civil War, and he it was who summoned the city of Coventry, the castle of Banbury, and the town of Warwick to surrender to the King. He was present at Edgehill but survived the war, the Protectorate, and the Restoration, to die quietly in his bed at Blythe Hall close by, two years before the coming of William and Mary.

He had married Margery Huntbach when she was 16 and he was 17, and they lived together nearly 60 years till their daughter died and broke her mother's heart. Then she died too, and four years later old William Dugdale died himself, in his chair. He lies beside her in this tomb. There is a tablet to two other Huntbachs, Thomas and Margaret, who died in the days of Queen Anne.

One other relic of the past the fire spared for this church, sparing it rather miraculously for it is of wood, an old dug-out chest nine feet long, the oldest thing in Shustoke, with three locks. One of the old bells had to be recast, but it rings out proudly now, declaring to the world:

> Untuned by lightning, flame, and fire,
> Again I lead the steeple choir.

A little way off is Botts Green House, stately with gables and porch and fine chimneys.

The new church has a lofty interior, simple but imposing, with a barrel roof, and its slender spire stands well on its hill-top. The font is a fine copy of the richly arcaded Norman style.

SHUTTINGTON. It has a fine view of Tamworth, dominated by its fine tower four miles away, and it has something fine of its own, a Norman doorway set up by the monks of Alvecote Priory. It is now in the church by the River Anker which has been restored in Norman style. The priory founded by William Burdet in 1159 is now a farmhouse, but many of its walls and the fishponds are here for us to see. Among the ruins near the house are carved doorways, fragments of windows, and a 13th-century stone dovecot, a sad building that has long been roofless.

The Village that Missed Shakespeare

SNITTERFIELD. Who has heard of it? And yet it might have been the most famous village in our Motherland. It might have had the fame that came to Stratford. For here long ago lived Richard Shakespeare with his two sons John and Henry. Henry stayed behind and died poor; he lies with his wife in the churchyard.

John the farmer's son left in 1551 for the rising town of Stratford. He married Mary Arden at Aston Cantlow, and 13 years after leaving Snitterfield their son William was born. A lucky 13 it was for Stratford, for had farming been better, or had John been a little less ambitious, those 13 years might have been spent at Snitterfield, and Shakespeare have been born there.

It is a charming place, with merits of its own without the help of Shakespeare. It stands so high that at its church door we are level with the top of the tower of St Mary's at Warwick. It has winding lanes and many good old houses, and its 14th-century church is ringed with fine elms. The churchyard has an avenue of firs, and close by, when we called, was a great elm avenue; we must say "when we called," for the axe was echoing sadly among the trees of Snitterfield and 250 acres of them had fallen, one of the trunks said to have been 40 feet round.

The church has some excellent craftsmanship. Very good is the woodwork of the chancel. The altar rails are carved with fine old scroll work, and the fronts of the stalls have been magnificent; they have seven little worn-out figures of angels under canopies. Two ancient bench-ends are treasures still, and the modern ones are not unworthy. Among the carving is the figure of a bishop, another of a boy with wings, and two figures of mermaids. The 17th-century pulpit has much good work in it. The east window, looking very well through the lofty chancel arch, has four Saxon bishops and saints (Dunstan, Wulfstan, Oswald, and King Edwin). Another window in the chancel has Faith, Hope, and Charity, and in place of a window in the south aisle is a painting, apparently on wood, of St James in a red cloak.

In this chancel lie five members of the Philips family. It is to Robert Philips and his two sons that the great obelisk near by was set up; we see it for miles round, for it rises 120 feet. Greatly these brothers loved each other. Mark was born in the first year of last century and Robert two days after Waterloo. Both sat in Parliament. When his brother died in 1873 Robert set up the great obelisk as a tribute to his brother and their father, of whom we are told that he was a good, wise, and brave man, a friend of liberty in evil days. In the chancel lies one of his little twin daughters; both twins died at 16, 66 years before the death of their brother Robert, who sleeps here too.

Standing at the foot of the nave is a noble font 500 years old; it has eight boldly carved heads, some of them of great dignity. A tiny treasure of the village hangs in the vestry, one of the smallest samplers we have seen, just five inches square. It was done by a child in the village school, and it is odd to think that the little fingers were working it in this quiet place in the year when Europe was in revolution, 1848.

Snitterfield missed Shakespeare, but her poet came along. Under the boards of the vestry floor is an inscription to an 18th-century poet whose name was Richard Jago. Some of his lines are quoted in the chancel, and his poem on the great view from Edgehill has kept his name alive.

What we like best of all of this place is just outside it; it is one of the most charmingly simple memorials we have seen to the men who died for us. Noble in its simplicity and its conception, an elegant cross stands at the end of a lane which brings us from the village to high ground looking out on the hamlets and fields round Stratford. Set in a panel in most admirable lettering are the names of the 35 men of Snitterfield who did not come back, and in front is a good stone seat from which we look out on a great horizon. Edgehill is on the left, and if the day is clear we can see the Wrekin. It is a noble prospect, and carved on the back of the seat are these fine words:

The noble expanse visible from this spot was Shakespeare's favourite countryside. The men whose names are inscribed on the neighbouring monument gave their lives for that England which never did nor never shall lie at the proud foot of a conqueror.

We leave it all feeling that Snitterfield would not have been unworthy of its great fame had John Shakespeare made his home with Mary Arden there.

Here, while his brother's son William was growing up at Stratford, Henry Shakespeare stayed behind as a poor relation.

Shakespeare's Poor Relation

HENRY was a stay-at-home member of the family Shakespeare; his brother John, father of the poet, had ventured as far as Stratford. Henry farmed as a tenant on the Hales manor from 1574 to his death in 1596. Like his brother, he left his record in the manor documents. In 1574 he was fined for an affray with Edward Cornwaile; 11 years later he was fined for not wearing a cap to church; and in 1596 for not "labouring with teams on the Queen's highway," and for having a ditch in want of repair.

The ecclesiastical courts got hold of him for not paying tithe and excommunicated him, the most tragic record telling of a case in the local court in which he was sued for £6 13s 4d owing to John Blythe of Allesley for two oxen.

The record shows that Henry Shakespeare fell ill when the money was due and that he died about the day payment should have been made, having the money by him in the house. With Henry Shakespeare lying dead in his bed, William Meades of Coleshall, a neighbour, broke into the house on pretence of recovering a debt, took away not only money but also a mare, the corn and hay from the barn, and all the goods and household stuff, and would not pay Blythe.

Meades declared that he only went to the house to ask the widow, Margaret Shakespeare, about £4 6s 8d due to him and went away quietly; and that William Rounde of Allesley, who was Henry's surety for the £6 13s 4d, had removed the oxen while Henry was in prison for debt, and had given them back to Blythe.

While this was happening at Snitterfield Henry's nephew was in London writing Henry the Fifth. Seeing that his uncle was so desperately impoverished, is it not reasonable to surmise that it was the poet who furnished the money which lay in the house of the poor farmer when death came upon him?

The Bowling Green Older than Francis Drake

SOLIHULL. The past and the present rub shoulders in this beautiful place, but a wealth of interest the centuries have left in the church, the old inns, and the splendid old homes and their gardens.

It is a pleasure to walk along the High Street and see between the young trees the old half-timbered dwellings and shops. Tudor England waits round nearly every corner in Solihull, and far older than Tudor England is the George Inn's magnificent bowling green. It was old when Francis Drake was playing bowls on Plymouth Hoe, and must be one of the oldest in England. It has a good companion of many centuries, a sturdy yew shaped as an arbour, in the shade of which twelve men can sit.

The church, on which a fortune of £20,000 was being spent when we called, has one of the best spires in Warwickshire, 168 feet high, with a peal of 10 bells. The chancel, built in the 13th century, has noble arches, and there are chapels to St Anthony, St Mary, St Catherine, St Thomas, and St Alphege; and under the chapel of St Alphege is a vaulted crypt with a rare altar stone older than the Reformation, and a stone cross in masonry. One of the chapels has an ancient altar, an old piscina, and a fine stone reredos. The pulpit is Jacobean, and there is an 18th-century candelabra adorned with shields. Two 16th-century tombstones of alabaster have engraved portraits of the Greswolde family, who were famous for centuries here. In the transept windows is a little 15th-century glass, and St Alphege chapel has a window of his martyrdom. There is a brass portrait of William Hill, who has with him two wives and three groups of 18 children, all as they were dressed in the childhood days of Queen Elizabeth.

Solihull is proud of its church, its school, and its old houses. The 15th-century Old Berry Hall still has its moat, and Malvern Hall, now a school, has a gateway to which it is said Inigo Jones contributed some of his genius, and two statues thought to be by the sculptor Cibber, who set the Phoenix 18 feet long over one of the doorways of St Paul's Cathedral.

Two items of history come to mind at the church and at the school. The church had John Feckenham as rector until the religious strife of the time took him farther afield, and he became chaplain to the terrible Mary Tudor. Elizabeth offered to make him Archbishop of Canterbury, but he refused to accept the Reformation and was sent to the Tower and kept a prisoner until he died in 1582. He was the last mitred abbot to sit in the House of Lords. The other item of history, linked with the grammar school, brings up our famous Dr Johnson. The school was here in Shakespeare's day, and among the scholars have been two of Warwickshire's smaller poets, William Shenstone and Richard Jago. About the time they were schoolboys here an uncouth and clumsy fellow applied for the post of master, and the authorities decided he should not be appointed, declaring that he had the character of being haughty and ill-natured and of distorting his face (which he could not help) so that it might affect the boys. He was Samuel Johnson, and so he lost the mastership of Solihull school, another of those disappointments which drove him to seek his fortune in London, where he arrived with David Garrick, "with twopence-halfpenny in my pocket, and thou, Davy, with three-halfpence in thine."

The Last Friend of Heroes

SOUTHAM. It has a holy well that never freezes and a street that always pleases. It was once so important that it was allowed to make coins of the realm, but its mint is now the inn. If it is not rich it is handsome, for it has a grand oak staircase, a gallery, and an old mounting-stone. Over the River Itchen is a bridge which has seen many centuries go by, and the handsome church with a big chencel, nave, and aisles has a spire 120 feet high and about 600 years old.

The nave, chiefly 15th century, has a graceful clerestory with carved faces; and there is a chapel in memory of a 17-year-old middy who went down in one of our battleships in 1914. A splendid oak roof with fine carving has been one of the glories here for 400 years; it is held up at the corners by stone angles with huge heads and foliage coming out of their mouths. In the south aisle is a quaint corbel of St Catherine holding the wheel of her martyrdom. The lectern is a winged angel. The piscina has a five-leaves drain, and let into the back of it is a strange little demon. The 16th-century oak pulpit has come back to a place of honour after being in a barn at Worm-leighton. There are two oak chests, one with five locks; and in the tower is a bell with a story. It did not ring for Charles Stuart the first time he came here, and its silence cost the Southam folk a fine. The king was here again on the eve of the Civil War, sleeping a night in a timbered house which is still standing.

In the churchyard is a magnificent chestnut and an avenue of limes planted in Waterloo year. We found a curious witness to a sad tragedy at the rectory about the time the trees were planted, for

Samuel Sandys took his own life on St George's Day in Waterloo year. The mason who carved his stone was clearly agitated at his work, for he misspelt a word and made a queer mess of it by trying to cover it over.

Moving stories come to mind at the sight of Augustine Bernher's name among the rectors here, for Bernher flits like an incredible apparition through the terrible pages of the martyrdoms under Mary Tudor. He was the servant and confidant of Latimer, and in good and evil report Latimer was saint and hero to him. When the bishop was arrested and sent to the Tower Bernher voluntarily attended him. When Latimer, Ridley, and Cranmer were removed to Oxford, there was Bernher ministering to them. Bishop Jewel, a father of the Reformation, about to be delivered to Bonner for burning as a heretic, fled from the University, on foot, penniless, and in dire peril. On the road, to his dismay, he saw a horseman riding towards him. It was the inestimable Bernher, who at once gave Jewel his horse and his money and sent him into hiding until he could reach London and fly the country. Throughout the persecution Bernher went from martyrdom to martyrdom, comforting and consoling the victims in prison and at the stake, and acting when the end had come, as Strype said, "as kind of overseer to the wives and fatherless children of those who died for religion."

The servant and solace of the bishops, he was the stay and comfort of many martyrs. To more than one of these heroes he was the last friend on earth. How he himself escaped is a mystery, for he thought only of others and counted his own life as nothing.

The Rector Who Went to Sea

SPERNALL. Its houses are few and far between and its church almost hidden in a corner of the rector's garden, where the River Arrow glides by the willows and under a tiny bridge. The simple Norman church has been much altered, but still has a window with fragments of ancient glass, and an old oak lectern. A man's head and a grotesque creature keep watch from an old studded door framed in a Tudor doorway.

There came here as rector in 1670 Henry Teonge, who stayed five years and then, being in need of money, took a chaplaincy in the navy, leaving his son as rector here. We may be sure that on coming back to Spernall in 1679 he told his people many good tales, for he was here another 21 years before he died. He left a diary of his years away, declaring that no life on shore was comparable to life at sea, "where we have good meat and good drink, and good company and good divertisements, without the least care, sorrow, or trouble." When a French man-of-war asked them if they wanted anything their captain said he wanted nothing that he "would be beholding to such rogues as they were for." One terrible page of the diary describes how a seaman was punished for going ashore without leave. His legs were tied together, his hands were tied to a rope, and he was set on the side of the ship to be hoisted up to the yard-arm, from which he was dropped into the water three times, "but he, looking so very pitifully, was spared."

STOCKTON. London walks on a bit of Stockton, for from pits here came the cement for the Thames Embankment. Hereabouts also are layers of blue lias where huge fossils have been found. The oldest possessions of the church are its 14th-century chancel arch and the tower, which has a cornice with grotesques of animals and men. On the roof beams are four old figures of mitred bishops, but everything else in the church is new.

The Philosophy of Lydia Eason

STOKE. Little it has except the memory of a village boy who grew up to hold high rank and to receive on behalf of his king the unwanted wife of Henry the Eighth; but there is a gravestone of a wife whose homely epitaph has been much quoted. It is on the grave of Lydia Eason, a queer rhyme reading oddly now:

> All who come my grave to see
> Avoid damp beds and think of me.

The village boy remembered here was apprenticed to a mercer, and made his way so well in London that he became Sir William Holles and was chosen as lord mayor. It was as lord mayor that he received Anne of Cleves on her way through London. He may have been christened at this font, for it is 14th century, as old as the church. The piscina is carved with a man's head, and five stone heads have been peeping from the corner of the south aisle for about 600 years. In fragments of old glass are small kneeling figures in blue robes, with six roundels of shields and heads of saints.

The lofty chancel screen has fine modern tracery in its open bays and along its canopy.

Proud Lady With a Bitter Story

STONELEIGH. It is one of the glories of Shakespeare's country. We should come to it from Leamington, for then the road brings us by Stoneleigh Park, through one of the loveliest wooded stretches in Warwickshire, a part of the old Forest of Arden, enchanting all the year. Oaks growing when Shakespeare was writing of Rosalind, old enough for Orlando to have hung her name on their branches, keep company with noble firs on bracken slopes, and the Avon winds along with delightful bends.

We have a glimpse of Stoneleigh Abbey near the old bridge the monks built when the Abbey was their home 700 years ago. In this great house the Leighs have lived since Queen Elizabeth's day. Charles Stuart stayed here with 600 horsemen on his way to set up his standard at Nottingham. He found the gates of Coventry closed to him and came here to find so warm a welcome that he gave his host a medal of himself, still here.

A little way on from the ancient bridge of the monks, kept not for traffic but as a lovely thing, is another bridge of eight arches close to the point where the Sowe pours into the Avon; it leads to one of the most attractive villages in the Midlands. It has kept the peace for ages, and still it seems an old-world place, with its rich red brick and its old black-timbered cottages facing the warmly tinted almshouses across the street. They have been looking at each other through the centuries, growing more beautiful as they were growing old. The almshouses, with their quaint roofs and double rows of high chimneys, and their dainty doorways, were built by Alice Leigh, whose father as Lord Mayor of London rode before Elizabeth when she was crowned at St Paul's.

But the pride of this proud village is its church. We found roses blooming in its churchyard and roses in its Norman doorway, over the blocked-up arch through which the Normans came. In its carved tympanum are two serpents coiled round each other, and two great beasts, one eating its own tail; and we noticed a fish, two roses, and a bunch of leaves. Like the capitals of the four Norman pillars the carving is crumbling away, but indoors the work of these sculptors has defied the hand of Time and is magnificent. The chancel arch is one of the noblest pieces of Norman work that we have seen, its massive pillars banded to the walls with 11 bands like arrowheads, carved discs of stone gradually lessening in size between the two main lines. The arch itself has four bands of moulding; it must be nearly five feet thick and has crude carvings of a serpent and a dove. It is all very beautiful. Beyond the arch is a group of pointed arches on the chancel walls, and halfway through the chancel are two Norman pillars with carved capitals. We may believe that they once bore a vaulted roof, or we may believe that the builders left them unfinished, being disturbed by some sudden call to arms.

In this handsome chancel lies a proud lady with a bitter story, one of the few Englishwomen made a duchess in her own right, Alice Leigh. She lies with her daughter, one below the other, both exquisitely carved in marble by the English craftsman Joshua Marshall, who drew aside the linen folds to show how white and serene their faces are. Gracious as these figures are, we could wish that so gentle a lady, looking so beautiful, had less oppressive weight of marble about her, so incongruous in this stately place.

Alice Leigh was one of the tragic figures of her time. She had married Sir Robert Dudley, son of Elizabeth's favourite Earl of Leicester, and at his father's death they lived with all the glory of Kenilworth Castle about them, he and she and their four daughters, as proud a family as Warwickshire had. At his father's death he tried to establish his noble birthright, that he might be not only Earl of Leicester but Earl of Warwick too; but he failed, and his failure was the end of the happiness of Alice Leigh. Robert Dudley left his wife and his home, taking with him a page boy who proved on their arrival in Italy to be none other than the beautiful Elizabeth Southwell, maid-of-honour to the queen. He never returned to his own country and his estates were forfeited and given to his wife. Alice found her consolation in building the almshouses we see here, and in enriching village churches with gifts of plate. She lived to a marvellous old age and Charles Stuart made her Duchess Dudley.

On one side of the chancel a Lord Leigh of the 19th century lies in a richly vaulted recess, his tomb beautiful with oak and ivy leaves; and on the other side sleeps an unknown priest, here as his people saw him 600 years ago. The east window, rich in crimsons, blues, and browns, shows Our Lord receiving to their rest those who labour and are heavy-laden. Below it are two fine old chairs, one with a man and a woman with flowing hair, the other with two children's faces.

We do not know how old the great beams in the roof may be, but they must have looked down for many generations on what is perhaps the oldest thing in Stoneleigh, the wonderful Norman font. It is a masterpiece of carving on a tiny scale. Round it are 12 arcaded niches with arches over them, and in the niches are the Twelve Apostles; in the tiny arches are rows of faces.

There is more Norman work in the tower, which rests in the earth as the Normans set it there. We found half hidden away two splendid Norman pillars with carved capitals in the west doorway. In the porch lies the strange nameless figure of a woman. Six centuries have robbed it of all chance of recognition, but still at her side lies her child. Its little life was rounded with a sleep, and now its little figure is rounded by the gentle hand of Time.

In the kindly world about Stoneleigh it is not surprising to come upon a tribute to a porter, a servant of Lord Leigh 250 years ago. A good fellow he must have been, for we read:

> Here lyes a faithful friend unto the poore,
> Who dealt large almes out of his lordship's store.
> Weepe not poore people tho' ye servant's dead
> The lord himselfe will give you dayly breade.
> If markets rise, raile not against their rates,
> The price is still the same at Stoneleigh gates.

The Stately House on the Banks of Shakespeare's River

STONELEIGH ABBEY enshrines the story of nearly 1000 years. It is said that Shakespeare walked under some of these old oaks; certainly it must be true that he knew this beautiful place less than half a day's walk from Stratford. He would know the bridge the monks built over the Avon, the church, and the Abbot's House.

Stoneleigh Abbey as we see it brings together the old and the new in striking contrast, though even the new part, the magnificent building of three storeys with tiers of windows and pillars, has seen 200 years. It shelters the original monastic buildings with their many gables, stone mullioned windows, and roofs of tiles which Time has painted with its lovely tints. A more charming place than the Abbot's House we have not seen in Warwickshire. It has a perfect setting of trees against a wide expanse of lawn, and it has great architectural interest also, for it shares with the remaining portions of the Abbey the possession of Norman arches and carved pillars.

The old stables, with their wide cobbled courtyard, are a sheer delight; one great coach is still here which calls to life the glory of the road of yesterday. We leave these stables to find arched doorways in old walls opening to entrancing gardens. At the end of shady walks, down by noble beech trees the Avon broadens to a pool and gathers itself to surge and sing over a weir. It is a place of unforgettable beauty at the very heart of England; who can forget these wondrous terraces, these gardens unsurpassed, these matchless scenes of one of our most loved rivers?

The house has more fine things than could be counted in a day, The windows have the royal arms since Henry the Eighth. The great gallery which confronts us at the entrance is believed to have been the south aisle of the Abbey Church. Its walls are splendidly panelled, the chimneypiece is a rare example of inlaid wood. In marble and stone, china and glass, in rare furniture and hundreds of pictures, the noble house brings before our eyes the beauty of centuries, unfolding like a pageant. In one exquisite window are over 30 heraldic shields. In other windows fragments of medieval glass shine as pure gems of colour. We can turn to the softer harmonies of ancient tapestries here and there, but scarcely can we turn anywhere without some face, solemn or serene, wistful or severe, peeping at us out of the centuries gone.

The house is rich in sculpture, in carved and panelled wood, in ancient chests from various parts of the world, in fine old tables, in old arms and armour, and in rare china. One splendid marqueterie table has inlaid panels representing the life of Columbus, another is enormously long and was probably the refectory table used by the monks of the Abbey. One of the bedrooms has the bed in which Charles Stuart slept. The chapel has some dazzling fragments of medieval glass.

But perhaps most wonderful to see are the decorations in the saloon, all by Cipriani, the ceiling showing the gods of Greek mythology receiving Hercules into the celestial regions, and medallions on the walls showing the Labours of Hercules—the taming of the bear and the slaying of the lion. On a panel over a mantelpiece the hero is leaning on his spear making his choice between Pallas and Aphrodite.

We take our leave by the fine gatehouse, with its great arch and huge doors of thickly studded oak that have been swinging to and fro 600 years. Easy it is to imagine the scene as it may have been on

Stratford-on-Avon   The Church where Shakespeare sleeps

Stratford-on-Avon   The National Theatre

The Birthplace

Site of Shakespeare's House

Harvard House

Tudor Front of Shakespeare Hotel

School and Aimshouses

Shakespeare's Schoolroom

Scenes in Stratford-on-Avon

The Font at which he was christened, the Room he was born in, and his Chair

Jug

Bust above his Grave

Trencher

His Signature

His Coat-of-Arms

His Signet Ring   Door Ring of the Church   His Brooch

The Desk he may have used in School   Old Door of his Home   The Cradle in which he was laid

Intimate Links with Shakespeare

Falstaff   Hamlet

Stratford-on-Avon   The Shakespeare Memorial

that August day of 1642, when the king a city had rejected stood here receiving the salutation of his host at this noble gateway crowded with his dashing Cavaliers.

The Very Heart of England

STRATFORD-ON-AVON. It is the heart of the heart of England. We look out upon this lovely countryside and feel as Shakespeare felt; it is a precious stone set in a silver sea. So near it is to him that we should hardly be surprised to see him walking here.

Here is the place where he was born, the very room. Here is the school in which he learned to write, the very room and perhaps the very desk. Here is the tower he looked upon as he sat in his garden, with the very metal of the bell still ringing out as it rang out the precious hours for him. Here is the river he loved, the banks where he would sit and watch the peaceful Avon rolling on. Here are the lanes in which he walked, the fields he crossed to see Anne Hathaway, the seat on which he sat to talk to her. Here is a note he had from a friend, the actual letter he held in his hand to read. Here is the bridge he crossed when he walked to London, widened but still with its old stones and still looking much as he saw it; he sits in bronze at the end of it, with a group of his characters about him. Then he crossed the bridge all unknown, but when he crossed it coming home again the seed was sown, the work was done, that was to make him better known than Caesar, more firmly set in fame than Socrates. Here are the visible foundations of the house he lived in then, still enclosing the very spot he died on. And here on the bank of the river he lies, his dust part of this earth, this blessed plot, this England. Well may we feel that there is no place like it anywhere for English folk, for us who speak the tongue that Shakespeare spoke.

There are not many towns in the world more delightful to visit or more easy to see. We begin, of course, with that most famous cottage in which his eyes first opened on the world. The very window is there through which he saw the light, the very fireplace—in which we hope a fire was burning on that April day. Above are the rafters under which he and his little brother must have often slept; he must have thought of it on that day when he stood far away by the Thames and laid his brother in his grave.

We could wish, as we stand in this birth-room of Shakespeare, that the trustees of this great place would take the view that must come to

233

many people here. The walls and ceiling and even the old glass in the window are crammed with countless names, scratched on them before this wretched habit was thought to be contemptible. We even find here the names of Walter Scott, Izaak Walton, Robert Browning, Thomas Carlyle, and Edmund Kean. It may be thought that these names justify this mass of scribbling on the walls, but surely it is wrong. It has nothing whatever to do with Shakespeare, and it must do great harm in seeming to condone the habits of litter louts and spoilers everywhere. The room should be as Shakespeare saw it, not with its walls scrawled on by every loon and lout who comes this way.

From the days of Shakespeare's father, John Shakespeare of Snitterfield, down almost to living memory, this house was owned by Shakespeares; it is now the possession of the Shakespeare Trustees, who hold it for us all by Act of Parliament. It is filled with interesting things belonging to Shakespeare and his day; they are in eight rooms, and there are about 400 treasures.

As far as possible the house has been restored to its old condition. Its living-room opens straight from the street, paved with stone. The kitchen fireplace has a great oak beam with a small cupboard on one side and a recess for a seat on the other. Behind the kitchen is a washhouse and a pantry. Upstairs is the birth-room, another room which was once two, a narrow staircase leading to an attic now closed, and the back stairs leading to the kitchen.

The rooms are full of interesting things. There are the marks of signatures actually made by Shakespeare's father and mother, his daughters Judith and Susanna, his younger brother Gilbert, and his friend Ben Jonson. There are documents and portraits and pictures of the deepest interest. There are all the coins mentioned in the plays. There are two fine oak chests with rich carving, both in the birth-room, along with an Elizabethan oak desk with carved ends. There is a sword and a ring said to have been Shakespeare's, the sign of the Falcon Tavern at Bidford which he must often have seen, and a carved chair in which he might have sat in the tavern. There are some oak carvings he may have seen on the walls of the Guild Chapel next door to his school, and some miserere seats, one of these, representing a mermaid with two tails, said to be the only one of its kind.

What will perhaps appeal to most of us among these treasures are two things—the desk from Shakespeare's old school, at which it has always been believed he stood at his lessons; and the actual letter sent to him by his friend Richard Quiney. It is the only letter in the world which is known to have been put into Shakespeare's hand by a messenger. In it Richard Quiney asks his loving good friend and countryman for a loan of £30 to pay his debts in London. It would much quiet his mind, he tells Shakespeare, and he promises that his friend shall neither lose credit nor money by him. "The Lord be with you and with us all, Amen," the letter ends. It is written from the Bell Inn in London, almost in the shadow of St Paul's.

We follow him to school. He would probably go the way we go and arrive in front of this fine piece of Tudor England which stands today as little Shakespeare saw it. Of all the sights in Stratford it may move us most, for this long line of Elizabethan England must have been familiar as a daily sight to this Warwickshire boy, and it has hardly changed since then. The old red roofs, the half-timbered fronts, and the little lead windows are here, much as he would see them. Within these walls he learned a little Latin and less Greek. Here he learned to love books, here especially he loved one book which came back to his mind as he sat writing his last play.

Here are two of the most thrilling little rooms that this world has: the schoolroom up the stairs, and under it the old Guildhall in which there may have come to him his first great dream, for in it he saw his first play. Does it not stir the imagination as we think of it? Again and again he must have been enchanted with these spectacles. Sitting in this room with the oak beams and the lovely windows, the imagination dawning within him must have been moved by the drama of life as the Strolling Players brought it before his eyes. Could that small Guildhall hold the vasty fields of France, or might they cram within that wooden O the battlefield of Agincourt? How often when his great days came, and he was shaping for the stage scenes that have thrilled men through the centuries, must he have thought of the plays he saw in this small room. Here his mind first thought of the stage; here the drama became real to him: in the room upstairs he learned his first history, felt his first consciousness of the power of knowledge, wrote perhaps the first words he ever put on paper. Dull would he be of soul who could stand here unmoved.

The Grammar School was built in 1428 as the home of a religious

Guild. On the wall of the ground-floor room is a painting with three figures fading away; they are what is left of a Crucifixion scene, with St John and the Madonna. A small doorway leading from the Guildhall takes us to the Armoury, a little room with Jacobean panelling, and a winding stairway leads up to the room where the town records were kept, and to the Council Chamber with the timber roof, and with Tudor roses on the wall, thought to have been here since the end of the Wars of the Roses in 1485. The Pedagogue's House in the playground is now used as classrooms; it has enormous beams.

The fine tower rising at the end of this long piece of Tudor England (about 100 yards long with the almshouses) is the tower of the old Guild Chapel, a plain place inside but a charming feature of this famous street. It is as Shakespeare saw it, built by Sir Hugh Clopton before Shakespeare was born. It has a fine set of elegant 15th-century windows, but the glass is modern. Over the north door are carved figures of two angels. The bell in the tower has been refashioned but is the same metal as in Shakespeare's day. The handle of the small door in the chancel is a splendid example of old ironwork.

This tower is one of the thrilling sights of Stratford because Shakespeare saw it from his garden and may have seen it from his window as one of his last glimpses of the world. We do not know, but he lived and died across the street and the shadow of the tower would fall upon his house.

It is one of the tragedies of Stratford that Shakespeare's house has gone. It was dire misfortune when Sir John Clopton rebuilt it in 1702, but although much altered it was still Shakespeare's house, and misfortune only became calamity when the sour-tempered Parson Gastrell came from Frodsham in Cheshire and bought this famous house. He had little of the spirit of his Master. He hated the people who peeped over his wall to see the mulberry-tree that Shakespeare planted, and he cut the tree down and sold it as firewood. He quarrelled with the town about his taxes, and in his temper he pulled down the house to spite the corporation. At last he left the town amid the ragings and cursings of its citizens, one of the most contemptible figures who ever strutted across Shakespeare's stage.

But none can take away from us this precious bit of earth where Shakespeare closed his life and fell asleep. In the garden facing the Guild Chapel are the foundations of the house he bought in 1597, altering it and calling it New Place. There are two descendants of the mulberry tree he planted. His grounds ran down perhaps as far as the Avon, and as we walk about these grounds, most beautifully laid out half in private gardens and half in public ones, we know that we are walking where Shakespeare would sit on a summer evening and think about his wondrous life in London Town. He had been half a century away from home, had gone away unknown and come back with immortality. He came back to live with his wife and two daughters. His father and mother were gone, dying in the cottage he was born in; they lie in the churchyard near Shakespeare's little son. We know nothing of this boy, and Shakespeare knew little more, but Hamnet lies near his twin sister Judith where the Avon ripples past.

The house next door to this great site, now called New Place, was standing in the days of Shakespeare, the home of Thomas Nash, who married Shakespeare's granddaughter and lies near Shakespeare's grave. Here Shakespeare must have often been. It has now been made part of the New Place Estate, and furnished as a museum with a remarkable collection of things of Shakespeare's time. In one room are fragments of Shakespeare's own home found during excavations, along with certain articles made from the wood of the famous mulberry tree that Shakespeare planted. In New Place Shakespeare lived for the last six years of his life; here his widow may have died, and here his daughter Susanna lived after him.

One memory there is of this small piece of England which lights up a page of history when Shakespeare was no longer here. Susanna was still living in his house when the Civil War brought its disturbing influence to Stratford, and here the daughter of Shakespeare entertained Henrietta Maria and soldiers of the Puritan Army. What a picture it is, Charles Stuart's wife and Shakespeare's daughter sitting by the fire before the Battle of Edgehill, and, when the battle was over, Shakespeare's daughter entertaining Cromwell's men in the house where Shakespeare died. Time rolls back his curtain and unveils the past, but was ever another little peep like this?

A mile away across the fields is a room which must appeal to a countless number as the most captivating of all the rooms in Shakespeare's town; it is the room where he would sit by the fire with Anne Hathaway. From that day to this, from 1470 to 1911, there were Hathaways living in this house at Shottery; there have been ten generations of them in Stratford and they are there today. It is a charming hamlet of thatched houses, but it lives on the map for one place only, the cottage which has been more visited than any palace in the world. Here was a bank where wild thyme grew, and a garden of rosemary, marigold, and lavender. William Shakespeare would open a gate in this garden and out would come Anne Hathaway, through this very door, along these walks. It is perhaps the most intimate place that remains in Shakespeare's world, unspoiled and full of things he saw.

There is an old carved bed that has never been out of the room for 400 years; it has five fine figures at the head, the original rush mat, and a needlework cover done by Anne Hathaway's sister. There is a table Shakespeare must have had his supper at, a wooden plate he may have eaten from, chairs he may have sat in, and, most wonderful of all, there is still by the great fireplace the old seat on which he would sit with Anne Hathaway in the happiest hours of his youth. A little uncomfortable it looks, but what was that to them?

The Hathaway kitchen is full of interest for those who love old domestic things. There is a tinder-box found at the back of the fire-place, and an old leathern jug used for ale, with a piece torn out— probably for mending somebody's boots. The dining-table has the bench he would sit on. There are plates showing 400 years of table history, plates of wood and pewter and china. There is the old rack where the bacon was stored; the oven by the fireplace with the great oak block for a door. It is easy to imagine that if Shakespeare came back to this fireside he would still feel very much at home.

Outside is the old manor house restored as he saw it; its old stone front is very dignified, and it has a fine large hall with a hammerbeam roof and massive timbers.

Very much at home, also, Shakespeare would feel standing in front of Harvard House, as fine a possession as Stratford has. Dear it is to Americans, for it was the maiden home of the mother of John Harvard. It was new when Shakespeare came back to Stratford with all his fame, for it was built in 1596 by Thomas and Alice Rogers, whose daughter Katharine married Robert Harvard in Southwark in 1605. Two years later John Harvard was born and he went to America, where he died before he was 30, having founded Harvard College by leaving a legacy of £779 17s 2d.

It is a gem of a house. This and Mary Arden's house at Wilmcote are as good as anything in Shakespeare's Warwickshire. The front is richly carved and has massive supports, a charming place with projecting windows. We enter straight from the street into a big room, and are fascinated by a lovely peep through a Tudor arch beyond which are three steps to a snug kitchen corner. The beams are extraordinarily rough and crude, and this fine little place, full of quaint passages and winding stairs and splendid windows, will probably be standing in 1000 years. It has a little old glass, and one of its curious possessions, interesting to Americans, is the walking stick of Jefferson Davis, the Southern leader in the Civil War.

The streets of Stratford are filled with old houses at which we want to stop, and it is to Miss Marie Corelli that we must always be grateful for uncovering many of their ancient timbers. We walk about again and again admiring them, round this most engaging town.

Perhaps we look in at the town hall, which Shakespeare never saw, for it was built in 1768 : all that is left of the old town hall is a column in the beautiful New Place Gardens, where also is a mulberry tree grown from a sapling from Shakespeare's. In a niche in the town hall is a statue of Shakespeare presented by David Garrick ; he is leaning against a pedestal, and about him are small busts of Henry the Fifth, Richard the Third, and Queen Elizabeth. There is a handsome oak staircase, and over the fireplace in an ante-room a curious monument in marble with a portrait of George the Third, and a miniature of Shakespeare with figures representing Tragedy and Comedy. Above this ornament is a small painting of Falstaff being carried away in the linen basket. In the great Reception Room is Gainsborough's portrait of Garrick, and a fancy portrait of Shakespeare. A queer painting by a local artist shows the old town crier in his scarlet coat and cocked hat, and another of his wife in her cap and apron, carrying a big spoon. Hanging on the wall among the charters is the town rent-roll of the days of Shakespeare, with holes cut in the parchment to show that the rents were paid.

Probably a century earlier than Shakespeare is the famous stone bridge across the Avon, built by Sir Hugh Clopton in place of a wooden one. It has 14 pointed arches, and is held to be the finest bridge in Warwickshire. Close by it is a tiny bridge built to carry one of the first railways. The scheme dropped through, but for years horses drew wagons this way with goods and passengers. It is now a footway only, from which we have a fine view of the Avon with the Shakespeare Memorial and the church behind it.

In front of this view, set in the gardens between the bridges, is the monument of the poet by Lord Ronald Gower, showing Shakespeare in bronze with four characters about him: Falstaff for Comedy, Prince Henry for History, Hamlet for Philosophy, and Lady Macbeth for Tragedy.

The Memorial is a red-brick block with a theatre, picture-gallery, museum, and library. The theatre is new in our time and (except for one view of it from the other side of the river) without architectural distinction. We should see it by night with its flood-lighting, from the meadows or from a boat by the vicarage gardens, if we would see how night may lend enchantment to a scene unattractive by day. But the theatre has perhaps the finest stage in England, with marvellous mechanical contrivances, and it is our first National Theatre, built from a public fund of about a quarter of a million pounds raised largely by Sir Archibald Flower, whose father founded the Memorial. The picture-gallery has pictures of Shakespeare and his characters. There are scenes from Measure for Measure and Much Ado, by Smirke; Miranda and Caliban by James Ward; a fine Zoffany portrait of Garrick and his wife; Lawrence's portrait of Mrs Kemble; Hugh Riviere's portrait of Genevieve Ward; Sir Peter Lely's Nell Gwynne; a fine picture of the Witches by H. Fuseli; a rather poor Reynolds of the Death of Cardinal Beaufort; Shakespeare before Sir Thomas Lucy; and a painting by Sir John Forbes-Robertson of Mary Anderson. Among the curiosities in the museum is a brooch made for Mrs Garrick from a piece of Shakespeare's mulberry tree. some bullets from Edgehill, and slippers worn by Mrs Siddons. More precious than all are Shakespeare's gloves and a chair he sat in. There is a death mask of Sir Henry Irving, a sculptured relief of the actress Helen Faucit, and a carving of a dragon by Grinling Gibbons. There are two sets of stained-glass windows, one showing the Seven Ages of Man, the other in a charming bay with 17 panels of Shakespeare's characters. One of the best of them is old Adam in As You Like It, a part which Shakespeare played. It was the thought of Shakespeare being carried on somebody's back in this play that stirred the indignation of the poet Coleridge.

The Memorial library has 7000 Shakespeare books, but the greatest of all the treasures of the Memorial is something more than these, for here is the original portrait of Shakespeare from which Martin Droeshout made the engraving for the First Folio. There seems little doubt that this is a portrait made from life, painted from a panel of elm, and that it is therefore the most precious thing we have concerning him who lies farther down the river. At the entrance to the Memorial, in the hall, is a copy of Shakespeare's statue from Poets Corner in the Abbey, and outside the entrance are three terracotta panels with scenes of Comedy, History, and Tragedy.

A little way along the river lies this wonderful man. It is a scene of perfect beauty, charming in its simplicity. It happens that the first thing we see at the gate, under a colossal elm, is a granite column to Kathleen Stoehr, who perished in the Persia, sunk by a submarine in the war; but all harsh thoughts are quieted as we come down this most lovely walk. The porch of the church is framed in a lovely avenue of limes, and everything about this place bids the traveller hush as he draws near. The massive panelled door, with much original ironwork still left on it, must have opened at Shakespeare's touch. He must have opened it with this magnificent bronze ring and have smiled at the curious face from which it hangs. The ring has been here about 700 years and is as old as anything in Stratford.

The church is fine and light. It has 11 great bays and is nearly 200 feet long, nearly 70 feet wide, and 50 feet high. Its outer walls and transepts are 700 years old. The aisle and tower and the piers of the nave have stood as they are since 1300. The chancel, the clerestory, and the west window came at the beginning of the century in which Shakespeare was born. They are largely built of Warwick stone and are therefore an integral part of Shakespeare's England. Each of the five bays in the chancel has a window, and on the outside wall the dividing buttresses are carved with foliage and dragons. There are many large and small gargoyles, sometimes seven in each bay. The north porch has two storeys; the door, with the lovely iron head older than itself, was set on its hinges about 1420, soon after Chaucer was laid in the Abbey.

Let us look round before we see what all the world comes here to see. The fine light from the great clerestory windows reveals a hundred beauties in this place. An angel supports each clustered column between the high windows, and there are rich carvings in wood and stone and a wealth of figures in glass. Painted on glass or carved in wood or stone in this great church are a thousand figures of angels, saints, and common folk.

In the nave is a window with four scenes from the life of St George, crowded with figures, the central scene crowned with a choir of angels. A window close by shows three epochs of poetry with portraits of Caedmon, Chaucer, and Milton, and a charming scene from each: Caedmon's vision, Chaucer's Pilgrims, and Milton dictating. Another window has three British saints. Another has a fine picture of Savonarola in Florence, and another St Francis of Assisi feeding the birds. The small figures in these scenes are remarkably good. Very interesting are the St Nicholas and St Christopher windows, the one of the three children in a tub, the other of the child with open arms begging Christopher to take him across. Very beautiful is the Soldiers Window in memory of Richard Fordham Flower, who gave his life for his country in the South African War; it shows three saints with scenes from their lives. Few churches can have so great a variety of historic figures in their windows; we find here such unexpected portraits as Charles Stuart, Archbishop Laud, Amerigo Vespucci, Columbus, and William Penn. High up in a window near the tower is a little old glass.

The two chapels off the nave are of very great interest. One is the Clopton Chapel, built for Sir Hugh who built the bridge, though he died in London and lies there. By the outer wall is a fascinating procession of small coloured figures of seven Clopton children, and close by them is a canopied monument to Sir George Carew and his wife, brightly painted and covered with military emblems; he lies in knightly robes of scarlet and fur, wearing a coronet. He married Anne Clopton and must have been familiar with Stratford, so that he would know Shakespeare. He was one of Sir Walter Raleigh's closest friends, and pleaded for his life with the king who threw him to the wolves. There is an old helmet and relics of fine funerals hanging on the walls. There is a grim tale of this vault which Shakespeare must have known. It is said that Lady Charlotte Clopton was buried alive in it in the time of the Black Plague. We do not know if it is true, but it must almost certainly be true that Shakespeare, knowing the story, would think of the vault of the Cloptons when he buried Juliet alive in the vault of the Capulets.

The other small chapel is St Peter's, and it has much to see. There are 10 painted panels of saints set here by a lady who wished to do something in memory of those who gave their lives for us in the Great War, and in memory of those heroes also is a plain stone beautifully cut by Sir George Frampton, the eminent sculptor, with these impressive words of Kipling on it:

> *We counterfeited once for your disport*
> *Men's joys and sorrows, but our day has passed.*
> *We pray you pardon all where we fell short,*
> *Seeing we were your servants to this last.*

Here hangs a Union Jack given by Edward the Seventh to the Shakespeare Club; elsewhere are flags of a Warwickshire regiment raised against Napoleon. St Peter's Chapel is screened off with a 17th-century screen, but facing it is the more beautiful screen of the 15th century once leading into the chancel and now hiding a vestry. It is beautifully carved and has two quaint faces.

But it is not for these things that we come to Stratford Church. We come to see the font in which a Stratford boy was baptised and the grave in which he lies. The font is by the door; it has been in use for 500 years. The register beside it is open at two pages, showing that Shakespeare was baptised here on April 26, 1564, and buried here in 1616.

We pass into the chancel where he sleeps, with beauty all about him. The windows are the best in the church. The east window is the Adoration of Christ Crucified, and on each side are five fine windows with ten Bible scenes. On the left are David playing his harp before Saul, Rebecca meeting Jacob, the Queen of Sheba visiting Solomon, and Elijah on Mount Carmel. On the right are the raising of Lazarus and Jairus's daughter, and Paul preaching at Athens. These gracious windows, modern and beautiful, look down on the spot where Shakespeare lies, nameless before the altar.

His wife is on one side and Susanna on the other. The row of plain stones behind the altar rails are: Shakespeare's widow, Shakespeare himself, Thomas Nash who married his granddaughter, John Hall who married his daughter, and Susanna. On the wall to the left is the poet's monument. It is not as we would like it but it comes down from his own time, and this half-length figure of him was made by a man who may have seen him walking by the Thames, Gerard Johnston, a Southwark mason. It was made within a few years of his death, so that it must have been accepted as a portrait. In Shakespeare's hand is a real quill pen, and below are these lines:

In wisdom a Nestor, in genius a Socrates, in art a Virgil,
The Earth shrouds him, the Nation mourns him, Olympus guards him,

and in six lines we are asked to believe that Nature died when Shakespeare breathed his last. The bust is now painted in its original colours, and above it are the arms of the poet, a skull, and a child on each side, one with a spade and one with a torch.

Where we expect to find his name on his plain stone is something that we feel is out of keeping in this place, and yet it is a dramatic flash of light on a world that has passed away. Here lies the master-poet of the world, and on his stone is a brass with four lines all unworthy to mark his tomb:

> *Good friend for Jesu's sake forbeare,*
> *To digg the dust encloasèd heare,*
> *Blest be the man that spares these stones,*
> *And curst be he that moves my bones.*

It is not impressive. It does not sound like Shakespeare. We should like to have had here something from Milton:

> *What needs my Shakespeare for his honoured bones,*
> *The labour of an age in pilèd stones?*
> *Thou in our wonder and astonishment*
> *Hast built thyself a live-long monument.*

Or something like the noble lines from Matthew Arnold's sonnet:

> *And thou, who didst the stars and sunbeams know,*
> *Self-schooled, self-scanned, self-honoured, self-secure,*
> *Didst walk on Earth unguessed at.*

Instead, we have this doggerel, and we wonder why. Perhaps we wonder less as we look at the little door by which he lies. It is blocked up now but the steps are there, and in Shakespeare's day they led down to the charnel house where dead men's bones were thrown.

Shakespeare had come back to his own people; he was a neighbour among men, and fame was nothing to him now. If it is true that he wrote this verse we may imagine he was thinking of the charnel house, and that he was writing, not for the world that would worship at his grave or the centuries that would wonder at his plays, but for vicars and sextons and gravediggers, superstitious folk, frightening them away from his bones. He would remember the gravedigger in Hamlet throwing up a skull; it had been Poor Yorick: "A fellow of infinite jest, of most excellent fancy; he hath borne me on his back a thousand times."

Next to these poor lines on Shakespeare's stone the most human words at this historic spot are the six lines which beg a tear for Shakespeare's daughter Susannah Hall:

> *Then, Passenger, hast ne'er a tear*
> *To weep for her that wept with all,*
> *That wept yet set herself to cheer*
> *Them all with comforts cordial?*
> *Her love shall live, her mercy spread,*
> *When thou hast ne'er a tear to shed.*

All about the Shakespeare graves are sculptured tombs, the best of them the rich altar tomb of Dean Balsall, who made the chancel beautiful and died in 1491. His tomb has nine panels richly carved with scenes from the last days of Christ. On the left of the altar lies a friend of Shakespeare who died two years before him, John Combe, and near him are busts of two other Combes, made during the Civil War. By the priest's door is a monument by Westmacott, and close by is another by Rysbrack. They can hardly be said to be beautiful. The most beautiful things in the chancel are the windows, the hammerbeam roof supported by angels, the choir stalls, and the sedilia. The canopies over the sedilia are handsome.

It is the carved choir stalls that we linger over here when we look about to see the kind of place our Shakespeare lies in. There are 13 on each side, all most beautiful. We remember the scolding wife pulling a man's beard, the two bears muzzled and chained, the monkey drinking from a jug, and the mermaid with a mirror combing her hair. We remember also the fine carving of St George and the dragon on one of these seats, and we look up to discover that St George stands by the east window too, guarding this place with the dragon at his feet. Between these two St Georges Shakespeare lies. He was born on St George's day; he died on St George's day; and here St George is guarding him, our master Englishman watched over by our patron saint.

The Avon by which Shakespeare was born is one of the most typical of our English rivers for beauty and historic interest.

The Long Journey of Shakespeare's River

SHAKESPEARE'S Avon is but a small river, a tributary of the kind one can feel more familiar with than with such a strong stream as the Severn into which it flows. From its source to where it loses itself in the Severn is about 60 miles direct as a bird might fly, or an easy-going half-hour as men now fly; but the frequent windings of its course make its journey almost 100 miles, and nearly all the while it is visiting places either renowned in history or delightful because of its surroundings.

From its start the river is remarkable. It rises in the upland part of Northamptonshire over 600 feet above sea-level, and falls nearly 500 feet before it joins the Severn. On the ridge above its source was fought, near Naseby, a battle which was a turning-point in English history, actually the last great battle fought by disciplined armies of Englishmen against Englishmen in England. There Cromwell finally overthrew the army of Charles Stuart under Prince Rupert. Afterwards the Civil War changed into the siege of castles which held out hopelessly for the King.

The infant Avon flows north-west to the boundary between Northamptonshire and Leicestershire and then turns south-west, and for about seven miles becomes the boundary till it crosses the Roman road of Watling Street and enters Warwickshire. Its course is now towards Rugby, whose ancient school has had a fine influence in helping to establish true honour in sportsmanship and in life. The Avon passes north of Rugby and immediately afterwards receives its first tributary the River Swift from Leicestershire. The Swift is an inconspicuous stream in itself; but it will ever be held in remembrance in England, for in 1428 it bore on its waters to the Avon, the Severn, and the Sea, the dust of John Wycliffe.

After receiving the Swift the Avon winds its way west through pleasant country, turns more south-west at Wolston, and is cut off from that remarkable city of romance and modern industry called Coventry, by the valley of the Sowe, which the Avon meets at Stoneleigh. Here the enlarged stream curls around the Stoneleigh Abbey estate, with its fine park and old oaks and its family now well on through the fourth century there.

From Stoneleigh to Charlecote the river's general direction is south with long sweeps to east and west, and what a wealth of antiquity is comprised in it! Kenilworth Castle with its 800 years of history is close by, one of the greatest ruins in all Shakespeare's countryside.

Perhaps the most beautiful bit of the river is where, before reaching Warwick, it runs close under Guy's Cliff and introduces us to an old romance which thrilled our forefathers, the legend that Sir Guy, a slaughtering adventurer, after visiting Holy Land, lived repentant here in a cave as a hermit, unrecognised by his wife who fed him daily. Nearer Warwick the river Leam joins the Avon as the first tributary on its left bank. It comes through Leamington, where its banks have been made delightful with spacious flower beds, terraced rockeries, and shady walks.

As for Warwick, it would be impossible to imagine a historic country town fitting more perfectly the part it has played. The tale it tells is as old as the tale of England. The preservation of the past is singularly complete. In some countries great care has been taken to reconstruct and rebuild the past, but the spirit of the past evaporates in such experiments. In Warwick the spirit persists. Its castle, its great church, its ancient hospital, its gates, its monuments, retain the source of antiquity, and Nature's setting perfects the picture.

At Charlecote the Avon takes a more definitely south-west course to its disappearance in the Severn. It laps the wall of the Charlecote grounds, where lived the Justice who drove young Shakespeare from Stratford, as it laps the churchyard bounds of the church where Shakespeare lies, drawing all the world to his grave. The river is the chain that binds all the interests of this lovely patch of England together.

On below Stratford the Avon continues its course with sustained quiet beauty. At one time it had locks which allowed some navigation up to Stratford, and still it has stretches allowing boating. It receives the river Stour from the south, becomes the county boundary between Warwickshire and Gloucestershire, returns to Warwickshire, and at Salford Priors receives from the north the rivers Alne and Arrow, which drain the almost fabled forest-land of Arden. Then it plunges into Worcestershire and becomes the lovely vale, reaching the historic town of Evesham, which still has relics of its ancient abbey.

Evesham has its lasting historic interest in having been the scene of the battle where Simon de Montfort was killed. Beyond the fertile orchards and gardens of Evesham the Avon turns north to find a way through the Worcestershire Cotswolds, and so reaches Pershore, a place with a noble church; then moving southward down the open Severn Plain, at the foot of the Cotswolds to the east and in view of the Malvern Hills to the west. So it reaches the end of its long journey in the Severn, opposite the magnificent abbey of Tewkesbury, a noble finish to a course which, taken as a whole, has no parallel in interest and quiet beauty among all the tributary rivers of our Motherland.

Three Old Neighbours Down the Lane

STUDLEY. It has lost its old priory, and what looks like a medieval castle is only just a centenarian, now a college set in lovely gardens. It is in the richly wooded country where the River Arrow flows to meet the Avon.

Three old neighbours have been together down a lane for centuries, a fine yew, a timbered and gabled house, and the 700-year-old church. The north doorway of the church is as the Normans left it, with an arch added when the south doorway was built 700 years ago. The old rood stairs are still here for us to see, and set against the chancel wall is the greatest treasure of the church, a stone coffin lid with a very beautiful cross. We might almost think it new, yet it was made for a prior six centuries ago, having been brought to light on the site of Studley Priory. It was one of the few priories where Henry the Eighth's Commissioners reported that all the priests were good men, but it came down with the rest, and only a few of its stones remain in the farmhouse walls.

The church has a Jacobean pulpit, an Elizabethan table, and a great dug-out chest. A brass tells us of a 17th-century man who left four dozen penny loaves for the poor, to be given out every Sunday. In one of the windows are the two conquering saints with their dragons, and in another, flying over the countryside with blue wings, is the Summoning Angel.

There are other old houses round about: Skilts with beautiful lawns and spacious views, and Gorcott Hall on the hill, delightful with timbered walls, gables, tall chimneys, and a window with as many panes as there are days in the year. A sundial throws its shadows on the floor of one of the rooms.

John Veysey Lies in the Place he Loved

SUTTON COLDFIELD. Who does not feel the friendliness of its long, bright, busy Parade, reminding us so much of the famous Richmond in Surrey? And who can forget the splendid park which makes this ancient place one of the most fortunate towns in all our land?

The park is the glory of Sutton, a place of inexhaustible delight. There are 2500 acres in it of wild and wooded country, of moorland

248

and meadow, of lakes and rills and shady groves. It has retained much of its loveliness unspoiled since the Normans hunted in it. A priceless boon it is to Birmingham and that vast industrial area of Staffordshire which begins a few miles away.

Fascinating it is to trace out the ridge of gravel which runs straight and narrow across the western side of it. This relic of a famous roadway moves us strangely, for thus it has remained untouched through centuries. Nowhere else may we see so much of the ancient Icknield Street, with nothing to mar its ageless character. British slaves and Roman soldiers knew it well, and here we tread where they trod, looking out over a piece of England very much as it must have been when they looked out. The park has this ancient way and a modern way, for a railway runs across it also.

A day's wandering in this park would scarcely be long enough to discover its great variety of scenery. Among the gorse and heather of its breezy heaths are expansive views. In the glade of massive oaks in Gumslade Valley is the feeling that we are in a deep forest, while the pools are charming with their reedy backwaters.

Pleasant it is to think Shakespeare probably knew this place. He had kinsmen at Sutton and perhaps (who knows?) he may have found inspiration here for the woodland scenes in A Midsummer Night's Dream. Certainly he brought to this place the pompous Falstaff's Ragged Army, for does not Sir John exclaim to Bardolph:

Get thee before to Coventry; fill me a bottle of sack; our soldiers shall march through. We'll to Sutton Coldfield tonight.

Shakespeare would have been free to roam in this fine park, for 36 years before he was born John Veysey, Sutton's most famous son, had obtained from the king the grant of all this land, which he bequeathed to the town for ever. A thrilling and joyous day it must have been for Sutton when the news was known. The park is his best memorial, but there is another memorial to John Veysey, to see which we must go to the church, standing nobly in a corner of the town which attracts by the quiet dignity of its streets and dwellings, some with hoary timbers peeping through the walls.

There is much to see. In all Warwickshire we have not come upon a church with so much extravagant finery. It has a great deal of elaborate decoration, and colour everywhere. But the porch gives us pause. A splendid old entrance it is, with oak canopies carved with

Tudor roses, and a great door with its face furrowed by the passage of the centuries. It is older than much of the church it guards.

We open the door to see a great contrast, for, while the porch has that simple charm which only Time can bring, the interior is bewilderingly rich. Paint and gilt have been lavished on it with great skill, and in many a cunningly wrought design. The roof of the nave has decorated panels, and 24 carved angels looking down, all with gleaming shields. The chancel and the chapel are brighter still. The chancel roof is adorned with bosses and heraldic shields, all shining with colour, and the organ screen is striking with its wrought-iron panels.

There are two brasses from Shakespeare's time. Here is Josias Bull in a gown of fur, with the small brasses of his five children. Barbara Eliot is in her hood and ruff and farthingale; she died at only 23 and has had the little figures of her two children to keep her company down the ages.

There are marble busts of Henry Pudsey and his wife, made by William Wilson, a young mason who worked for Sir Christopher Wren. When Pudsey died his widow scandalised her relatives by marrying the humble mason. It is a strange story. Wilson built the house in which they were to live, which made his wife so proud of him that she obtained a knighthood for him. The King asked what his income was. "He has £3 and his wife £800," he was told. When his wife died Sir William laughed at his title and turned to his mason's tools again. When he grew old he wished to be buried by his wife, but her kinsfolk would not hear of it, and Wilson bought a piece of land in the churchyard adjoining the Pudsey vault. "There will only be a wall between us," he said, "and as I am a mason there will be no trouble in cutting my way through." By the church door a tablet tells of Wilson's love for his great lady, and of the vanity of her relations.

The font is Norman, probably the oldest thing here. It has four crudely sculptured heads, with scroll-work and interlaced arcading, and has served both man and beast, for it was used for years as a mounting-block outside an inn, and was once a flower-vase in a Sutton garden.

The old church has a great wealth of carving. Under the tower is much Jacobean oak, some from Worcester Cathedral; it has grotesques curling round its columns. The choir seats are 17th-century Italian work; the tall pulpit with a handsome canopy of inlaid wood

Coughton: Sir George Throckmorton
and his wife, 1535

Exhall: John and Eleanor Walsingham,
1590

Compton Verney
Anne Oddyngsdale, 1523

Meriden
Elizabeth Rotton, 1638

Coventry
Anne Sewell, 1609

Sutton Coldfield: Barbara Eliot and her
two children, 1606

Shuckburgh
1500 (partly on slate)

OLD WARWICKSHIRE FOLK ENGRAVED ON BRASSES

is 18th century. In the chancel is a very old screen, with scrolls and fishes and set with painted shields. Under a row of seats are some gems of ancient carving, with figures of a man plucking grapes, another carrying a basket, and a third sitting with the empty basket over his head. But the finest of all the old carving is in the wonderful oak screen between the chancel and the Veysey Chapel. It has a host of queer figures of animals and faces, and slender columns and arches carved with fruit and leaves.

The Veysey Chapel, a bright and lovely place, is the shrine of the man whom Sutton can never forget. Its ceiling is rich with painted panels of roses and thistles, and carved and painted angels. All round it runs a cornice of oak leaves, with birds and squirrels among foliage, charmingly coloured and seeming to bring the spirit of the forest into this hallowed place. The light falls through a window adorned with the emblems of four bishops connected with Sutton, and in the midst of all this beauty Bishop Veysey lies.

He died about 400 years ago, but they have not tired of honouring him in his native town. His tomb is the spot at which all visitors must pause. He lies in painted splendour, his figure so wonderfully kept in all its detail that it looks but a few years old. John Veysey is said to have lived to be 103, but here he is a young man, fresh and alert, as smart, we may think, as a bishop may look. He is in all the glory of his robes, his gloves tasselled at the wrists, his mitre studded with jewels, and shod with square-toed sandals, carrying his staff.

He has squirrels, birds, and oak leaves above him, and it is fitting that this touch of Nature should be, for he loved all natural things. Few people have done more than he did for their native place. Not content with giving his park to the town, he fenced its woods and stocked the open heaths with horses. He paved the town, founded a school which remains to this day, and built a market hall. He built two stone bridges and 50 stone houses. He was born, it is said, in a house on the site of Moor Hall, one of the modern houses of Sutton, and there he kept his servants in scarlet caps and gowns. Being made Warden of the Marches of Wales he held court at Ludlow with great pomp. He was with the king at the Field of the Cloth of Gold.

Greatly Sutton has changed since his day, but it does not forget him. It is a fine modern town, but it keeps some good old houses, the oldest among them, oddly enough, being New Hall, which is said to have stood 700 years. It has also a small touch of nature outside its park which we loved to see, for at its Baptist Chapel we found a Garden of Thankfulness to God for his gift of animals and birds.

SUTTON-UNDER-BRAILES. Its centuries of peace seem to have been unbroken, and every traveller will remember the beauty of the lofty church seen from the road, set among the fine old tombs under a spreading chestnut tree. There is a simple Norman doorway in the nave, and the porch in the 15th-century tower has a canopied stone seat. The chancel has some splendid medieval windows, one with richly coloured figures of James and John in modern glass, and from its walls men and women and many strange beasts have gazed in stony silence through the centuries.

The Last of a Great Family

TANWORTH-IN-ARDEN It has glades about it with trees that call to mind Shakespeare's Forest of Arden, and a church which is like a small cathedral, much of its beauty regained last century. It is sad to think that it would have been more beautiful still if much of its 13th-century work had not been destroyed when Christopher Wren's great-grandson was vicar.

It is said that the rough stones in the north wall are 800 years old. The fine tower and the spacious chancel with its lofty arch are 14th century. In a corner of the sanctuary are tiles from a 14th-century pavement, and on each side of the altar are charming medieval stone pedestals on slender shafts still with traces of colour. The great east window has elegant tracery and modern glass of the Crucifixion and other scenes. In other windows are the wise and foolish virgins, a pretty scene of Christ with children and their mothers on a hillside, and delightful figures of Dorcas with her satchel and Elizabeth laden with roses, while 14 saints fill the windows of the south aisle.

There is an old chest which has seen 700 years come round. Eight feet long with three locks, it has six iron bands enriched with scrolls. Half as old is another chest in the vestry. The oak chancel screen has tracery matching the east window. The choir stalls and the pulpit have admirable work of our own time. Even the organ is fine here, with its clustered silver pipes on both sides of the chancel resting on vaulted brackets. It is richly carved and has two angels, with a canopy like a bower with vine and grapes under which the organist sits.

There is a handsome village hall in memory of a wife, a peace memorial by a splendid chestnut tree, and a mile-long avenue bringing us to Umberslade Hall, built in 1680 as the home of the Archers, barons of Umberslade. Simon Archer spent much of his life in Shakespeare's day collecting rare manuscripts of Warwickshire; another Archer built an obelisk in the park 200 years ago. The Archers of Umberslade sleep in the shelter of this church, and here the family passed away. There is a marble monument with a woman leaning on a pedestal in memory of the last of the family, which came over with the Conqueror. A brass of 1614, framed in ancient oak, has a fine portrait of Andrew Archer's wife, kneeling before a stool with an open book. A "gentle wife and a helper of the poor," she wears a Paris hood, a ruff, and a richly brocaded gown. An odd little treasure is a fragment of another brass showing ten children whose names have been forgotten.

Old Ladies in Poke Bonnets

TEMPLE BALSALL. There is no other place in Warwickshire quite like it. We step from the 20th century into the days of the Crusaders. Its 13th-century church, with two old yews growing by it, belonged to the Knights Templars, whose refectory is close by; they have stamped their memory on this quiet place.

Delightful it is to walk by the long box hedge of the almshouses, with their trim little gardens, and to come to the splendid old gateway and the hospital founded in 1670 by Katherine Leveson, granddaughter of Elizabeth's favourite Robert Dudley. Its almshouses, school, and the fine old house with two towers (one with a clock, the other with a sundial) run round three sides of the lawns of a quadrangle. Here we shall always find old ladies dressed as 250 years ago, in poke bonnets and shawls. Perhaps we may envy them the peace and beauty of this place.

Simplicity, height, and a glowing freshness give the church a charm within, and it has unusual features. There is no chancel arch, no window is like its neighbour, the floors are in varied levels, the nave ascends in broad and shallow steps. Each rank in the Order had its appropriate place in the varying levels of the nave. Imagination fills it with the pageantry of ancient knights, and we see them in the great east window, the striking feature of the chancel, with modern figures of knights and saints. Over 30 feet high, it has fine modern glass showing Christ in glory with a great company of angels: Gabriel bringing the good news to the Madonna, Crusader knights, saints and shields. There is a lovely three-stepped sedilia, and the piscina, with its clustered shafts and beautiful tracery, is considered one of the best in the country. The richly carved stone pulpit has modern statues of Our Lord holding a sphere and the Evangelists sitting at desks.

The church is little changed since the days of the Templars. Near the altar is a stone cross they would have known. Nine windows with richly varied stone tracery are memorials to the founders of the Hospitallers, and probably it was the knights who put the crouching figures of animals on the buttresses of the nave and the carved faces on the parapet. The fine roof by Sir Gilbert Scott has 10 knights supporting some of its arches and bishops and kings supporting others.

It seemed incredible that nearly 700 years have not worn a smile off the faces looking out from its walls. How many there are we do not know, but not less than 78 run along the cornice under the roofs, all sorts and conditions, those at the west end laughing and smiling. They are the artisans and retainers of the Templars, and on the top of some of the buttresses are their dogs clinging precariously. Also there are eight small heads round each pinnacle along the roof.

Who Was Anne Whateley?

TEMPLE GRAFTON. It is the hungry Grafton of the rhyme about Shakespeare's villages (hungry on account of its poor soil), but at any rate it has fine views towards Cheltenham and the Cotswolds. It is one of the villages that might have been much visited if what some people think was known to be the truth, for it is one of the places where Shakespeare is said to have married Anne Hathaway. There is a licence granted by the Bishop of Worcester in 1582 for the marriage of a William Shakespeare to Anne Whateley of Temple Grafton, and the suggestion that Whateley may have been a misreading of Hathaway is the one slender link for Temple Grafton's story. In any case the old church in which Anne Whateley may have married another William Shakespeare has gone, and a 19th-century church has taken its place.

It has a tower with a timbered belfry and shingled spire, and a lofty cedar shading the south side. In the brightly coloured west window are a Knight Templar and a Knight Hospitaller, both in chain mail, appropriate here because the church was owned by these knights. At the sides a Templar is giving shelter to a stranger and a Hospitaller tends the sick, while below are groups of the hungry, thirsty, and other needy folk to whom these knights were benefactors. Another window has attractive glowing pictures of Jacob's Dream, angels and shepherds, and children about Our Lord amusing themselves by making daisy chains.

The only touch we found of Shakespeare here was in the windows of Temple Grafton Court, the handsome brick-and-timber house in a finely wooded park, with stained-glass scenes from the plays of Shakespeare and from the Canterbury Tales of Chaucer. A little walk from here and we are in a hamlet which rejoices in the proud name of Little Britain.

TIDMINGTON. It is so tiny that many a car must miss it, yet it has a rare Norman tower by the great house, and the Stour is flowing a stone's throw off. The tower has a ring of faces under the eaves. The nave is Norman and the chancel 16th century. The little ones of Tidmington are still baptised at the same font as the little Normans; it is carved with a triumphant picture of Christ. The piscina has been here for 700 years, and some of the bench-ends 500; they are carved. The chest is 17th century.

Alfred's England

TREDINGTON. Who, being an artist, would not long to paint it, with its charming grey walls and thatched roofs and the impressive spire of the old church the Saxons loved? It has lost its marvellous rectory, of which an old writer begged his readers "not to be dazzled with the glory of it," although the old rectory barn has still the enormous fireplace in which we imagine 20 people could stand. The old stepping-stone is still outside a cottage near the church, and the magnificent old door of the church is still swinging on its hinges after 400 years. It has bullet marks all over it and seven bullets of the Civil War still bedded in it; we touched some of them with our fingers. We imagine that the door must be unique with its seven witnesses of Cromwell's day.

Here also is another door that has been swinging on its hinges through all these generations, for the parson would open it in the days before the Reformation to mount the rood loft stairs and declare the good news every morning from the loft.

And yet Time takes us farther down its corridors at Tredington,

Shakespeare's Grave

His bust looks down on the spot where he lies, marked by the middle brass

Warwick   West Gate and Leycester Hospital

Warwick   Entrance to the Courtyard of Leycester Hospital

for here we held in our hands a piece of wood which, for all we know, may have been handled by a carpenter in Alfred's England. It came from a window above the chancel arch before the Normans altered it, and it is pitted with the little holes bored by the death-watch beetle centuries ago.

High up in the walls of the nave are more enduring witnesses of Saxon England. The work of the Saxon builders is before us, stones in walls and windows as they left them, high up below the rough clerestory windows. The remains of four deeply splayed windows and two doorways appear in the walls above the arcades, a curious spectacle indeed, for they suggest that on the level of the ground in the Saxon church there were no doors, but to enter the church wooden stairs were set up on each side which could be removed at will, so that the church became a place of refuge from raiding Danes.

Very impressive is this old place with the story of 1000 years in its walls, a veritable museum of interesting possessions. It has 12th-century arches on Norman piers, a 14th-century screen, benches that 20 generations of village folk have known, and a magnificent font raised on two steps in the middle of the aisle, with arcaded panels and the marks of the old staples by which it was guarded against witches.

The canopied pulpit came in Cromwell's century, the reading desk has still the old chain which held the Bible long ago, and on it when we called was a book of sermons printed in Shakespeare's day. In the tower, with its low screen made from the Jacobean altar rails, was an old wooden clock made by a village blacksmith, and side by side in one of the aisles we found the top of the old steeple and the great beam of the old stocks. For generation after generation a man held captive in the one must have looked up wearily at the other.

There are three portraits in brass of people who knew this church, two of priests who served at its altar and one of a lady who sat in its pews. Richard Cassey, who had a new dignity conferred on him by Henry the Fifth in York Minster, is here in his priestly robes; Henry Sampson, a 15th-century rector, is kneeling; and Alice Barnes is wearing a gown with the puffed sleeves of the 16th century.

St Gregory is wearing away in his niche at the porch after centuries of wind and rain, but the old church stands strong and well beloved. We found it being cared for by a good lady whose ancestor's name is on a stone above the fireplace of a cottage with the date 1631, Richard Rawlings. For 200 years the clerks of this church have been Rawlings; they are the oldest family in the village. Now a generation has come which will break the long line, for there is no successor to tend this ancient church. But it may stand another 1000 years, for its walls are sturdy, as strong a refuge for its people in these days as when the Saxons sought security in it against the Danes.

Its porch has two stone-mullioned windows, with a room over it with ancient beams and a window covered up for centuries. It is a monument of which a village may be rightly proud, and it has come into Warwickshire in our time, for only the other day it was in Worcestershire. A noble newcomer it is into Shakespeare's county.

The Three Tysoes

TYSOE. It is three places. Lower Tysoe has a few houses; Upper Tysoe has a great hollow tree in which a dozen men can stand; Middle Tysoe has a handsome church full of wonderful things. Within its parish stands the famous house called Compton Wynyates, one of the most historic homes in Warwickshire, set in a lovely scene.

Under the floor of the manor house when we called men had just found an interesting document saying that in 1834, on August 15, a man was hanged for setting fire to 13 hayricks there. Times have changed since then, but not in Tysoe church.

Saxon and Norman and English it is; it has Norman columns and a fine Norman doorway. The 14th-century clerestory, crowned with a decorated parapet, may have seen the old cross set up in the churchyard; compared with both the thatched cottages gathered about are young indeed.

About 20 stone faces look down from the wall inside, some grotesque and some very fine. Perhaps the rarest possession of the church is a number of the very oldest benches known, surely as old as the church itself, and down one aisle, keeping company with them, are fine pews carved by Jacobean craftsmen. There are three brasses: Thomas Mastropp, a 15th-century vicar holding a chalice; a fine small brass to Jane Browne of 1598; and another small brass of 1611 to Tomizane Browne, which has three horses' heads on it. There are three other monuments of stone. One is a coffin lid under a canopy, with the sunken face of a man in the centre of a cross; another is an

odd 14th-century figure on a tomb in which only the head and
feet are visible, and the third is a stone figure of William Clarke,
an authentic portrait of the time of Shakespeare. He lies in the
chancel, bareheaded, with a ruff round his neck, a belted doublet
with close-cuffed sleeves, and wearing shoes and stockings. There
are two ancient fonts, a plain one and another carved 600 years ago
with sculptured panels of six familiar figures—Mary Magdalene with
long hair, the Madonna crowned, Saint Catherine on the wheel,
Saint Peter with the keys, Paul with the sword, and Saint Michael
weighing the souls of men. In one of the windows is a charming
picture of a mother and two children.

The Kneelers Round the Tomb

UFTON. A small place with a great view of the Avon Valley,
we found here a simple stone coffin for a child, resting on a
windowsill in the 13th-century church.

In the churchyard is a richly carved head of a cross which may
have been new when they laid the little one hereabouts. On a brass
in the wall is a family of Queen Elizabeth's day with the wife and
seven children of Richard Woddhomes; they are all kneeling on a
tiled floor round a table tomb, the wife with a broad-brimmed hat
and the daughters in bonnets. In the windows are the Little Child of
Bethlehem, the Good Shepherd, a reaper and a gleaner in a cornfield,
and the scene of Joseph before his brethren. Looking down from the
roof are three crude faces and a lion with great claws.

Two tributes we found in the nave, one to Francis Augustus
Chatwin who loved all that is beautiful, the other to Robert Field,
a faithful labourer who for good deeds won two prizes of the Royal
Agricultural Society and was at last crushed by a steam windlass.

The Hostess Charming

ULLENHALL. We should see it from a hill above the village,
the slender spire of the new church rising above the trees, the
blue Cotswolds and the darker Malvern Hills beyond.

At Barrels Hall below, its 18th-century walls hidden in trees,
lived a Lady Bountiful, Henrietta Knight, who made her house the
meeting-place of poets and artists. She wrote letters which have since
thrown light on notable people of her day. To this house came William
Shenstone and Richard Jago, good friends who praised each other's
poems, and William Somerville, the scholar who became a ne'er-do-

well and died of drink, after a short life as a squire and poet. Of Shenstone our great lady said that his conversation strewed the rugged road of life with flowers.

The charming hostess sleeps in the old church at the end of a lane, with a few cottages for company. The chancel is all that is left of the 13th-century walls and has windows with some golden fleur-de-lys centuries old. The font has been here 600 years. There are 18th-century altar rails of iron, a sundial on the bellcot, and a bell believed to have been ringing here in the days of Cardinal Wolsey.

Most of the Throckmortons sleep at Coughton, but one lies here under a coloured monument with Corinthian columns. He is Francis, who, born in Italy, came here to receive from Mary Tudor the gift of Ullenhall and several other manors. It was his family which gave England more than one conspirator.

The new church is more impressive with its array of arches running down the nave and chancel, even framing the windows of the apse, all covered by one great roof looking like an upturned boat. The chancel floor has a great circle of mosaic, the altar in the middle.

WALSGRAVE-ON-SOWE. A village on the road from Coventry, it has the rough 14th-century walls of Caludon Castle and yews in the churchyard planted in Tudor days. The church has 14th-century arches, eight stone faces watching over the chancel, and an arcaded Norman font. There is a big 18th-century chest, like a forerunner of the Victorian family trunk, and a Jacobean chair. One of the aisle windows has old glass in the tracery, perhaps three centuries old, with a quaint company of curly-haired angels and a modern picture of the Madonna in blue.

Village Delight

WALTON. Its cottages are a delight; its secluded byways are enchanting. The great house and little church are side by side, as fair a sight as we could wish to see. The Saxon and the Norman knew it; Saxon jewels have been dug up, and the 18th-century church stands where the Normans built. Only the Norman font remains from old days, in the dimness of light passing through richly coloured windows. They have scenes from the life of Christ, and a Good Shepherd in memory of Charles Mordaunt of the great house.

Walton Hall was built by Sir Gilbert Scott. In the house before it lived the Mordaunts in the time of Henry the Eighth, and Mordaunts were here still when we called. The Hall stands in 250 acres, the graceful slopes of its spacious lawns coming down to a lake fed by the Dene. Here are noble cedars and firs in lofty groups and avenues.

The Plough Has Levelled the Forts

WAPPENBURY. Who would think of these fruitful fields with their winding river as a place of arms? Yet it was once fortified and great earthworks encompassed it about. Little remains of them, for the plough has levelled the earth.

The River Leam is crossed by old stepping-stones, and, having crossed it, the way leads easily to the church, passing in the churchyard, at the top of mossy steps, the remains of an old stone cross. A 15th-century tower watches over the peaceful countryside, but the glory of it all is the charming chancel, with nine tall lancets in its red and grey walls of mottled stone. The east window is a fine triple lancet, slender and graceful, and has glass of a singular style which adds to its charm with splashes of vivid colour, showing Christ in glory, the Crucifixion, John the Baptist, and the Four Evangelists. Very striking, too, is the west window seen from the chancel.

The nave has an arcade of three arches, with which the tower arch works in oddly at the west end, one left arch continuing the arcade, one across the aisle, and corner buttresses projecting into the nave and through the wall into the porch. At the top of three steps in the tower is a big font, and in this corner are the oldest stones the village has—two coffin lids. There is a gnarled oak chest. A bearded head with face all awry is looking down from an arch. A canopied wall monument with a woman sitting sadly in a harvest field, with a plough near her, is in memory of a zealous friend of scientific agriculture last century, Thomas Urnbers.

The Queer Man in the Vestry

WARMINGTON. The traveller here on a summer's day will not forget it, climbing up its flagged pathway lined with mauve nepeta, under a great cedar and through firs and pines.

The village is in a hollow, the church is on a height. One of the loftiest churches in the county, it stands sentinel over the battlefield of Edgehill, the spacious countryside in which lie buried many of the dead. The battle is mentioned in the registers.

From two ways long flagged steps bring us up to this 14th-century shrine, which still keeps something from its Norman days. The nave has three Norman arches and six Norman pillars, all different, with simple dignified capitals. The stone seats for priests are richly carved, with four tiny heads on the canopies; and there is a Norman tub font, a Bible box, and an enormous crudely made chest. A lovely doorway from the chancel, with two fine heads, leads us into the vestry; the door has five hinges bearing its heavy weight. Behind it is another medieval door opening on a stairway leading to a room above, where hangs a third old door into a chamber with a fireplace, which may have been a shelter for a hermit or a priest. It has a peephole through which the altar can be seen.

We found lying about in the vestry three extraordinary stone faces, one of a man with his mouth wide open, showing all his teeth, and with a movable tongue which can be taken out.

Warwick and Its Treasures

WARWICK. It is the county town of the Shakespeare Country, and it is a beauty. Let him who would feel the thrill of England come here. Not in all England are more historic interest and beauty crowded into so small a space.

Here at the gate at the top of the hill are 12 old men in a house kept for them through the centuries. Here is as fair a castle as ever was built in England, and a bridge with an incomparable peep of it. Here is one of the rarest little chapels in Europe, and in it, set as in a jewel in this fair house, lies that proud earl who in the name of England burned the Stainless Maid. Across a noble chancel and down some steps lies Philip Sidney's friend, his sword still on his tomb.

It is all near the very heart of England; it is of the stuff of which our history is made, and it is fair and beautiful. Those who are wise will walk about these streets an hour or two before they see the famous places—the Leycester Hospital by the West Gate, the Castle on the hill, and the Beauchamp Chapel in the impressive church of St Mary. There are streets made glorious with old houses, one of them (Mill Street) with a marvellous row of black and white Tudor fronts running down to the foot of the Castle Rock. The view of the Castle from the bridge, with its span of over 100 feet, is one of the great sights of England, hardly to be surpassed in the countryside.

There is the 15th-century house by the East Gate in which was born Walter Savage Landor, sleeping now on another hill in Florence after a life summed up in those four perfect lines :

> *I strove with none for none was worth my strife;*
> *Nature I loved and, next to Nature, Art;*
> *I warmed both hands before the fire of Life,*
> *It sinks, and I am ready to depart.*

In the garden of the house, which is now a school, is a great tree the poet must often have sat under.

There is the church of St Nicholas by the East Gate, now rebuilt but still with the brass portrait of old Robert Willardsey, the first vicar of the vanished church, as he stood in his vestments in 1423. There is a Grammar School with documents which show that it has been a school since Edward the Confessor; one of its boys was John Masefield. There is the county hall, with a crypt which has a cell with posts and chains to which prisoners were fastened in the days when Quakers languished here. There is a most charming gabled Jacobean house, and a blacksmith's shop which has all that is left of the hospital of St Michael, grown from a leper's house of 800 years ago. The Great Fire of Warwick which burned down 250 houses in 1694 happily left standing much that was loveliest in this famous city, and everywhere we come upon some splendid place, narrow ways and quaint corners, and cottages half built from trees.

Let us climb the hill to St Mary's great tower, 174 feet to the top of its 16 pinnacles. It calls us to Warwick from miles around, and it looks out on country tramped by Shakespeare, much of it as he saw it. It is a handsome church, light and spacious, 180 feet long, standing where a Saxon church once stood. The tower, nave, aisles, and transepts were all destroyed by the great fire, which sent its flames into the chancel and blackened the tomb of Thomas Beauchamp. What is new since 1694 is not unworthy of what is old—the Norman crypt, the 14th-century chancel, and the 15th-century Beauchamp Chapel.

The roof of the nave has angels at the base of the vaulting, and the columns have finely carved capitals. In a niche in one column is a bust of Walter Savage Landor, Warwick's poet son. The beautiful pulpit is modern, carved in wood from Stoneleigh Park; the canopy has finely carved tracery. Hanging on the wall are the Warwickshire colours of the Volunteers raised against Napoleon, and in the north transept is a stone to Richard Perry, a sergeant who saved the colours at the Battle of Chillianwalla and is buried in the churchyard.

But most charming of all as we come into this place is a thing made in our time, the alabaster memorial of 11,445 men of all ranks of the Royal Warwickshire Regiment who gave their lives for us. On a floor of black-and-white marble stands a cenotaph with four angels on the sides, one with a lamp, one with a cross, two with a spray of palm, and let into the cenotaph is a beautiful book with the names that live for evermore.

There are two splendid brasses which survived the great fire, both rescued from the flames. One, begging us to remember the charity of the poor for ever, shows Thomas Oken in his civic gown, with his wife Joan. He was a rich mercer who died in 1573, leaving some houses for charity which are still largely as he saw them, one row forming a quaint little passage in sight from the church door. His old chest is still in the court house. The other brass is Thomas Beauchamp's. It shows him with his wife. They were the father and mother of Richard Beauchamp, and the brass is on the wall outside the wonderful door of their son's chapel. It is as if they were looking down on the ceaseless throng of people who from the 15th century to this day have come to Richard Beauchamp's tomb.

The very handsome chancel, approached through fine iron gates made by Nicholas Paris, whose work we have seen at South Kensington, has eight painted windows high up on the walls, and a great east window. Lying proudly in alabaster in the middle of the chancel is the first Thomas Beauchamp, Earl of Warwick, his wife at his side and his family about him. He died in 1369, in the same year as his wife, and they have lain here clasping hands for more than 500 years. He is in armour; she has a girdle studded with jewels; and in niches all round are 36 small figures of the Beauchamp family. It is one of the finest galleries of costume available for artists anywhere.

At the foot of the old steps which lead down to the crypt, we read of an old housekeeper of the Castle, Maria Home, who lived to be 93 and died on the eve of the Victorian Era.

On the way to the crypt from the chancel we pass through the vestry, rich with its windows of ancient glass. Eight figures at the top are English work of the 14th century, and there are 13 medallions by Flemish and German craftsmen from Elizabethan times. Two of them, showing feasts, are excellent, one being the Last Supper. Through another door and we are in the small and ancient

Tomb of Richard Beauchamp

Head of Richard Beauchamp

Dog at feet of Ambrose Dudley

Warwick   The Beauchamp Chapel

| Angel | Robert Dudley and his Wife | Angel |

| Angel and Saint | Ambrose Dudley | St Catherine and Angel |

Sculptures of the Beauchamp Chapel, Warwick

Weepers on the Tomb

Warwick　　　　　　Weepers on Richard Beauchamp's Tomb

Warwick Musical Angels in the Beauchamp Chapel

Coventry Richard I, Edward III, and Henry V in St Mary's Hall

Windows in Coventry and Warwick

chapter house in which Fulke Greville lies. He set up this tomb for himself, and under its heavy canopy he lies wrapped in lead with those famous words paying tribute to him:

> *Servant to Queen Elizabeth*
> *Counsellor to King James*
> *Friend to Sir Philip Sidney*

On his tomb lie three swords and a dagger; they were on his coffin at his funeral. Many a time Philip Sidney must have seen them, for Sidney was to Greville closer than a brother. He must have known Shakespeare too, for he was Recorder of Stratford and would doubtless be at Shakespeare's funeral. Down more steps and we are in the crypt, with three great columns still where the Normans put them, and (a queer possession for this great place) one of the old ducking-stools which they kept in those days for scolding wives.

But it is, of course, the Beauchamp Chapel that all come here to see, and it is not through its fine doorway but down the chancel steps that some of us would choose to enter it; a glorious approach it is, with the archway framing the golden figures round Richard Beauchamp's tomb. It is one of England's most famous places. In this small house, crammed with glory from floor to roof, lies Richard Beauchamp, the man who stood for England at the burning of Joan of Arc. He saw three kings on the English throne. He lived through the reign of Henry the Fourth; he looked on the wild youth of Henry the Fifth and saw him rise to be the idol of the people; and he lived long enough into the reign of Henry the Sixth to see our flag stained with an infamy that time will not forget. The first earl lies in the chapel just up the steps, the second is on the brass outside this chapel door, and the third is he who built this place as his last house. He left a fortune for it equalling £40,000 today, and the builders and craftsmen were at work for 20 years on this wonder they left us in bronze and iron and wood and stone and glass.

He lies amid all this loveliness with 14 kinsmen and 18 angels round his tomb—and yet we wonder if he does lie here? For there is a story which some believe and some do not. He died in Rouen as Joan did, but her ashes are blown about the fields of France and her tomb is in the hearts of men. He has this splendid tomb, they say, and here it is true he slept about 200 years, but it is recorded that the floor of the chapel then fell in and Richard Beauchamp was seen again, fresh and perfect for a moment as in sleep, and then a heap of dust. It is said that the ladies of Warwick made rings with the locks of his hair.

So it is said, but in fact his bones still lie within this tomb, and here above them he lies magnificent in bronze, one of the most perfect figures fashioned in an age when craftsmen were artists indeed. He is armoured and wearing a garter, his head resting on his helmet and his feet against a griffin and a bear. In 32 canopied niches stand the Beauchamps, all with their coats-of-arms, with angels between them, an impressive gallery of golden figures.

This rich tomb was made in London by a Dutch goldsmith, with the help of a barber surgeon who was engaged to make it correct to the smallest detail of anatomy. Seen and unseen, all its parts are finely done, every buckle, strap, and hinge perfect. The inscription round it tells us that Richard Beauchamp was one of the most worshipful knights of his day for manhood and cunning, and truly we feel that, as an old writer has said, the knight rests in a "full fair vault of stone set on a rock." He is looking up at the Madonna enthroned in the roof in red and gold as Queen of Heaven. She wears a simple dress and mantle, and her crown is a narrow band of pearls. Behind her, the keystone of this roof, is the symbol of the Almighty surrounded with the hierarchy of Heaven, Paul's thrones, dominations, principalities, and powers. The impressive scheme runs down the mullions of the east window, which are hollowed out, painted red and blue, and filled with 30 figures of saints and angels. Some of the colour is as vivid as when put on 450 years ago.

The roof itself, enriched with about fifty gilded bosses (no two alike), is vaulted in three bays, each bay having in its centre an irregular panel with heraldic carving. In one of the three panels is a swan's head ringed with a coronet, in another is an angel; the third has the Queen of Heaven.

High up near the roof is something almost unique in England, a gallery of musical angels painted in glass in the middle of the 15th-century. The music is printed on a scroll and is a genuine old version of the song sung to the Shepherds. In providing for this chapel in his will Richard Beauchamp called for the finest glass, the best and cleanest and strongest that could be had beyond the sea, set in lead as well as any glass in England; and it was given to John Prudde of Westminster to find it. They made what we may call their

Te Deum, for the angels are playing musical instruments and singing and dancing to them. There are violins, harps, organs, and musical glasses. There are pipes and bagpipes, and the angels have before them a continuous scroll of music with the notes picked out. The windows are all remarkably correct; one shows an angel playing a clavicord on which we can see the keys and strings; another shows what is probably the finest example we have of a richly ornamented clavicymbal, on which we can count the 19 strings. It is a fascinating collection of saints, angels, and cherubs, and it is thought they may be actually older than the chapel, having been brought from the wreck of some other place. John Prudde was paid two shillings a foot for putting it all here.

Very impressive is the great east window, with the glass which has kept these angels company through the centuries. It has been broken to pieces but is complete again. One of its figures has never been broken, and it is a precious thing, one of the best and oldest pictures we have of Thomas Becket. He is in the act of blessing. His robe is set with hundreds of pearls and gems. In his mitre the pearls are set in a background of gold without the aid of lead, holes being bored in the glass and the pearls set in them. The front of the beautiful red robe is bordered with double rows of pearls and jewels, and the ornamented band on the cope is one of the loveliest gems in any stained window in England. Set in this narrow band are three figures under canopies, all very charming.

Richard Beauchamp left in his will four images of himself in gold to the four shrines of St Thomas, St Alban, St Winifred of Shrewsbury, and St John of Bridlington, and it was decided to put these four saints in this window. They stand side by side, St Alban with a jewelled mantle over his armour; St Winifred in black relieved with ermine and jewels, holding an open book; and St John dressed as a monk.

Three small places open off the Beauchamp Chapel. Stone steps lead us into a tiny chantry rich with fan tracery and a fine stone screen. A superb place it is, with what must be one of the tiniest fan-vaulting roofs in existence. There was once a little wren which chose a crevice at the top of a canopy over this altar to build its nest and bring up its family in.

Out of this chantry stone steps worn by a multitude of feet bring us to a still tinier place, a narrow chamber with peepholes to the altar, a private pew probably for the dean. The third small room is the passage called the library, which when we called had just been enriched with new windows of fine old glass, part of the original treasure of this place. It had been found under the richly carved oak stalls by the door—we should not miss their fine arm-rests with lions, griffins, and bears. The floor of one of these stalls was being repaired, and on raising the boards they found the joists charred with fire, the work of molten lead falling from the roof in 1694. A short length of one of the vanished brasses was found, and a tiny pilgrim's badge, but more precious than all were 3000 fragments of old glass, one of them an angel's face. Charming it is to see these fragments, buried in darkness for centuries, with the sunlight coming through them again.

Three sleepers there are keeping Richard company. Close by him lies Ambrose Dudley, the good Earl of Warwick; he lies in armour and wears his coronet. Facing him is a huge tomb 25 feet high crowned with a bear in chains, supposed to have come from the same workshop as Shakespeare's bust at Stratford. In it lies Queen Elizabeth's Sweet Robin, Robert Dudley, Earl of Leicester, husband of Amy Robsart, the man of whom a historian has said that he was without courage, without talent, and without virtue. His last wife Lettice lies by him, having lived 46 years after him, dying at 94. Very amusing are two small bears looking down on these proud sleepers.

Pathetic is the figure of Robert Dudley's little son lying here in a rich coat; he died when he was three, and is called on his tomb the Noble Imp. He has a bear at his feet and two others with his shield, and we are moved to read that he was

Of great parentage and of far greater hope, taken from this transitory into the everlasting life at his tender age at Wanstead in Essex, and in this place laid up among his noble ancestors.

But at least he is innocent, and therefore worthy of the beauty all about him. We are astonished at the fineness of it all, at the minuteness of the splendour of these craftsmen. If we look at the inscription on Richard Beauchamp's tomb we find tiny animals engraved among the words. Richard's figure lies inside six hoops connected by poles, and in the round bronze terminals of the poles are set in enamel, an inch or two across, the arms of England and France and the badge of the Garter. On the doors of the three small chambers opening off the chapel are tiny carved wheels with bear's heads as handles.

Nothing, it seems, could be too ingenious, too difficult, or too rich for this place, and we leave it for the streets of Warwick as leaving one world for another.

We come from this realm of the past to the living world of the Leycester Hospital by the West Gate of Warwick; some of its 12 old men will be sitting on the terrace when you call.

Its chapel crowns the gateway built on a rock in the 14th century; it stands on the fortifications of the 12th century; we can see the iron stanchions of the old gate. The balcony gives us a vision of the Cotswold Hills. Facing it is an Elizabethan house with a black-and-white front which escaped from the fire, as this place did. Built as a religious house early in the 15th century, it was made a hospital by Robert Dudley in 1571, and its tiny courtyard with the oriel windows, the overhanging balcony, the carved gables, the queer wooden faces, and the dozens of heraldic crests are all Elizabethan.

It has three fine places to see—the chapel, the kitchen and the banqueting hall. In the banqueting hall Fulke Greville entertained King James; in the kitchen is the chair the king sat in. The roof timbers are Spanish chestnut. In the kitchen is the wardrobe Queen Elizabeth used at Kenilworth, and hanging on the wall are two pieces of work done by Amy Robsart, a piece of needlework in coloured thread and the Warwick Bear embroidered in silk. There is the sword of the last king of Poland, the king of Dahomey's execution sword, a cannon-ball fired in the Battle of Edgehill, and some Balaclava helmets; but by far the most interesting possessions of this place are the medieval mace and an ancient chair used by the town watchman centuries ago.

The chapel has been refashioned in our time. We pass through iron gates made by Coventry men, charming with lilies, and the modern woodwork is admirable too, six stalls at the west end having splendid arm-rests carved with animals and 22 other seats being carved with heraldic heads. There are two ancient oak chairs in the sanctuary. The east window is modern, but the south window has six angels in 17th-century glass.

Perhaps the oldest possession of this place is the little oak door in the turret, which leads us into a room where the deeds are kept; it has been opening and shutting for at least 600 years.

Of Warwick Castle, the great glory about which all this other glory has grown up, it was Sir Walter Scott who said the right word:

it is "that fairest monument of ancient and chivalrous splendour which yet remains uninjured by time." There is nothing like it; it is the house magnificent. Whether we see it from the bridge with the Avon flowing beneath it, or walk along the winding way cut for 100 yards through solid rock and stand entranced by this vast place across the lawns, we feel that we are looking down the corridor of time through English history. Both these towers were fashioned in the 14th century. Guy's Tower is 128 feet and Caesar's 147 feet high.

These walls have seen something of the splendour of every generation of our story since Richard Beauchamp entertained Henry of Agincourt here; and their rooms are open to all who will. They are rich in treasure beyond the dreams of avarice, and glorious with peeps of as fair a landscape as England has. Through room after room we pass. The State Bedroom has lovely views of the winding Avon with cedars of Lebanon under the windows. Its walls are covered with Brussels tapestry made soon after the death of Queen Elizabeth. The Cedar Drawing Room, about 50 feet long, is panelled with carved cedar. It has a fine music table from Florence, a bust of one of the earls by Nollekens, a lovely ebony casket, and a small statue of Venus in wax. The Red Drawing Room, panelled in deep red with the ceiling picked out in white and gold, has a fine cabinet of ebony and tortoiseshell inlaid with ivory. One of the windows of the chapel is filled with old glass, and there is some good Flemish glass in what is called the Compass Room. Close by the chapel, in a passage, is a clever wood carving of the Battle of the Amazons, copied from the painting by Rubens.

The impressive Great Hall, over 60 feet long and nearly 40 high, has lovely views of the Avon running 100 feet below and a fine landscape of Shakespeare's England. We can see a 100-yards length of the castle from its windows. The floor is of red and white marble from Verona. In an earlier hall here Piers Gaveston was probably tried in 1312, before he was executed at Guy's Cliffe.

There are not many rooms richer in treasure than this; it is filled with things precious or curious or beautiful. One of the things is what is called Guy's Porridge Pot, probably made in the 14th century as a garrison cooking pot; it holds 120 gallons. There is an oak dower chest belonging to Izaak Walton and Rachel Floyd, a very richly carved oak bench, and a head of the extinct elk recovered from Irish bogs.

There is a sword said to have belonged to Henry the Eighth and something said to have been his walking-stick. Pathetic is the tiny suit of armour belonging to Robert Dudley. Here and everywhere, of course, are magnificent pictures—Mrs Siddons by Sir Joshua Reynolds, Holbein's Henry the Eighth and Anne Boleyn, Murillo's Laughing Boy, Van Dyck's portraits of Strafford and Charles Stuart and St Sebastian, The Card Players by Teniers, The Emperor Maximilian and his sister by Louis Cranech, and portraits of Henrietta Maria by Reynolds and Van Dyck. The castle is indeed a museum. There is a fine tapestry of the Gardens of Versailles. There is Cromwell's helmet, Queen Anne's travelling trunk, and Marie Antoinette's clock with 12 scenes from the life of Jesus worked in enamel. We can see all these, for this marvellous castle is the great show place of Warwick, inside and out.

The lawn in front of the castle is about two acres and the grounds cover about a square mile, with 36 acres laid out as gardens. The Normans had a fortress here, and probably the Saxons had, for the mound in front of the castle was named after Alfred's daughter, and the castle was fortified by order of the Conqueror. A marvellous example of a comfortable house and a fortified place, the castle has seen 20 generations of men come and go. How many volleys of arrows have been shot from the parapet of Caesar's tower, as solid as the rock on which it has stood 600 years! From the top are seen the spires of Coventry, the ruins of Kenilworth, the hills of Shropshire, and the battlefield of Edgehill.

Amid this great scene of English history and English beauty stands something of the grandeur that was Greece, a marvellous vase found in the bed of a lake at Tivoli. It is believed to have been made by one of the master sculptors of all time, Lysippus. It is fashioned in white marble, stands as high as a man, and holds 163 gallons. For 22 centuries this wonder has been in the world, and for half of them it has lain at the bottom of a lake, thrown there, it is thought, to save it from destruction when the Goths were at the Gate of Rome. It is a superb piece of work, with vine stems for handles and bunches of grapes forming a frieze round the edge. It has sculptures all over it something like tiger skins, with splendid carvings of the heads and paws, and arranged along these skins are heads of attendants on Bacchus, for whose temple it is thought the vase may have been made.

The gardens of the castle are marvellous with yew hedges, and the lawns were alive with peacocks when we called. Well do we understand the pride of that George Greville who laid out these grounds and made them fit for kings; it is like reading of the glory of Solomon to read the proud boast of this Earl of Warwick.

I PURCHASED a magnificent collection of pictures not equalled perhaps in the kingdom. I made a noble approach to the Castle through the solid rock, and founded a library full of books.

I made an armoury, and built walls round the court and pleasure-gardens. I built a noble greenhouse, and filled it with beautiful plants; I placed in it a vase, considered the finest remains of Grecian Art for its size and beauty. I made a noble lake, from 300 to 400 feet broad, and a mile long.

I planted trees, now worth £100,000, besides 100 acres of ash. I built a stone bridge of 105 feet in span, every stone from 2000 to 3800 pounds weight; the weight of the first tier on the centre was estimated at 100 tons. I gave the bridge to the town with no toll on it.

I will not enumerate a great many other things done by me. Let Warwick Castle speak for itself.

We leave it all feeling that Shakespeare's England has indeed not passed away. A mile or two from this great place was born John Rous, Warwick's historian and antiquarian. He lived at a house at Guy's Cliffe about 500 years ago, and he is remembered in St Mary's. For five centuries since then Warwick has been in the midst of English history, but much of his old town John Rous would know if he came back, for Warwick has almost defied the spirit of Change. Time comes and goes, but she remains.

Perhaps the most interesting man sleeping here is Fulke Greville, servant of monarchs and friend of Sir Philip Sidney.

Friend of Sir Philip Sidney

THE Fulke Greville we all admire was the grandson of the Fulke upon whom Henry the Eighth bestowed the site of the old monastery, and so was one of the greatest landowners in the county. He was born in 1554, the same year as Sir Philip Sidney, entered Shrewsbury school the same day with him, and formed a friendship with him that only death could sever. Greville, who was knighted in 1597 and created Baron Brooke in 1620, was another Sidney in spirit and instincts, a lesser Sidney in poetical talent. He grew up

Warwick
St Mary's

Warwick
West Gate

Warwick

Mill Street

Long Itchington
14th Century Screen

Astley
Medieval Stalls

Southam
16th Century Pulpit

Wolfhamcote
Ancient Screen

Wootton Wawen
15th Century Pulpit

Knowle
16th Century Screen

Wootton Wawen
15th Century Screen

Ancient Pulpits, Screens, and Stalls

the very mirror and pattern of chivalry, high-minded, scholarly, as ready with a sonnet as with his lance in the tilt yard, where he was a magnificent figure. Ten years older than Shakespeare, he was 21 years the junior of Elizabeth, who loved to have him with Sidney about her court. Although she permitted the two to visit Heidelberg in 1577, she forbade Fulke to wander farther. To attach him to England she made him Secretary for Wales before he was 30, and, 10 years after the Armada, Treasurer of the Navy. James, who gave him his peerage, trusted him and made him his Chancellor of the Exchequer.

But it is as the friend of learning and as a writer that Fulke Greville is dear to us; above all, he was Sidney's friend and biographer. It was to Greville and their friend Dyer that Sidney left his books, to them that he addressed his re-union poem beginning:

> Join, mates, in mirth to me,
> Grant pleasure to our meeting;
> Join hearts and hands so let it be;
> Make but one mind in bodies three.

The death of Sidney shook Greville to the soul; there is a letter he wrote at the time which can hardly be read without tears. He wrote his friend's life, a noble, loving tribute; and with radiant vision as to posterity's estimate of him he graduated his claim to esteem in an epitaph he wrote for himself:

> Fulke Grevil, Servant to Queen Elizabeth
> Counsellor to King James
> Friend to Sir Philip Sidney

His end was as melancholy as Sidney's, but less glorious. A trusted old servant, believing him about to die without having included him in his will, stabbed him to death, and then took his own life.

If Sherwood has its Robin Hood, here we have a still older legendary figure, the redoubtable Guy of Warwick.

Guy of Warwick

DURING the immortal ride to Canterbury Chaucer, rallied into telling a tale, introduces Guy of Warwick to the Pilgrims in a poem so tedious that the host shouts him down and scoffs him into prose.

Norman-English ballads are less brief in their treatment of Sir Guy, but for all their heroics and loquacity we really get no more authentic history from them than from the Father of English Poetry. The romantics make him a tremendous fellow in all respects, and local tradition through the centuries has built about the legend a structure which only the daring will question.

We are to believe that Guy of Warwick was the son of a steward to the Earl of Warwick in the time of Athelstan, and that to win the love of Felice, his master's daughter, he followed classical precedent by undertaking heroic labours, first fighting the Saracens at Constantinople, then returning to slay the dragon that was devastating northern England. His valour, approved by Athelstan, won him his bride, but his adventures continued, for there was fighting for him to do in Holy Land, and after that a Danish giant, Colbrand, to encounter at home. With war between the English and the invading Danes dependent on the result, Guy met Colbrand in single combat, slew him, and gave his country peace. Thereupon, in remorse for the blood he had shed, he retired to Guy's Cliffe, hewed out the cave we see there, passed the rest of his days in rigorous seclusion, and did not communicate with Felice again except to summon her to his deathbed by sending a herdsman with a ring.

Poetry and legend will not have our David too minute a hero against the Danish Goliath; here is his Porridge Pot, a staggering cauldron that holds 120 gallons. The rib of the dun cow that he killed and ate at a sitting is so prodigious that science must be forgiven for proving it to be the rib of a whale. His walking staff, fit support for a giant indeed, is in reality the shaft of a lance made six centuries after the good Guy's era. The armour shown as his in the castle is made of pieces from several reigns, all long after the days of Guy.

There may have been a Saxon prototype of Guy; there may have been shrewd blows at social evils that live picturesquely to posterity in the name and semblance of a dragon. There may have been a battle against Danes in Warwickshire whose happy issue seemed fitly to blend in the laurels of the mystic hero of the Anglo-Saxon poets. There may have been all these. For eight centuries and more the feats of Guy have formed part of our literature, and when Thomas Beauchamp added a new tower to the castle in 1394 he honoured tradition and its hero by naming it Guy's Tower. Guy is one with our Treasury of song and romance.

Warwick is the most intimate meeting-place we have with that volcanic genius, Carlyle's "unsubduable old Roman," Walter Savage Landor.

The King Lear of the Nineteenth Century

LANDOR is an almost legendary figure, to scholars one of the great masters of English literature, to the general public only a name. One of his friends was the daughter of Addison, who was born in 1672; he himself, born 100 years later, lived to praise Byron, to proclaim the genius of Shelley and Keats, to be the hero of Lamb, Southey, and Dickens, and to see the dedication to himself of Atalanta in Calydon by Swinburne, to whom he was "the old demigod with the heart and head of a lion." His life covered all but 90 years, and he drew his admirers from the elect of three generations in succession.

His father was a Warwick doctor who married twice, each wife bringing him a fortune, the second of which was inherited by the poet. Landor inherited not only an estate, but genius which flowered from a spirit fundamentally haughty, fierce, and rebellious, modified by an exquisite tenderness which manifested itself in generosity to friends and kindred and to all dumb creatures.

He was a scholar almost by intuition, for he was expelled from Rugby and rusticated at Oxford for insubordination; yet he was the first classical scholar of his age, the courted companion of gifted seniors. The quarrels begun at home and continued with all sorts and conditions of men throughout his life involved his being sent from home to Wales, where he met his first love, Rose Aylmer, whose untimely death inspired one of the shortest and tenderest elegies in English literature:

> Ah, what avails the sceptred race?
> Ah, what the form divine?
> What every virtue, every grace?
> Rose Aylmer, all were thine.
>
> Rose Aylmer, whom these wakeful eyes
> May weep, but never see,
> A night of memories and sighs
> I consecrate to thee.

Early established as a poet of genius appealing to the elect, Landor was an aristocratic republican who despised the mob but worshipped liberty. He bought Llanthony Abbey and planned an earthly paradise, but found that he had called a social inferno into being. Worse still, at 36 he married an unintellectual beauty of twenty, from whom he was soon glad to part. He was writing and publishing for 70 years, poems in English and Latin, dramas, and, among his rich and splendid prose, the incomparable Imaginary Conversations, dialogues between sovereigns and statesmen, poets and philosophers, slaves and beauties, a unique gallery unmatched in dramatic presentation of character and in nobility and beauty of diction.

He neither sought nor desired popularity. "I shall dine late," he said with an eye to posterity, "but the dining-room will be well lighted, the guests few and select." He had another 14 years to live, and he strove, quarrelled, and battled with everybody, his vehement fury and ungovernable whims estranging nearly all his friends. An unpardonable libel drove him finally to Florence, and to wretchedness.

Like King Lear, he disposed of his property to his children, and they turned on him and left him homeless and beggared. It was only through the agency of Browning that an annuity from the old poet's brothers was forthcoming to keep a roof over the veteran's head. "Mr Browning," said his daughter, "if my father lay dying in that ditch, I would not lift a finger to save him!"

To the end, impoverished and enfeebled, he was unconquered. The British Minister in Florence offended him, and he wrote, "You by the favour of a Minister are Marquis of Normanby; I by the grace of God am Walter Savage Landor." It was at Florence he died, and he sleeps there on a little hilltop, close to Mrs Browning.

The Merry Craftsmen

WASPERTON. A meadow by the Avon brings us to a 17th-century dovecot fallen on evil times, much decayed and with a hatchway for the hundreds of birds once kept here for the parson or the squire.

The lovely garden of the parsonage, gay with flowers when we called, is neighbour to a church made new by Sir Gilbert Scott. Its east window is said to have been the last designed by Pugin, one of the forerunners of the English Gothic revival.

The merry craftsmen who made the iron altar rails finished off their foliage with quaint heads of birds, while on the gate are two winged mermen. There is a plain old chest with two locks, a brass inscription assuring us that Honest Henry Collins of 1664, who lived on earth so well, has gone already in heaven to dwell, and an oak lectern with lions at the foot and saints on the pedestal. But the most interesting thing is the pulpit, which has finely carved panels of Adam and Eve in the garden, John the Baptist, Abraham about to sacrifice Isaac, and Jacob wrestling with the angel.

The Angel on the Bridge

WATER ORTON. The best scene of all here is a little way from the village, the glimpse of a black-and-white cottage and a lovely old bridge over the Tame. It is a charming peep of this countryside of the days when Warwickshire gave England her most famous son. Long and narrow with quaint recesses, the bridge for 400 years has seen people come and go, and we find it very much as it stood in Tudor days, its stone beautifully weathered. For centuries the bridge was watched over by an angel, which at last lost its head and has now found shelter in Curdworth church. Its own neat church with a slender spire is not yet 100 years old. Over its font is a finely carved figure of the Good Shepherd, lantern in hand.

WEDDINGTON. Nuneaton is coming to meet it and new houses are nearing its little grey church, rebuilt 200 years ago on Norman foundations. It has a fine oak screen by a modern craftsman with 16 birds peeping from the foliage on its cornice, and an oak reredos with an old painting of the Crucifixion and four guardian angels. There is a monument to Humphrey Adderley, lord of the manor in Henry the Eighth's day, and an arcaded font with a pattern of stars at which Weddington's children have been christened for about 800 years.

The Storm That Wrecked the Armada

WELFORD-ON-AVON. It is close to a lovely stretch of the Avon near Stratford, and has a charming row of old timbered and thatched cottages, an ancient mill still working, a new maypole, and a lychgate Shakespeare must have known. The gate is as he would see it, with splendid beams full of the scars of time; and hundreds of artists have put it into pictures.

Much of the church is as the Normans left it. The lower part of the tower, the north and south doorways with their chevron carving, the massive arcades with wide arches, are all 800 years old. There is a 15th-century sanctus bellcot. The font was made by the first English builders 700 years ago, and has a round bowl on a round pillar. There

277

is a 14th-century piscina, a few fragments of medieval glass, and a Jacobean pulpit.

In the register is a thrilling page recording the flooding of the Avon in the summer of Armada year, due to the storm that wrecked the Armada, and Shakespeare, it is thought, had it in mind when he wrote these lines in Midsummer Night's Dream:

> *The winds, piping to us in vain,*
> *As in revenge, have sucked up from the sea*
> *Contagious fogs; which falling in the land*
> *Have every pelting river made so proud*
> *That they have overborne their continents:*
> *The ox hath therefore stretched his yoke in vain,*
> *The ploughman lost his sweat, and the green corn*
> *Hath rotted . . .*

The oak chancel screen is the peace memorial, and the names of the fallen are on a stone tablet. The east window, with an Ascension scene, has a little portrait of Basil Arthur Davis, son of the rector here; he was killed in a motor accident.

A little way on the road to Stratford is an inn called the Four Alls with a curious old painting by the porch, showing four characters;

> *The king who rules over all*
> *The parson who prays for all*
> *The soldier who fights for all*
> *The farmer who pays for all*

Politics in the Candle Age

WELLESBOURNE. Old people here remember the days when the village was the centre of a movement for improving the life of the agricultural labourer. Meetings were held in the evenings by the light of candles stuck in the bark of old trees, and it was all so interesting in those days that the London papers sent artists down to draw pictures of it. When we called there were still one or two people who remembered the candlelight which brought a little fame to this quaint place.

The church, restored about 100 years ago, has little of its beauty left except an arch in the chancel. Amongits good modern possessions are mosaics behind the altar in memory of Lord Charles Paulet, who died in 1870 and was vicar here for 40 years. There is beautiful glass in a window of the chancel, and a memorial to Francis Dipple tells us that he was a faithful servant in one family for about half of the 19th century. Perhaps the most precious possession is a small brass showing Thomas le Strange in the armour he wore about the time of Agincourt. He was Constable of Ireland and his brass is one of the oldest and one of the best kept in all Warwickshire.

John Trapp of Shakespeare's School

WESTON-ON-AVON. A thatched-cottage village by the river, it has a man blowing a trumpet at the top of its 15th-century tower. In the sanctuary are two fighting men in armour, their portraits in enduring brass. One, Sir John Grevill, is shown with his head resting on a horned sheep, and his feet on a grassy mound with flowers; his son, who fought at the Battle of the Spurs in 1513, is in a heraldic coat, his hands at prayer.

The great feature of the church is its grand array of north windows, all of the 15th century and remarkably close together. Two are crowded with fragments of old glass in small leaded panes, among them pictures of little golden ark-like ships, quaint and pleasing.

We like to remember old John Trapp who was vicar here for ten years in Charles Stuart's day, and again for nine years of the Restoration. For about 12 years he was a master of Stratford grammar school and, though he first went to Stratford six years after Shakespeare died, he must have known the family; his wife, a Stratford girl, must often have seen Shakespeare in her younger days.

The Physician Slain

WESTON-UNDER-WETHERLEY. It has everything to make a typical English village, lovely timbered cottages with thatched roofs, an old forge and farm buildings, gardens that were a picture when we called, and a splendid church with a sturdy tower.

The tower and the red sandstone walls of the church take us back 700 years. Two solemn faces over the porch have the mark of ages on them, and other faces, small and much worn by the rain, look out into the churchyard from the windows. There are also heads on the 600-year-old font, which has a curiously irregular shape, with concave sides.

As old as the tower, perhaps, are three arches in the nave; and there is an arch to a tiny chapel, with some of the old stonework cut away for a screen of oak, hoary with age and carved at the top with two leaves and a rose. In two windows are fragments of medieval glass; and there are three small pieces of brass of much interest to antiquarians, some of the oldest inscriptions in Warwickshire. One is to Anne Danet, who died in 1497, and above it, engraved with tiny flowers and scrolls, is a brass of the 16th century to Joyce Tomer, whose skill in physic failed him at the end:

> *Here lieth Joyce Tomer, slain at death,*
> *That had of physic skill.*

Another 16th-century inscription informs us that Margery Saunders was a perfect wife; and near it lies another Saunders, Sir Edward, a judge of Shakespeare's day, kneeling with his wife on a stone tomb under a tiny arch. Both have lost their heads. Above them are two sculptured scenes of the Resurrection, with Roman soldiers at the tomb, and the Ascension.

One of the old walls of the chancel leans outward, and the crude masonry seems just as it was in the 12th or 13th century. This wall has two windows, one square and deep, both topped with beams of ancient oak. There is a piscina and a small priest's doorway. The west window has Michael with a sword in one hand and a cross in the other, a dragon writhing at his feet; it is a splendid harmony of colour when the sun comes streaming through.

The Grand Old Man of Whatcote

WHATCOTE. At this charming little place so remote from the world we came upon a Grand Old Man, John Davenport, who preached in this church for 70 years and lived to be over 100. He lived through the whole reign of Queen Elizabeth, he knew all about Shakespeare and Francis Drake, he saw the coming of the Stuarts and the gift of the Authorised Version of the Bible to the English people; he lived through the Civil War and saw Cromwell Protector, and he saw the Stuarts back again. His stone is in the chancel, and he is one of about a dozen people we have found who preached in one place so long.

The church still keeps much that he knew so well; there is a Norman doorway, a font with a Norman bowl, and a 13th-century porch. The tower has been here 600 or 700 years, the chancel 500.

Two other rectors are remembered in stone and brass; Thomas Nelle by a 15th-century stone engraved with a chalice and a cross, and William Auldyngton, a headless figure in parson's robes on a brass of 1511. On another brass are the names of two men who never came back, and a little window has a scene in richly coloured glass showing Christ appearing to Peter on the first Easter morn.

In the churchyard is a sundial set on the ancient cross.

A Pair of Spectacles

WHICHFORD. Its cottage windows look over lovely gardens and into Oxfordshire, and amid the loveliness of this charming village is a church with a 15th-century nave and tower, a 13th-century chancel, and a fine doorway the Normans made with bold zigzag, a column on each side, and carved capitals. Five queer stone faces look down from the walls, and there is a sanctus bell.

The treasure of the church is a fine portrait of John Mertun, one of the best for miles around, engraved in alabaster, about 1537. He is in rich robes under an elaborate canopy with a book and a chalice. resting on a stone tomb a century older than the portrait itself. In the middle of a panel at one end of the tomb is a rare curiosity in sculpture, a pair of spectacles. They are carved with a book. We have come upon carvings of men wearing spectacles in one or two churches (once again in this county at Wormleighton), but we have never seen a pair of spectacles like these, and they are among the oldest in the land, coming from the early days of the 16th century.

Under an arch is the fine coffin lid of Sir John Mohun of Dunster who fought at the battle of Boroughbridge in 1322 and died soon after. By the altar lies Nicholas Asheton, in a richly carved tomb with his brass portrait set in the top and his arms at the back. A priest of Elizabethan England, he is shown in a beautiful robe with his hands at prayer.

There is a little old glass from the 14th century with a Crucifixion, Gabriel and the Madonna, and saints at prayer, and good modern glass with Michael and his angels casting out the dark-winged knight of evil. The east window (which has a fine hood outside with two rows of ballflowers) has glass of rich colour showing the Shepherds and the Wise Men at Bethlehem and other early scenes in Galilee. The massive font is Norman, the chalice is Elizabethan. The pulpit is reached from a doorway in the wall of a chapel.

Beside the Still Waters

WHITCHURCH. It has been made to lie down in green pastures, beside the still waters. It has a church tucked away among the trees, a lonely place reached only by those who love the footpath way, but very well worth finding. Here the little Stour runs through the fields.

The church has a simple Norman doorway with a holy lamb over it. A painted sundial marks the hours as we approach; it has been marking them since 1646. Immense old beams look down on the nave, but far older are its walls; they are Norman. The early lancets and 15th-century windows are the glory of the chancel. The modern east window has a figure of Christ enthroned, and two panels of old heraldic glass with lions in its tracery; at the sides are fragments of fine canopied brackets. Other windows also have some bits of old glass—shields and stars and sacred monograms in red, blue, and gold. In this chancel comes to mind a tragic bit of history, for a stone in the floor is in memory of Dame Overbury who died in 1686; she was the wife of Sir Thomas Overbury, whose famous uncle was poisoned in the Tower of London.

There is a pulpit with arcaded Jacobean panels and a fine cross with a heart at its base, a chalice and a book at the sides. It is on the tomb of William Smyth, who was rector here and chaplain to the Guild of the Holy Cross at Stratford 100 years before Shakespeare was born.

WHITNASH. Its pleasant black-and-white houses and barns are in the shade of tall elms, and in its church, which has a 15th-century tower, three people are specially remembered. They are Benedict Medley, who has been here with his wife in brass since 1504, he in a long gown and she with a hood and sleeves with embroidered cuffs; Richard Bennett, who was preaching here 400 years ago and has a brass showing him with a chalice; and Nicholas Greenhill, who was rector for 40 years in the 17th century, coming to Whitnash from Rugby, where he had been one of the two youngest headmasters of that famous school.

The Captain Bold

WILLOUGHBY. Near lovely Dunchurch, it hides from the busy road and offers a little world of quiet to those who turn the corner.

The 14th-century church has a splendid tower and a nave with lofty arches sweeping smoothly down without capitals. On the age-worn Norman font are two curious little men with lilies instead of

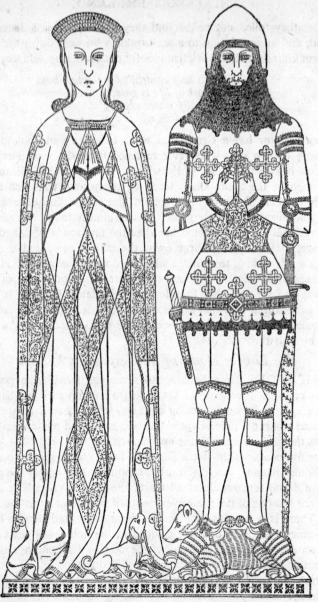

Warwick: The splendid 15th-century brass of Thomas Beauchamp and his wife.

hands; they toiled not neither did they spin. There is a Jacobean pulpit, and an inscription to a sea-captain who went down near the coast of Guinea in 1674. He left money for poor folk here, and we read:

> Death hath controlled a Captain bold
> Yet loss of life is gain,
> Especially where charity
> For ever doth remain.

One window has a Crucifixion scene in green and gold to the memory of two men who never returned from the war. The east window has a white-robed Christ with St Nicholas and St Elizabeth; St Nicholas, the Santa Claus loved by the young, rests one hand gently on a child's head, while behind him sails a fine Elizabethan ship; St Elizabeth, whose golden tresses almost touch her ankles, holds a chalice, while behind her rises the fine tower of Magdalen College, Oxford. This college owns the manor here, and thereby hangs a tale linking this village with the downfall of a king. Henry Clerke, whose marble monument is here, was long lord of the manor, and he was also President of Magdalen College. It was after his death in 1687 that James the Second tried to give the college a Roman Catholic president, one of the many foolish acts which cost him his throne.

The Lovely Home of Shakespeare's Mother

WILMCOTE. Here Shakespeare's mother lived, in a perfect cottage. The house of Mary Arden is almost all the hamlet has except for its neighbouring cottages, which should be seen in lilac and laburnum time. Captivating is its black-and-white front seen across the green from near the new church.

For five centuries the house has stood here, and its mighty beams, we should imagine, would stand 100 centuries. It is one of the most beautiful and remarkable of all the Shakespeare cottages. Its huge fireplace has one of the great oven doors of which not many are now left. There is a monk's table made about 1480, and herring-bone timbering in the roof of a wing added to the house 400 years ago. It is an old farmhouse, and one of the best of its buildings is the ancient dovecot, with nesting-places for 650 doves.

From this delightful place went Mary Arden to Aston Cantlow, where she found John Shakespeare waiting for her. The lanes are pretty much today as she would know them when she rode to meet her bridegroom. What she cannot have known is that her name and her home would one day be preserved for ever among the famous and beautiful things of the world.

WISHAW. The path to the lonely church brings us to its oldest inhabitant, a great yew 16 feet round and still vigorous. There are other magnificent trees in the park of the great house, but none so venerable.

The small 15th-century church has lofty arcades, a low chancel arch, and a peephole for the altar. There is an elaborate monument to an ardent Royalist of the Civil War, and of Mary Lisle, who lived to see the Restoration, we read that even an age can scarce raise such another saint. St Peter with his keys and Cornelius, the devout Roman centurion, with his sword and shield, are companions in modern glass. In tiny niches in the splendid peace memorial are figures of St George with his dragon and St Chad of Lichfield with his cathedral, companions in alabaster.

Village Portraits

WITHYBROOK. It is as pleasing as its name, with a dignified little church in a field beside a brook. The centuries have dealt gently with it, and the old stonework in the nave looks almost new. Faces peep from its arches and a chain of flowers encircles one of the capitals.

The roofs keep a few of their old beams and some of the windows have fragments of medieval glass, in which we noticed three heads and a robed figure. In the chancel is a rare sort of Easter sepulchre which must have looked fine when it was new. It has two worn figures and an angel. There is a battered brass portrait of a man in civilian robes who has been here since the 15th century, and engraved on an altar tomb are portraits of Christopher Wright in armour and his wife, who have been sleeping here for over three centuries.

Old Yew on Its Crutches

WIXFORD. Perhaps it is the shining white tower on the hill with the red roofs grouped about it that sets us wondering, but it is the church in its solitude that keeps us. The white tower belongs to an ancient building made into a charming modern house by Mr David Greig. It looks out across a noble piece of Shakespeare's countryside, with its village below it running along the sunken road called Icknield Street in the days before history.

Here the black-and-white almshouses built by Sir William Throckmorton make a charming terrace on their raised pavement by the road to Alcester, and across the fields are the rest of the timbered cottages, with nothing between them and the church except the arms of one of the greatest inhabitants of Shakespeare's country spreading out like an octopus. We took at least 100 paces round Old Yew and could have taken more. Some of its limbs are more than 10 yards long and we can understand the impression this tree makes on the people hereabouts; but they think it much older than it is.

It is remarkable not for its age but for its shape, for it has grown straight out horizontally so that we can walk under it as under a flat roof. It is said that there was trouble about this tree in Shakespeare's time, for it is recorded that the village folk feared that the parson meant to cut it down and petitioned the bishop to prevent him, only to find that he loved Old Yew as much as they. Now its weary limbs rest on dozens of crutches, and one of the finest spreading yews in England (though not one of the oldest) is safe from harm.

Three old things to see has this church outside, almost all that is left of its antiquity. One is the plain Norman doorway on two round shafts, one is the great beauty of the stonework of the east window, and the other is a pair of tiny windows which captivate the eye in the north wall, looking like two well-sharpened pencils, with a tiny head between them.

The old-looking door brings us into the nave, and we find ourselves in an interior rich with interest. The oak-barrel roofs have about 400 delicately carved bosses with a narrow little cornice running above the sanctuary. The east window has in it St Christopher in gold and the patron saint Milburga in a rich blue cloak; and the window in the medieval chantry chapel has about 40 fragments of old heraldic glass, in which we noticed small figures of musical angels. There is a medieval font no longer used, pieces of the heavy old screen, and a six-foot chest with the mark of the axe all over it.

But Wixford has a treasure which a cathedral might envy, for it has one of the most magnificent brasses of the 15th century that we have come upon, more than nine feet long and splendidly preserved, showing an attorney and his wife on their great altar tomb. He is Thomas Crewe, who looked after the affairs of the Countess of Warwick in 1400, in the days when plate armour was taking the place of chain mail. Was ever a man more securely protected against the buffetings of his enemies? His throat and shoulders, his legs and feet, his arms and his hands, are all encased. The engraver has decorated him with the cross of St George, the Warwick arms, and a lion. His wife has a long flowing robe with tight sleeves, a mantle tied with tassel cords, and a jewelled band to keep her hair in place. A scarf falls over her shoulders, and her dog nestles at her feet.

This superb brass, covering the tomb in which they sleep, has a pinnacled canopy above the figures, and between the words running round it all are odd emblems we have not been able to understand, the badge of a human foot, many times repeated. There is another brass of a kneeling little one, Rise Griffin, who died in 1597 when he was "but three-quarters old," and another to Jane Alline and her 10 children with an inscription of those days. We may imagine that Jane's little ones would often be sent to tell the time by one of the mass dials still on the walls.

WOLFHAMCOTE. The trains rush by and leave it undisturbed, and the simple church with its sturdy tower stands lonely in the fields. It has a very primitive font, unmounted and unadorned. Nobody knows its age, but it may well be Saxon, for a church stood here 1000 years ago. The arcades are 13th and 14th century; the screen has been here 600 years. On seven crude benches the people of this small place have sat from generation to generation.

The stocks are by the pond, not far from a house built when Charles the Second came back.

The Secret Printers of Armada Year

WOLSTON. Hereabouts are a few fragments of masonry and many earthworks of what was an important castle in Richard Lionheart's day, and here is a church with something of nearly every century from the Conqueror's day to ours. The south doorway, some of the small windows, and three of the tower arches are Norman. One arch has curious capitals with crudely carved men on each side of a cross and a man holding the arm of a kneeling figure.

Little faces peep from the richly canopied sedilia and piscina, three of them smiling, and there are more quaint heads on the bowl of the 14th-century font. A rich canopy shelters the worn stone figure of a man who may have been baptised when the font was new. The chancel roof is painted in many colours, and one of its fine windows

287

shows Luke the physician with a mother and sick daughter, given by the grateful patients of a village doctor.

A stone in the churchyard has an inscription saying:

> Tell me which is best:
> The toilsome journey or the traveller's rest?

There is a memorial to a boy who was drowned near Cape Horn and lies in a lonely grave in America's Farthest South, and one to the old boys of Priory Hill School with the fine words:

> They gave their youth that
> we might grow old in peace.

Not far off is Priory Farm, chiefly Elizabethan, though it still has stones of a priory founded about 20 years after the Battle of Hastings. A 15th-century doorway brings us to what has long been known as the chapel, and there is a 13th-century piscina, a Tudor doorway with a massive old door, and a cellar where a little company of printers was working as long ago as Armada year.

Here for a season, nearly three and a half centuries ago, was the hidden hub of the intellectual world, the mystic cradle of some of the most famous tracts of the Martin Marprelate controversy.

Elizabeth was on the throne, Whitgift was Primate, Puritanism was raising its voice against abuses in the Church, when John Penry, Father of Welsh Nonconformity, who was born in Brecknockshire in 1559, focussed attention on himself by a petition to Parliament pointing to the deplorable state of religion in Wales.

The petition spoke of the idolatrous superstitions and Roman Catholic practices of the Welsh, and of the silence and greed of their clergy; and its author received a month's imprisonment. At that time Whitgift, a furious opponent of Puritanism, succeeded in getting an Act forbidding publication of any unlicensed writings by members of that sect.

The answer was the appearance of the raciest and most brilliant satirical tracts in the controversial literature of the time. Their author, declared to be Martin Marprelate, was in reality John Penry, with a clergyman, John Udall, as assistant contributor. With keen wit and sarcasm the tracts exposed the anomalies, intolerance, and misdoings in the Church, and each publication was, of course, in defiance of the new Act, so that the pamphlets were secretly printed, with successive flights and removals of the press.

Security and a home were found first at Kingston, then at Fawsley in Northants, where Puritan Penry went about disguised in the finery of a dashing Court gallant. To elude the arm of the law the press was moved to Coventry and finally found a home at the priory here, where the pamphlets at last came to an end amid excursions, alarums, and perils enough to furnish a drama.

Penry fled to Scotland and his printer to France, while Udall was arrested and imprisoned for life. With the press seized here, authority lay in wait for Penry, and when he returned from Scotland he was arrested, tried on a false charge of treason, and in May 1593 was hanged. Udall died in prison.

Of his many pamphlets seven survive, with the replies called forth by famous writers. Among the best known of all are three which were printed here, entitled for short, Martin Junior, Martin Senior, and The Protestation, all famous in their day and unrivalled as prose satires in the Elizabethan age.

The Dove and the Serpent

WOLVERTON. The centuries have left much unspoiled beauty here, and it is a great delight to walk through the rectory garden and along the tree-shaded path to the church. It has a quaint wooden tower and a richly timbered old porch, with this cunning fragment of wisdom for all who come:

> That thou injure no man, dovelike be,
> And serpentlike that no man injure thee.

The windows are interesting for their new glass and for their old. In the chancel are figures of Mary and Jesus, and Elizabeth with the young Baptist, thought to be one of the youthful works of Burne-Jones, and the east window has fragments of a 14th-century Doom in which we can recognise some small heads and an angel. Elsewhere is a fragment with the heraldry of Warwick the Kingmaker, and other medieval glass shows a man in a red tunic, an angel, a bellman, and St Anthony's pig with a bell round its neck.

It is known that this beautiful church was made new about 1208, and it has a list of rectors from 1283. The triple sedilia and the piscina are still in the ancient walls. There is an old chest with three locks, and modern choir stalls with misereres finely carved by a man from the neighbouring village of Snitterfield, some with shields, others with St George, a crowing cock, and the Madonna with her two boys.

U   289

Captive King Edward

WOLVEY. It was a thriving town of knitters and millers in the Middle Ages, with 27 windmills vaunting their sails; but these trades have marched away with the regiment of mills and today it is a village on a hill away from the throbbing centres of life.

It takes us back to the Wars of the Roses, and we think here of a king taken captive by those to whom he had looked for succour. It was on Wolvey Heath, some of our historians say, that Edward the Fourth camped in those unhappy days when his friends lay dead and scattered, and it was while he slept here that Warwick the Kingmaker surrounded his camp, overpowered his guard, and took him captive. One other memory of unhappy far-off days has this place, for on a little mound near Wolvey Lady Dorothy Smythe is said to have been burned at the stake in 1555 for having encompassed the death of her husband.

The splendid church which stands grey and beautiful by a bend of the road is chiefly 14th century, but it has a Norman doorway with a curious moulding, a design like the letter M gracefully repeated; perhaps we like to think it stood for the Madonna. Above this is the familiar zigzag, and there is a plain outer arch with grotesque creatures on its capitals. A pity it is to see the fine columns of such an arch deeply scored by the sharpening marks of arrows, so deeply that at one point the stone is nearly worn through. Small heads look down from the lofty 15th-century tower, and in it hangs a bell which has been ringing for 500 years; it is said to have come from Nuneaton Priory, the villagers fetching it away at dead of night in a farm cart.

The spacious dignity of the interior is impressive. The old rood stairs and the fine canopied sedilia are still here, but it is the monuments which attract all eyes. On one tomb near the tower, the light falling on them through 14th-century windows, lie Thomas Wolvey and his wife. In this church they have lain 600 years, he wearing armour and a sword, his lady in a rich headdress clasping a heart. From Shakespeare's day are the alabaster figures on the tomb of Thomas Astley and his wife. Very fine they must have looked before the roof fell on them in the 17th century, some of the fragments lying about them still.

Near the village is Wolvey Hall, built in 1676 on the site of an older house, with patches of medieval glass in its windows.

The Oldest Church in Shakespeare's Country

WOOTTON WAWEN. We may doubt if there is a more fascinating village in all Warwickshire than this. Certainly we have seen none more rich in the beauty of many centuries. The 20th century rushes past in its cars, but Time stands still in the church, where the Past has a thousand symbols. Said to be the oldest church in Warwickshire, it takes us back to Saxon days. We pause to admire it from the lovely path among the ancient tombstones, attracted by the battlemented tower, the crocketed pinnacles, the parapets of the nave and aisle, the tracery of the windows, and the remarkable array of carving on the walls. There is a sundial which was telling the hours in Shakespeare's England.

Thrilling it is to enter through this fine old timbered porch, to open this old door with its ancient iron ring, and inside we are bewildered, for here is something like three churches in one. The altar is under the tower, approached through a chantry chapel, the chancel lies farther east behind it, while on the south is an aisle like another chapel, all these places packed with interest and beauty.

We stand in the chantry chapel, looking past the altar into the chancel, and think we have never seen a village church in Warwickshire with more quaintness to show, or one with more antiquity. We go to the lower part of the tower to see up as far as the belfry storey what is believed to be Saxon work; one of the windows they left is like a pencil. The tower rests on four small Saxon arches which are gems of their kind, one with a modern iron gate admitting to the chancel being among the smallest in England, less than five feet wide. Very old it all is here, so that the handsome Jacobean chair in one of the arches seems young in years.

There is fine carving in a 15th-century oak screen and in the dainty pulpit probably made by the same men. If it were for nothing but these this church would be memorable. One screen has a superbly pointed arch, and there is more 15th-century carving in the pews. There are ancient timbers in the barn-like roofs of the chapel and the chancel, probably untouched since they were hewn.

The west window has two sentinels, great sculptured heads of stone, one on either side and both wearing crowns. They may be Edward the Third and Queen Philippa, but in comparison with the rest of the church they look new. In the glass are 10 apostles and martyrs. The chancel has a splendid 14th-century window with seven lights in which are fragments of ancient painted glass, but its most curious feature is the ornamentation of crockets in a hollow moulding. An east window in an aisle, filled with plain glass, is one of the loftiest we have seen. On a high tomb in the chancel lies the alabaster figure of a man in armour with a dog at his feet, and under his head is a marvellously sculptured figure of a hare which must have been here 500 years, for the figure is probably of John Harewell who died at the time of Agincourt. Another John Harewell of 1505 is seen in a fine brass set in grey marble on a high tomb, he wearing his armour, his wife wearing a beautiful gown and a strange head-dress, with a scent bottle hanging from her girdle. At their feet are little brasses of five sons and five daughters.

The tomb of George Dunscombe, a priest of Shakespeare's time, tells us that he was his people's joy. Very elaborate is the high canopied tomb on which lies the extraordinary painted stone figure of Francis Smith, with a beard nine inches long; he is in armour as he wore it in the 16th century, but has lost his sword.

The church has two splendid old chests, both richly ornamented with wrought iron, a desk containing some old chained books, and an excellently preserved Bible of 1640. The font is of the 14th century and rests on eight lovely heads. In the nave lies William Somerville, a hunting squire and poet of the 18th century. A tablet on the wall has on it the epitaph he wrote for himself.

If you discover any virtue in me, imitate it.
If you detect any failing, shun it with your utmost strength.

Two of his huntsmen lie near him in the churchyard, and of one we read:

Here Hoitt, all his sports and labours past,
Joined his loved master Somerville at last.

We leave this absorbing place and find in the village a bronze statue of a mother and a child, a beautiful sculpture of our own time. They look out towards the busy road from the green and quiet courtyard of some new almshouses, and the figures are of Lucy Fieldhouse and Seymour her son, who was killed in a riding accident. William John Fieldhouse, who put the statue here, lived at Austy Manor, a handsome place on the hill towards Stratford.

We may go that way, passing a weir which is a lovely picture beside the road, and an old red mill-house; but first we see Wootton Wawen's old cottages, which give the village so much of its charm, and the timbered inn where men were probably sitting when news arrived in this countryside that the Earl of Warwick had burned Joan of Arc.

George Washington and William Shakespeare

WORMLEIGHTON. In this charming hilltop village, with greens shaded by noble trees, we stand in surprise before the great gateway of the house built for John Spencer when Henry the Eighth was king, or by John Spencer's cottages. He built the gatehouse for himself and the cottages for his people, and both have come down to us as perfect bits of Tudor England.

The children now play under the gateway which once saw Prince Rupert riding off to Edgehill; it is the centrepiece of a scene where Time has greatly healed the damage wrought in the Civil War. Enough dignity the gatehouse has still, with its fine archway and its parapeted tower, to remind us of Wadham College, Oxford. On its walls are panels of the royal arms, with thistle, rose, and the date 1613; and higher up is the stone of an ancient sundial.

More sculptured panels adorn the house, with attractive chimneys, mullioned windows, and fine doorways making it one of the most notable examples of the domestic architecture of late Tudor days. It is now a farmhouse.

Delightful is the walk from the gatehouse to the church. It has a low cornice round its squat tower, from which faces have been looking down for perhaps 700 years. The nave has 13th-century pillars and arches, and a 15th-century clerestory. In the 13th-century doorway is an ancient studded door, and in the roof are many old beams. There is a founder's recess in the north aisle, ancient tiles in the floor, and fragments of old glass.

The font is centuries old, the chest Jacobean, but the most impressive possession of the church is the oak screen in the chancel, a magnificent specimen of 15th-century work, lofty and richly carved, with a beautiful vaulted canopy looking east. Wonderfully preserved are its details, and we see in it a finely carved stag as small as a half-crown. The little heads of men, some laughing, some solemn, others wearing crowns, are modern. One of the heads wears spectacles, very rare in sculpture at any time. It is thought the screen may have come from a great priory.

Keeping it company in this fascinating chancel is the fine old panelling round the altar, and seats with old ends; on them is an eagle and a winged man, two unfriendly bishops sitting back to back, and a savage dog on the priest's seat standing with its tongue out. Among the memorials is one to a John Spencer who died in his youth a few years before Shakespeare. He has a fine stone monument with painted heraldry, and we are told he was 19 years, eight months, and some odd days old. Under a round stone of the 16th century, near the altar rails, rests the remains of Robert Spencer, said to have been the richest man in England.

Thus the Spencers are remembered, but we look in vain for a memorial to a more illustrious name. The Washingtons were allied to the Spencers by marriage. We know that their name was entered in the register here in 1595. Here one of George Washington's ancestral family was married and another George Washington was baptised. Strange that in this corner of the world there should be living at that time, only a few miles apart, a George Washington and a William Shakespeare.

Christopher Wren, Junior

WROXALL. We pass through a splendid park to a beautiful scene linked with a name we must always honour. For here came Christopher Wren, seeking rest in this lovely retreat three years after finishing St Paul's. He bought Wroxall Abbey from the Burgoynes when his son Christopher married Sir Roger Burgoyne's widow. It was this son who laid the last stone of the lantern above the dome of St Paul's in the presence of his father.

A great affection our immortal Wren must have had for this charming church and the few remains of Wroxall Priory. It is said that he built the red-brick wall of the gardens here with a series of alcoves sheltering delightful nooks. Some portion of this wall, we were told, always catches the setting sun. The wall has two magnificent pillars and an iron gate put here since Wren's time, but most of what we see he would see. Here we may be sure he loved to walk on summer evenings, and we go in fancy with him through the old lychgate, with an old cross above it, to the church among the yew trees which would shade him as he passed.

In one of the walls of the church is a filled-up doorway with a perfect little arch of ballflower ornament, very worn. The nave is 14th century, long and grey and well cared for. The brick tower has glorious old beams. The church is rich in things old and new. There are several marble memorials of the Wrens, one to Christopher and his wife, and a big marble monument to the Burgoynes, who held the priory in the time of Henry the Eighth. On one of the walls of the nave is a solitary figure, an ancient brass portrait of a lady, which is among the best we have seen in Warwickshire. She wears a flowing headdress and is at prayer. Perhaps older than the brass are the figures of saints in medieval glass set in some of the modern windows. Particularly fine is the east window with scenes of the early life of Christ, the Madonna, and four saints in red, blue, and gold.

There is a wealth of modern carving here; we see it in the choir stalls, with a great variety of human faces, gems of their kind. No bigger than a man's closed hand is a pelican feeding her young. It is good to look on these new carvings and on the old panels in the modern pulpit, and to reflect that the love of creating such beautiful things has persisted through so many centuries. Hardly less impressive is the stone reredos with a canopied Crucifixion, four angels, and the Evangelists.

We pass from this scene of much masterly work to the grey walls of the priory close by. Time and Nature have wrought beauty here. The moss grows in the ancient font in the midst of what was once the chapter house, flowers peep like jewels from nooks and crannies of sculptured stone, and the faces of men and the forms of animals surprise us among the ferns. It is an entrancing place. A stone coffin lid has its ancient cross embossed in moss, and there is another stone richly carved, both probably 600 years old. How often Sir Christopher must have stood here and lamented that so much ancient beauty should decay! It was all new about 800 years ago when, legend tells us, the owner of the manor, taken prisoner in the Crusades, built it in thanks to St Leonard for his deliverance.

In these lonely ruins we found two small stones inscribed to two dogs, and on one the inscription runs:

> *The tombstone here doth mark the place*
> *Of Mona, purest of her race,*
> *Whose winning ways and looks refined*
> *Proved her descent of highest kind.*
> *From purest stock both long and true*
> *With blood a shade of bluest blue,*
> *She died as all good dogs must die,*
> *Leaving a tear in friendship's eye.*

All round the ruins are the glorious gardens of Wroxall Abbey, and we wonder what Wren would have thought of it, for the abbey in which he lived was pulled down and the new house built in its place. Some of the lawns are as old as the ruins, shaded by old cedars, bordered by clipped yews, while the pools and flower beds make it a place of blazing colour on a summer's day. The park has fine avenues, and we may say of all this, indeed, that it was a worthy place for Christopher Wren to spend some of his resting days in, and that it is a worthy place for any pilgrim of our day in search of what is beautiful and enduring in our countryside.

The Astonishing Chair from Flanders

WYKEN. A lonely little place among the fields round Coventry, it has a church and two cottages, the church with a very low tower that has stood 500 years. The light has been falling through some of its windows much longer still, for there are three Norman lancets. Men and women have been coming through its western doorway for 25 generations, for this is also Norman.

The astonishing thing that Wyken has for us to see is its great carved chair, a very quaint thing from Flanders. Who was sitting in it, we wonder, 400 years ago? It has two crudely fashioned winged men with pouches hanging from their shoulders. They are riding on dragons, sitting backwards on the beasts, whose heads are turned round to bite their wings. Above all this unfriendly scene presides a little cherub! We have seen some curious chairs, but never one like this.

The Widow's Mite

YARDLEY. We see it first as a busy piece of a city teeming with life, with multitudes of people and hosts of modern houses, and all the liveliness of 20th-century Birmingham about it—in all its parts but one.

The spire of the church seems to beckon us on. We pass the rows of bright new houses, and the old brown cottages begin. In a second we have left the modern world behind. We stand in a corner of Old England, perfect and complete, as beautiful a place as we shall find within the bounds of any industrial city. Here in Birmingham we can forget the city.

The church takes us back 1000 years or more. The splendid little timbered school beside it is a link with Shakespeare's time. The smithy, the inn, the cottages, and the charming rectory all give a sense of beauty and peace living on through the centuries. Far above the roofs rises the battlemented tower, with a spire 150 feet above the pavement. It was here before anyone had heard of America, a silent watcher while green fields have changed to busy streets. The nave was here when Wycliffe was a boy, the chancel is older still, and the walls are believed to stand on the foundations of a Saxon church.

There are mason's marks on stones in the tower and deep grooves here and there made in the days when bowmen and weavers came to church to sharpen their arrows and shuttles. A west doorway which has been here since the 15th century has faces probably meant for kings. A north doorway no more used has a Tudor rose and a Spanish pomegranate, perhaps symbols of that marriage of Catherine of Aragon with Prince Arthur which changed the face of the world before its final chapter was told. There is a priest's door in a graceful little arch, and the south porch is one of the loveliest for miles round, its massive beams dark with the passage of five centuries. Outside the north wall are modern bosses linking our own day with the Saxon beginnings of this place. One shows King Alfred, to whose granddaughter Edburgha this church is dedicated, and another has the Saxon spelling of Yardley (Gyrdeleahe), a word forgotten centuries before Birmingham was known.

Inside we are impressed with the beauty of the church. Years ago it was in danger from the death-watch beetle, which made havoc of the beams in the roof, but a courageous rector who loved old things raised £7000 and saved it. Some of the money came in small amounts, the smallest being a halfpenny from a poor woman to whose home a church worker walked a long way to give her a receipt, that she might know the great appreciation of the widow's mite. We are told the poor woman burst into tears. Very fine is the timbering of the roofs, old and new; and it is good to see it floodlit, as has been made possible in this noble and nobly managed church.

Under the chancel sleep many who loved this place centuries ago. There are fine sculptured stones in the floor with the arms of the Greswoldes, a family long known here. Isabel Wheeler is kneeling on a brass between her two husbands, one in civil robes, the other in Tudor armour. Henry Greswolde, a 16th-century rector at Solihull, has a great monument of white marble on which we see him with neatly curled hair beside his wife, while round them in medallions of marble are portraits of their 11 children.

The windows are glorious. One shows the chalice and book and sandal of the patron saint Edburgha, whose remains, it is thought, lie under the chancel floor. In this same window are panels of old glass showing scenes of the Nativity and the Crucifixion. Another window has magnificent glass of our own time, showing a woman with two children offering a coat to a beggar. It is in lovely blues, reds, and purples, with delightful little flowers, and is a memorial by a son to his mother. The east window is rich with modern glass, and under the tower arch is a splendid Te Deum window with scores of angels, saints, and kings.

With the dainty silver cross on the altar are elegant candlesticks bearing symbols of Saint Edburgha in enamel. They are the work of artists at Birmingham's School of Art; so also is the lectern Bible with Saint Edburgha on its beautiful cover. The lectern itself was exquisitely carved by a modern craftsman out of a beam 500 years old. It has two small figures of women, and is worthy of everything in this lovely church. The carved oak pulpit is 17th century. The piscina has traces of colour. The Becket chapel has old beams with carved bosses in its open timber roof. The walls of the nave have two small panels of painting fading away.

Embedded in the wall of the tower arch is one of the oldest possessions of the church, a huge white stone from the tomb of Thomas Est and his wife, sleeping under the Gilby Chapel. It is engraved with figures much spoiled, showing Est in the armour he wore in the wars of the 15th century. He was Governor of Kenilworth Castle in its great days.

From the church it is but a step to the old school and its master's house, with roofs of tiles and heavily timbered walls, giving it all a gracious harmony of antiquity. Inside are huge beams from oaks that were growing long before Shakespeare was born, but the building as we see it is 16th century. It is used by the people. The gardens are delightful, and remind us a little of Anne Hathaway's home.

Hay Hall, the old home of the Ests, is still to be seen surrounded by factories; an Elizabethan house, it was empty with an uncertain future when we called. But we found one of the oldest houses in Birmingham, Blakesley Hall, with a new lease of life and happiness. It stands a few minutes from the church and has been made into a city museum. It was here in Elizabeth's day and is still an imposing sight, with two gables and a projecting porch of two storeys all framed with beams remarkably well preserved. The effect of its diagonal braces springing from upright beams is charming. The ceilings have massive beams, and floors and doors and walls all tell of the days when there was oak enough and to spare in Arden's glades.

Alfred's Granddaughter

IT is believed that Alfred's granddaughter lies here before the altar. Her grandfather was Alfred, her father King Eadward, her brothers Athelstan, Eadmund, and Eadred became kings. Six of her sisters were married to foreign princes, but she who might have been a queen did the work of a servant girl and became a saint instead.

This is the story that is told of her. She was but a babe of three when her father took her on his knee and placed within her reach the Gospels, a chalice, and a handful of glittering jewels. The little hands, we are told, stretched forth and grasped the chalice and the book, an act hailed by her delighted parents as a divine sign that Edburgha was called upon to devote her life to God.

She was sent to Winchester as a girl, to become a nun. We know that later she went to Pershore Abbey, and there became Abbess. Such was her humility and piety, it is said, that she washed the garments of the nuns at night while they slept. In everything she did she inspired those around her to do good. When she died they took her home to Winchester, where Alfred and her father lie and where Alfred had been crowned. Many years afterwards they took her in solemn procession back to Pershore, and it is believed that some portion of her remains was brought to the church at Yardley, then connected with the Abbey at Pershore, and buried here under the chancel.

WARWICKSHIRE'S TOWNS AND VILLAGES

In this key to our map of Warwickshire are all the towns and villages treated in this book. If (as may rarely happen) a place is not on the map by name, its square is given here, so that the way to it is easily found, each square being five miles. One or two hamlets are with their neighbouring villages; for these see Index.

WARWICKSHIRE'S TOWNS AND VILLAGES

Solihull	C5	Temple Balsall C5	Warmington	F9	Willoughby	G6
Southam	F7	Temple	Warwick	D7	Wilmcote	C7
Spernall	B7	Grafton B8	Wasperton	D7	Wishaw	C3
Stockton	F7	Tidmington D10	Water Orton	C3	Withybrook	F4
Stoke	E5	Tredington D9	Weddington	E3	Wixford	B8
Stoneleigh	E6	Tysoe E9	Welford-on-		Wolfhamcote	G7
Stratford-on-			Avon	B8	Wolston	F5
Avon	C8		Wellesbourne	D8	Wolverton	C7
Studley	B7	Ufton E7	Weston-on-		Wolvey	F4
Sutton		Ullenhall B6	Avon	C8	Wootton	
Coldfield	B3		Weston-under-		Wawen	B7
Sutton-under-			Wetherley	E6	Wormleighton	F8
Brailes	D10	Walsgrave-on-	Whatcote	D9	Wroxall	C6
		Sowe E5	Whichford	D10	Wyken	E5
Tanworth-in-		Walton D8	Whitchurch	C9		
Arden	B6	Wappenbury E6	Whitnash	E7	Yardley	B4

INDEX

This index includes all notable subjects and people likely to be sought for. The special index of pictures is at the beginning of the volume.

INDEX

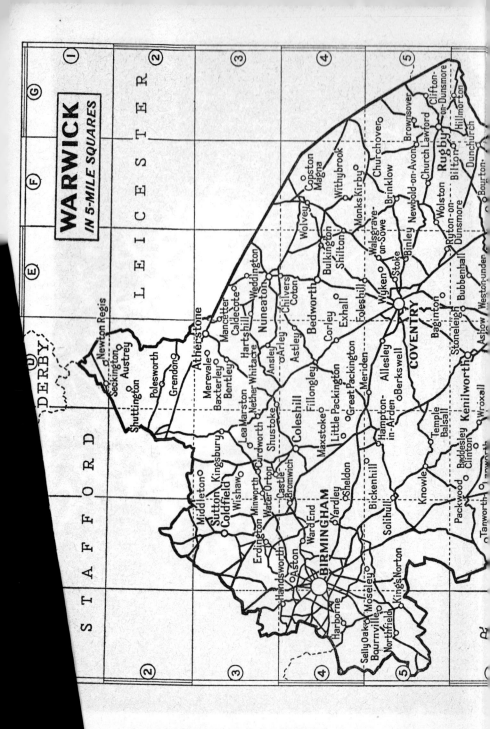

WARWICK
IN 5-MILE SQUARES

STAFFORD

DERBY

LEICESTER

Newton Regis
Seckington
Austrey
Shuttington
Polesworth
Grendon
Atherstone
Merevale
Bentley
Baxterley
Mancetter
Caldecote
Hartshill
Nether Whitacre
Weddington
Nuneaton
Ansley
Arley
Astley
Chilvers Coton
Bedworth
Corley
Exhall
Foleshill
Wolvey
Copston Magna
Withybrook
Monks Kirby
Brinklow
Churchover
Brownsover
Clifton-on-Dunsmore
Bulkington
Shilton
Walsgrave-on-Sowe
Wyken
Stoke
Binley
Newbold-on-Avon
Church Lawford
Rugby
Bilton-on-Dunsmore
Hillmorton
Dunchurch
Bourton
Wolston
Ryton-on-Dunsmore
Weston-under-
Middleton
Kingsbury
Sutton Coldfield
Wishaw
Lea Marston
Curdworth
Shustoke
Coleshill
Fillongley
Maxstoke
Little Packington
Great Packington
Meriden
Allesley
Berkswell
COVENTRY
Baginton
Bubbenhall
Stoneleigh
Ashow
Erdington
Minworth
Water Orton
Castle Bromwich
Handsworth
Aston
BIRMINGHAM
Ward End
Yardley
Sheldon
Bickenhill
Solihull
Hampton-in-Arden
Temple Balsall
Knowle
Kenilworth
Wroxall
Baddesley Clinton
Packwood
Tanworth
Harborne
Selly Oak
Bournville
Northfield
Moseley
Kings Norton